First World War
and Army of Occupation
War Diary
France, Belgium and Germany

24 DIVISION
17 Infantry Brigade,
Brigade Machine Gun Company
29 June 1915 - 28 February 1918

WO95/2209/1

The Naval & Military Press Ltd
www.nmarchive.com
Published in association with The National Archives

Published by

The Naval & Military Press Ltd

Unit 10 Ridgewood Industrial Park,

Uckfield, East Sussex,

TN22 5QE England

Tel: +44 (0) 1825 749494

www.naval-military-press.com

www.nmarchive.com

This diary has been reprinted in facsimile from the original. Any imperfections are inevitably reproduced and the quality may fall short of modern type and cartographic standards.

© **Crown Copyright**
Images reproduced by permission of The National Archives, London, England, 2015.

Contents

Document type	Place/Title	Date From	Date To
Heading	WO95/2209/1		
Heading	17th Machine Gun Coy. Jan 1916-Feb 1918		
Heading	17th Machine Gun Company 17th-30 January 1916		
War Diary	Poperinghe	17/01/1916	30/01/1916
Heading	17th Machine Gun Company February 1916 (31.1.16-1.3.16)		
War Diary	Zillebeke	31/01/1916	16/02/1916
War Diary	Ypres	17/02/1916	24/02/1916
War Diary	Poperinghe G.8.b.4.0	25/02/1916	26/02/1916
War Diary	Poperinge	27/02/1916	27/02/1916
War Diary	Poperinghe	28/02/1916	29/02/1916
War Diary	Ypres	01/03/1916	01/03/1916
Heading	17th Machine Gun Company March 1916 (2-31.3.16)		
War Diary	Ypres	02/03/1916	25/03/1916
War Diary	Poperinghe	26/03/1916	27/03/1916
War Diary	Goddaeswelde	28/03/1916	29/03/1916
War Diary	Petit Pont	30/03/1916	31/03/1916
Heading	17th Machine Gun Company. April 1916 (31.3.16-30.4.16)		
Miscellaneous	D.A.G. 3rd Echelon		
War Diary	Petit Pont	31/03/1916	05/04/1916
War Diary	Courte Dreve Farm (ref. X.I.d.3.3.)	06/04/1916	06/04/1916
War Diary	Courte Dreve	07/04/1916	30/04/1916
Heading	17th Machine Gun Company. May 1916		
War Diary	Court Dreve	01/05/1916	31/05/1916
Heading	17th Machine Gun Company. June 1916		
War Diary	Courte Dreve	01/06/1916	24/06/1916
War Diary	X.5.X.3.5. Belg & France Sheet 28.	25/06/1916	25/06/1916
War Diary	X.5.C.3.5.	26/06/1916	27/06/1916
War Diary	M.30.b.3.4 Bel & France Sheet 28	28/06/1916	28/06/1916
War Diary	M.30.b.3.4	29/06/1915	30/06/1915
Heading	17th Machine Gun Company July 1916		
War Diary	M.34.B.3.4	01/07/1916	01/07/1916
War Diary	N.31.b.1/2.5.	02/07/1916	20/07/1916
War Diary	St. Jean	21/07/1916	21/07/1916
War Diary	St Jean Cappel	22/07/1916	22/07/1916
War Diary	Meut Boom	23/07/1916	23/07/1916
War Diary	Riencourt	24/07/1916	30/07/1916
War Diary	Bois Des Tailles Ch. 12.B. Sheet 62 D	31/07/1916	31/07/1916
Heading	17th Machine Gun Company August 1916		
Miscellaneous	A Form. Messages And Signals.	15/09/1916	15/09/1916
War Diary	Sant Pit (E.18.D)	01/08/1916	04/08/1916
War Diary	Carnoy	08/08/1916	17/08/1916
War Diary	Bernafay Wood (Coy HQ)	18/08/1916	22/08/1916
War Diary	Happes Dulley	23/08/1916	24/08/1916
War Diary	V. Albert D 12 C	25/08/1916	27/08/1916
War Diary	D.12.C	28/08/1916	30/08/1916
War Diary	Fricourt	31/08/1916	31/08/1916
Miscellaneous	24th Divn. G. 320	09/08/1916	09/08/1916
Miscellaneous	To Headquarters 17th Infantry Brigade.	27/08/1916	27/08/1916

Type	Description	Start	End
Miscellaneous	Headquarters 24th Division.	28/08/1916	28/08/1916
Heading	17th Machine Gun Company. September 1916		
Miscellaneous	A Form Messages And Signals.	30/09/1916	30/09/1916
War Diary	Montauban	01/09/1916	05/09/1916
War Diary	Near Fricourt	06/09/1916	06/09/1916
War Diary	Near Albert Camp D.12.C.	07/09/1916	07/09/1916
War Diary	Ergnies	08/09/1916	19/09/1916
War Diary	Pernes	20/09/1916	23/09/1916
War Diary	Ruitz	24/09/1916	24/09/1916
War Diary	Camblain L'Abbe	25/09/1916	26/09/1916
War Diary	Villers Bois	27/09/1916	30/09/1916
Heading	17th Machine Gun Company October 1916		
War Diary	Villers Bois	01/10/1916	03/10/1916
War Diary	Camblain L'Abbe	04/10/1916	11/10/1916
War Diary	Villers Bois	12/10/1916	25/10/1916
War Diary	Gouy Servins	26/10/1916	26/10/1916
War Diary	Mazingarbe	27/10/1916	29/10/1916
War Diary	Lee Brebis	30/10/1916	31/10/1916
Heading	17th Machine Gun Company. November 1916		
Miscellaneous		02/12/1916	02/12/1916
War Diary	Les Brebis	01/11/1916	30/11/1916
Heading	17th Machine Gun Company December 1916		
Miscellaneous	A Form. Messages And Signals.	02/01/1917	02/01/1917
War Diary	Les Brebis	01/12/1916	13/02/1917
War Diary	Noeux-Les-Mines	14/02/1917	02/03/1917
War Diary	Fosse 10	03/03/1917	03/03/1917
War Diary	Bully Grenay	04/03/1917	31/03/1917
Heading	17th Brigade Machine Gun Company 24th Division April 1917		
War Diary	Bully Grenay	01/04/1917	13/04/1917
War Diary	Lievin	14/04/1917	19/04/1917
War Diary	Bully Grenay	19/04/1917	19/04/1917
War Diary	Noeux-Les-Mines	20/04/1917	20/04/1917
War Diary	St. Hilaire	21/04/1917	24/04/1917
War Diary	Greuppe	25/04/1917	26/04/1917
War Diary	Les Pesses	26/04/1917	27/04/1917
War Diary	Bethune	28/04/1917	30/04/1917
Map	Lens		
Miscellaneous	17th I. Bde. O.O.138/3	08/04/1917	08/04/1917
Miscellaneous	Smoke Operations		
Miscellaneous	Appendix 1 (Issued with 17th Inf. Bde O.O. 138).	08/04/1917	08/04/1917
Operation(al) Order(s)	17th Infantry Brigade Operation Order No 138	07/04/1917	07/04/1917
Miscellaneous			
Map	Machine Gun Barrage Map		
Map	Givenchy And Souchez.		
Miscellaneous	8/Bde. Inf.	12/04/1917	12/04/1917
Miscellaneous		10/04/1917	10/04/1917
Miscellaneous	Section in the event of the Enemy with drawel opposite the 24th Division Front.		
Miscellaneous	Appendix "A"		
Map			
War Diary	Bethune	01/05/1917	02/05/1917
War Diary	Fouqueril	03/05/1917	09/05/1917
War Diary	Robecq	10/05/1917	11/05/1917
War Diary	Hazebrouk	12/05/1917	12/05/1917
War Diary	Steenvoorde	13/05/1917	15/05/1917

War Diary	Brandhoek	16/05/1917	27/05/1917
War Diary	C 20 C 4.4. Sheet 28 N.W.	28/05/1917	31/05/1917
Heading	War Diary June 1917 17th Machine Gun Company Volume No. XVII (24th Division.)		
War Diary	K.15 D.4.3.	01/06/1917	04/06/1917
War Diary	M 36 C 15.25	05/06/1917	05/06/1917
War Diary	N 1 Central	06/06/1917	06/06/1917
War Diary	Assembly Frenches near Veoormezle	07/06/1917	07/06/1917
War Diary	O 9 C 2.8	08/06/1917	08/06/1917
War Diary	O 9 C. 2.8 (Damm Strasse)	08/06/1917	10/06/1917
War Diary	Quebec Camp	11/06/1917	15/06/1917
War Diary	Micmac South	16/06/1917	29/06/1917
War Diary	Lumbres	30/06/1917	30/06/1917
Miscellaneous	A Form. Messages And Signals.		
Heading	War Diary of the 17th Machine Gun Company July 1917 Volume No. 19		
War Diary	Nabrinchem	01/07/1917	09/07/1917
War Diary	Ecault	10/07/1917	11/07/1917
War Diary	Nabringhem	12/07/1917	17/07/1917
War Diary	Watterdal	18/07/1917	18/07/1917
War Diary	Bayenghem	19/07/1917	19/07/1917
War Diary	Reniscure	20/07/1917	20/07/1917
War Diary	Caestre	21/07/1917	21/07/1917
War Diary	Steenvoorde	22/07/1917	22/07/1917
War Diary	Steenvorde (K 26d 8.9)	23/07/1917	25/07/1917
War Diary	Micmac Camp H 31d d 8	26/07/1917	30/07/1917
War Diary	Hedge St I 24 d 6.0	30/07/1917	31/07/1917
Map			
Miscellaneous	Address to:	31/07/1917	31/07/1917
Miscellaneous	17th Machine Gun Company	21/07/1917	21/07/1917
Map			
Miscellaneous	Appendix "B"		
Miscellaneous	Appendix "C"		
Miscellaneous	Machine Gun/Barrage: Final Time Table.		
Heading	War Diary 17th Machine Gun Company for month of August 1917 Volume No. 20		
War Diary	Micmac Camp H 3.d.4.8	01/08/1917	06/08/1917
War Diary	Dickebusch	07/08/1917	07/08/1917
War Diary	Micmac Camp	08/08/1917	15/08/1917
War Diary	Dickebusch	16/08/1917	19/08/1917
War Diary	Micmac Camp	20/08/1917	31/08/1917
Heading	War Diary 17th Machine Gun Company September 1917 Volume No. 21		
War Diary	Hedge St Trenches	01/09/1917	03/09/1917
War Diary	Micmac Camp	04/09/1917	07/09/1917
War Diary	Dickebusch	08/09/1917	11/09/1917
War Diary	Hedge St	12/09/1917	15/09/1917
War Diary	Dickebusch	16/09/1917	16/09/1917
War Diary	Merris area (F2d 4.8)	17/09/1917	20/09/1917
War Diary	Bapaume	21/09/1917	21/09/1917
War Diary	Bus	22/09/1917	22/09/1917
War Diary	Bus M.C. Camp	23/09/1917	27/09/1917
War Diary	Haut Allaines C 29b 3.1	28/09/1917	29/09/1917
War Diary	Bernes	29/09/1917	30/09/1917
Heading	War Diary 17th Machine Gun Company October 1917 Volume 22		

War Diary	Bernes	01/10/1917	31/10/1917
War Diary	Bernes (Q4) Sheet 62C	01/11/1917	01/11/1917
Heading	War Diary 17th Machine Gun Company November 1917 Volume No. 23		
War Diary	Bernes	02/11/1917	06/11/1917
War Diary	Hancourt	07/11/1917	30/11/1917
Heading	War Diary 17th Machine Gun Company December 1917 Volume No. 24		
War Diary	Hancourt	01/12/1917	17/12/1917
War Diary	Vraignes	08/12/1917	18/12/1917
War Diary	Bernes	19/12/1917	27/12/1917
War Diary	Hervilly	28/12/1917	31/12/1917
Heading	War Diary 17th Machine Gun Company January 1918 Volume No. 25		
War Diary	Hervilly	01/01/1918	02/01/1918
War Diary	Vraignes	03/01/1918	08/01/1918
War Diary	Hervilly	09/01/1918	12/01/1918
War Diary	Bernes	13/01/1918	20/01/1918
War Diary	Vraignes	21/01/1918	31/01/1918
Heading	War Diary 17th Machine Gun Company February 1918 Volume No. 26		
War Diary	Vraignes (Q.19d 90.50)	01/02/1918	06/02/1918
War Diary	Bernes Q4 C. 90.28	07/02/1918	15/02/1918
War Diary	Hervilly K 23d 8.4	15/02/1918	28/02/1918
Operation(al) Order(s)	17th Machine Gun Coy. Operation Order No. 3		
Miscellaneous	Table to O.O. No. 3-17th Machine Gun Company.		
Operation(al) Order(s)	17th M.G. Company Operation Order No. 4	21/02/1918	21/02/1918
Miscellaneous	8 Company H.Q.		
Miscellaneous	A		
Miscellaneous	B		
Miscellaneous	C		
Operation(al) Order(s)	17th Machine Gun Company Operation Order No. 5		
Miscellaneous	Appendix A		

WO 95/2209/1

24TH DIVISION
17TH INFY BDE

17TH MACHINE GUN COY.
JAN 1916-FEB 1918.

24TH DIVISION
17TH INFY BDE

17th Brigade.
24th Division.

17th MACHINE GUN COMPANY.

17th - 30th January 1916

Feb '18

17th Brigade.
24th Division.

WAR DIARY or INTELLIGENCE SUMMARY

Army Form C. 2118.

of the 19th Brigade Machine Gun Company from 17th January 1916 to 1st August 1916

Place	Date	Hour	Summary of Events and Information	Remarks and references to Appendices
POPERINGHE	17/1/16	—	January 17th 1916. The 19th Brigade Machine Gun Company officially formed the personnel and material being drawn from the following regiments :— 1st Royal Fusiliers, 1st North Stafford Regt, 2nd Leinster Regt, 3rd Rifle Brigade (these being the original Battalions of the 19th Brigade) and the 2nd London Regt. The Company finds eight guns in the line, RAILWAY WOOD – H.0.0.62, relieved by the 24th Division. Casualties :— Nil	I.R.B.
POPERINGHE	18/1/16		Situation Normal. Casualties :— Nil	I.R.B.
POPERINGHE	19/1/16		Situation Normal Casualties :— 1 Driver killed	I.R.B.
POPERINGHE	20/1/16		January 20th 1916. Four guns in left sector, RAILWAY WOOD, relieved by the Company. Casualties :- nil	I.R.B.

Army Form C. 2118.

WAR DIARY
or
INTELLIGENCE SUMMARY.
(Erase heading not required.)

Instructions regarding War Diaries and Intelligence Summaries are contained in F.S. Regs., Part II. and the Staff Manual respectively. Title pages will be prepared in manuscript.

Place	Date	Hour	Summary of Events and Information	Remarks and references to Appendices
POPERINGHE	21/1/16		January 21st 1916. Situation Normal. Casualties: Nil.	J.R.B.
POPERINGHE	22/1/16		January 22nd 1916. Situation Normal. Casualties: Nil.	J.R.B.
POPERINGHE	23/1/16		January 23rd. Four guns J.R.B. right brigade 17th Brigade relieved by the 72nd Brigade in Left Sector, RAILWAY WOOD. Eight guns of the Company in the Line. Casualties: Nil.	J.R.B.
POPERINGHE	24/1/16		January 24th 1916. Situation Normal. Casualties: Nil.	J.R.B.
POPERINGHE	25/1/16		January 25th 1916. Situation Normal. Casualties: Nil.	J.R.B.

Army Form C. 2118.

WAR DIARY
or
INTELLIGENCE SUMMARY.
(Erase heading not required.)

Instructions regarding War Diaries and Intelligence Summaries are contained in F. S. Regs., Part II. and the Staff Manual respectively. Title pages will be prepared in manuscript.

Place	Date	Hour	Summary of Events and Information	Remarks and references to Appendices
POPERINGHE	26/1/16		January 26th 1916. Situation Normal. Casualties :- Nil	J.R.B.
POPERINGHE	27/1/16		January 27th 1916. Four guns relieved in YEOMANRY POST by the Company. Casualties :- Nil	J.R.B.
POPERINGHE	28/1/16		January 28th 1916 Situation Normal. Casualties :- Nil	J.R.B.
POPERINGHE	29/1/16		January 29th 1916. Situation Normal. Casualties :- Nil	J.R.B.
POPERINGHE	30/1/16		January 30th 1916 Situation Normal Casualties :- Nil	J.R.B.

17th Brigade.
24th Division.

17th MACHINE GUN COMPANY.

February 1916

(31.1.16 - 1.3.16)

WAR DIARY
or
INTELLIGENCE SUMMARY.
(Erase heading not required.)

Army Form C. 2118.

Place	Date	Hour	Summary of Events and Information	Remarks and references to Appendices
ZILLEBEKE	31st Jan		January 31st The Brigade relieved the 73rd Brigade in the night Sector in the night of Jan 31st Feb 1st Brigade Hqrs in ZILLEBEKE dug-outs & HOOGE Sector. Casualties:- Nil.	P.R.B.
ZILLEBEKE	1st Feb		February 1st 1916. Heavy bombardment by an 9.2" howitzer on Enemy's trenches J.13.c. Much damage was done, & enemy was heard calling for stretcher bearers. Enemy retaliated on the HOOGE trenches with shell effect. Casualties:- Nil.	T.R.B.
ZILLEBEKE	2nd Feb		February 2nd 1916. Situation Unchanged. Casualties:- Nil.	T.R.B.
ZILLEBEKE	3rd Feb		February 3rd 1916. Situation Unchanged. Casualties:- Nil.	T.R.B.

Army Form C. 2118.

WAR DIARY
or
INTELLIGENCE SUMMARY.
(Erase heading not required.)

Instructions regarding War Diaries and Intelligence Summaries are contained in F.S. Regs., Part II. and the Staff Manual respectively. Title pages will be prepared in manuscript.

Place	Date	Hour	Summary of Events and Information	Remarks and references to Appendices
ZILLEBEKE	4th Feb		YEOMANRY POST and GORDON HOUSE shelled. Casualties :- Nil	T.R.B
ZILLEBEKE	5th Feb		YEOMANRY POST and ground near heavily shelled. Some S.A.A discharged. Casualties :- Nil	T.R.B
ZILLEBEKE	6th Feb		Artillery on both sides active. Casualties :- Nil	T.R.B
ZILLEBEKE	7th Feb		Considerable aeroplane activity on both sides in early morning. Own artillery shelled heavily the enemy's trenches N° 6 of ROVER'S RY. Enemy retaliated heavily. ZILLEBEKE dug-outs & our various shelters at night. T.R.B Casualties :- Nil	
ZILLEBEKE	8th Feb		Enemy's artillery very active during day and at night on roads round YPRES and DICKEBUSCH were heavily shelled. Casualties :- Nil	T.R.B

Army Form C. 2118.

WAR DIARY
or
INTELLIGENCE SUMMARY.
(Erase heading not required.)

Instructions regarding War Diaries and Intelligence Summaries are contained in F. S. Regs., Part II. and the Staff Manual respectively. Title pages will be prepared in manuscript.

Place	Date	Hour	Summary of Events and Information	Remarks and references to Appendices
ZILLEBEKE	9th Feb		Situation normal during the day. Our trenches heavily shelled at night. Casualties: Nil	T.R.B.
ZILLEBEKE	10th Feb		Artillery activity on both sides. Casualties – nil	T.R.B.
ZILLEBEKE	11th Feb		Artillery active on both sides. Casualties: 1 man wounded	T.R.B.
ZILLEBEKE	12th Feb		Heavy artillery fire during night of 11th/12th. Enemy worked on trenches near PICK M Hut. No more shown out. Great artillery activity during the whole of the day.	T.R.B.
ZILLEBEKE	13th Feb		Heavy artillery round HOOGE/enemy. Casualties: Nil	T.R.B.
ZILLEBEKE	14th Feb		Enemy heavily shelled the whole of the trenches. Enemy attack reported at HOOGE. All the spare guns of the Company brought up and placed at the disposal of Brigadier Commanding right and left sector. Enemy did not press an attack owing to the steadiness of our infantry and the prompt and accurate fire of our artillery. Losses inflicted by enemy in our sector. One of our men killed. Casualties: 6 men killed	T.R.B.

T2134. Wt. W708–776. 500000. 4/15. Str J. C. & S.

Army Form C. 2118.

WAR DIARY
or
INTELLIGENCE SUMMARY.
(Erase heading not required.)

Instructions regarding War Diaries and Intelligence Summaries are contained in F.S. Regs., Part II. and the Staff Manual respectively. Title pages will be prepared in manuscript.

Place	Date	Hour	Summary of Events and Information	Remarks and references to Appendices
ZILLEBEKE	15th Feb		Situation normal. Casualties:- Nil	T.R.B.
ZILLEBEKE	16th Feb	2 am	Aeroplane bombs dropped near billet at G.6.b.4.0. Situation normal. Casualties:- Nil	T.R.B.
YPRES	17th Feb		Situation normal. Quiet day. Casualties:- Nil	T.R.B.
YPRES	18th Feb		Enemy shelled H.20 in LEFT SECTOR (RAILWAY WOOD). Company relief in RIGHT & LEFT SECTORS, RAILWAY WOOD & HOOGE. 8 guns in the line; teams only relieved. Very hot night. Casualties:- Nil	T.R.B.
YPRES	19th Feb		Enemy shelled H.20, S.21 and RAILWAY WOOD. Casualties:- Nil.	L.R.B.
		9 am	Enemy aeroplane dropped bombs near billet at G.6.b.4.0. No damage done. Casualties:- Nil	
YPRES	20th Feb		Situation normal. Wind beginning W. Screen W.E. and turned E. Gas alert "off". Casualties:- Nil	L.R.B.
			Aeroplane bombs dropped on billet at G.6.b.40. Casualties:- Nil	

WAR DIARY
or
INTELLIGENCE SUMMARY.
(Erase heading not required.)

Army Form C. 2118.

Place	Date	Hour	Summary of Events and Information	Remarks and references to Appendices
YPRES	21st Feb	4 am	Enemy shelled billet at G.8.b.4.0. Shells came very near the house & home farm; I have moved in. In the salient artillery activity on both sides. Casualties:- Nil.	T.R.B.
YPRES	22nd Feb	Midnight	Great artillery activity on both sides in left of salient. Hostile aeroplane again dropped bombs near company H.Q. at G.8.b.4.0. I fell within 50 yards of the house. Casualties:- Nil.	T.R.B.
YPRES	23rd Feb		Situation Normal. Casualties Nil.	T.R.B.
YPRES	24th Feb		Situation Normal. Two heavy artillery shelled enemy's trenches near the "Bluff" between 5.30 pm & 6 am. Casualties:- Nil.	T.R.B.
POPERINGHE G.8.b.4.0	25th Feb		Situation Normal. Snow and frost.	T.R.B.
POPERINGHE G.8.b.4.0	26th Feb		Situation Normal. 4 guns & teams in RAILWAY WOOD SECTOR relieved by guns & teams of 16 Bde. M.G.C.	T.R.B.

WAR DIARY of the 17th Brigade Machine Gun Company

or INTELLIGENCE SUMMARY. from Jan 17th 1916 to March 1st 1916

Army Form C. 2118.

(Erase heading not required.)

Instructions regarding War Diaries and Intelligence Summaries are contained in F. S. Regs., Part II. and the Staff Manual respectively. Title pages will be prepared in manuscript.

Place	Date	Hour	Summary of Events and Information	Remarks and references to Appendices
YPT POPERINGHE	27th Feb		Situation normal. 6 guns and 4 teams rely of the Company in the line – HOOGE SECTOR. Remainder of guns and teams at Company Billet. B8645. Casualties:- Nil	B8B. B25
POPERINGHE	28th Feb		Situation normal. Company in billets formed and taken on to range. Casualties:- Nil	B&B.
POPERINGHE	29th Feb		Two Officers, Lieut Rodcott and 2/Lieut Pigott attached from the M.G. Corps as supernumery to the Company. First reinforcements from the M.G. Corps.	
		10.45 pm	Received orders from the Division to man all available guns and teams up to YPRES at dusk and to report to B.B.C. 72nd Brigade	
		3.30 pm	Teams & guns moved off.	T&B.
		8.30 pm	14 guns in the line – HOOGE SECTOR - 11 teams. Casualties:- Nil	
YPRES/RAMP	March 1st	11.30 am	Artillery activity on both sides. Enemy shelled KRUISTRAAT with tachymetry shells. An artillery encounter a heavy straf in enemy's front line trenches in the HOOGE v	T&B.
		5 pm	ST. ELOI SECTOR. 14 of our aeroplanes up over YPRES; enemy hurried scattered Platelet wards.	

T2134. Wt. W708 – 776. 500000. 4/15. Sir J. C. & S.

17th Brigade.
24th Division.

17th MACHINE GUN COMPANY.

March 1916
(2 - 31. 3. 16)

WAR DIARY or INTELLIGENCE SUMMARY

Army Form C. 2118.

Place	Date	Hour	Summary of Events and Information	Remarks and references to Appendices
YPRES	2nd March		Artillery active all day. Enemy put a barrage of shells on SHRAPNELL CORNER and shelled ZILLEBEKE BUND and HOOGE at intervals. Divisional artillery retaliated principally in the direction of BELLEWAARDE LAKE. Casualties:- Nil	SRB
YPRES	3rd March		Enemy shelled HOOGE and ZILLEBEKE BUND on artillery retaliated. On I. Oy. a.5. RE machine guns still in the 24th Div. Line. Three officers of the Company viz. Lieut Stephens, Lieut Franklin and 2/Lieut Coleman. Two officers, Lieut Antrush and Lieut Pigott from the M.G. Corps attached to the Company as supernumeraries. 2/Lieut Gromie in m M.G. Course, only 5 officers on duty - last billet attached to HQ 42nd Brigade. Casualties :- Nil	SRB
YPRES	4th March		Quiet day on both sides. Casualties :- Nil	SRB
YPRES	5th March		Quiet day. Seven teams and 10 guns now withdrawn from HOOGE SECTOR, leaving 4 teams and 6 guns in the line. Casualties :- Nil	SRB

Army Form C. 2118.

WAR DIARY
or
INTELLIGENCE SUMMARY.
(Erase heading not required.)

Instructions regarding War Diaries and Intelligence Summaries are contained in F. S. Regs., Part II. and the Staff Manual respectively. Title pages will be prepared in manuscript.

Place	Date	Hour	Summary of Events and Information	Remarks and references to Appendices
YPRES	6th March		Quiet day. Casualties :- Nil	ILB
YPRES	7th March		Situation normal. Casualties :- Nil	ILS
YPRES	8th March		Enemy's artillery active, shelled round WATER TOWER, YPRES STATION, SQUARE and LILLE GATE from 7.05 to 10.0 hrs. HELLFIRE CORNER and neighbourhood also shelled between 7.30 and 9.35 hrs. Casualties :- Nil	RRB
YPRES	9th March		Enemy's artillery action on Divisional Front. Right of the 9th/15th the 14th Bgd. Bde. relieved the 150th Bde. 51st Division in SANCTUARY WOOD SECTOR. The 14th B.M.G.C. relieved the 150th B.M.G.C. Eight pistols were taken over and 6 teams and 6 guns were placed in the Brigade line and two guns in some at ZILLEBEKE. The Company had then all its effective personnel in the line and all its guns. 6 guns and 4 teams in the HOOGE SECTOR and 10 guns and eight teams in SANCTUARY WOOD SECTOR. Casualties :- Nil	8KB

Army Form C. 2118.

WAR DIARY
or
INTELLIGENCE SUMMARY.
(Erase heading not required.)

Place	Date	Hour	Summary of Events and Information	Remarks and references to Appendices
YPRES	March 10th		Quiet day on the whole. Enemy's machine guns were active in SANCTUARY WOOD. One of their guns was silenced by a retaliation from our Hotchkiss G.S. Casualties: Nil.	J.R.B.
YPRES	March 11th		To-day at 5.15am the enemy shelled YEOMANRY POST with shrapnel. At 2pm HOOGE was heavily shelled with over 95 9".H.E. Our artillery retaliated with very good results. From 3.65 to 6.45am its enemy fired about 200 rounds H.E. and a high bursting shrapnel from OBSERVATORY RIDGE from RUDKIN HOUSE to VALLEY COTTAGES. Casualties: Nil	J.R.B.
YPRES	March 12th		Enemy's artillery was active up to 4 a.m. on OBSERVATORY RIDGE area, MAPLE COPSE, YEOMANRY POST, and ZOUAVE WOOD, hereafter favourite targets during the day. Casualties: Nil	J.R.B.

Army Form C. 2118.

WAR DIARY
or
INTELLIGENCE SUMMARY.
(Erase heading not required.)

Instructions regarding War Diaries and Intelligence Summaries are contained in F. S. Regs., Part II. and the Staff Manual respectively. Title pages will be prepared in manuscript.

Place	Date	Hour	Summary of Events and Information	Remarks and references to Appendices
YPRES	13th March		Artillery activity on both sides. The "C" trenches in the HILL 60 sector were heavily shelled during the afternoon and at 11 p.m. at night. Casualties :- Nil	TRB
YPRES	14th March		From 7.45 am to 8.45 am the enemy shelled round about ZOUAVE WOOD and in the afternoon T.8, S.8, C.12, R.S.2 and GOVERN ROAD were heavily shelled and considerable damage was done. Casualties; Nil	TRB
YPRES	15th March		HOOGE was heavily bombarded by the enemy in the afternoon. Our artillery retaliated with effect. Casualties: Nil	TRB
YPRES	16th March		Enemy's artillery very active. WARRINGTON AVENUE was shelled from 1.30 pm to 4.30 pm with concentration between B.4 & CONSETT DUGOUTS. I.2. &c. Cpl Glancy's team in WARRINGTON AVENUE suffered severely through shelling. The Corporal and 2 men were killed, 2 men wounded and the remainder suffering from shock. One man of Sgt Heighs team was killed. Two guns were injured. Casualties: 1 Cpl and 3 men killed, 2 men wounded.	TRB

T2134. Wt. W708-776. 500000. 4/15. Sir J. C. & S.

WAR DIARY
or
INTELLIGENCE SUMMARY.

Army Form C. 2118.

Place	Date	Hour	Summary of Events and Information	Remarks and references to Appendices
YPRES	May 15th		Enemy's artillery during the day; YEOMANRY POST and R.S.8 were shelled. KRUISTRAAT - YPRES ROAD. WOODCOTE HOUSE to S. of RAILWAY by RAILWAY DUGOUTS and ZILLEBEKE BUND were shelled with gas crumps H.E. shrapnel & gas shell from 2.30 to 5.30 p.m. Very little damage done. Casualties - nil	TKS
YPRES	16th		Artillery on both sides inactive. Casualties (1 man wounded)	TKS
YPRES	19th		Situation normal. During the past 5 days several changes among the officers of the company have taken place. Lieuts Rothwell & Lieut Argent who were attached were posted to the 41st M.G.C. 16th Division. Lieut Wilkinson during work with the 4th & 5th Bdgs & Lieut Morris from the M.G. Corps have taken his place. Officers of the company are :- Capt Bird, Lieut Wright, Lieut Stephens, Lieut Sommer 2/Lieut Coleman, 2/Lieut Coleman, 2/Lieut Morris and 2/Lieut Stansend, 2/Lieut Franklin. 2/Lieut Young. After the following non-comd and officers :- Lieut Stephens Lieut Franklin, 2/Lieut Coleman, 2/Lieut Young to 2/Lieut Stansend all in Coy Bugle Sect Sergt Others leaving to The Ende	TKS

WAR DIARY or INTELLIGENCE SUMMARY

Army Form C. 2118.

Place	Date	Hour	Summary of Events and Information	Remarks and references to Appendices
YPRES	20th March		Quiet day. 24th Division to be relieved by the 2nd Canadian Division. All guns of the 17th B.M.G.C. to remain in the line for 3 days. Half the personnel of the company returns by half personnel of 42nd B.M.G.C. Teams made up by 17th and 72nd B.M.G.C. Three officers of 72nd M.G.C. came up on night of 20/21st and went into the line; half personnel of 17th B.M.G. handing over billets at MOERINGHE on 20th inst. the 17th B.M.G.C. is attached to the 2nd Canadian Division. The 42nd Inf. Bde. marched a night of 20th/21st to proceed to rest camps near POPERINGHE; they the relieving Brigade was the 8th Canadian I.B. Casualties - nil	SR3
YPRES	21st March		Quiet day. The 17th Brigade was relieved by the 4th Canadian Brigade on the night of the 21st/22nd. The machine gun company was not relieved and the guns were available in the line. The 26th Divisional relief was completed on the night of 21st/22nd. Casualties - nil	SR3

Army Form C. 2118.

WAR DIARY
or
INTELLIGENCE SUMMARY.
(Erase heading not required.)

Instructions regarding War Diaries and Intelligence Summaries are contained in F.S. Regs., Part II. and the Staff Manual respectively. Title pages will be prepared in manuscript.

Place	Date	Hour	Summary of Events and Information	Remarks and references to Appendices
YPRES	22nd March		Situation normal. Our artillery active, enemy put a number of whizz-bangs in front of his trenches between Ar'tang & 10. Unknown components arrived from the M.G. Corps, Base. Casualties - Nil	T.R.B.
YPRES	23rd March		Situation normal. Quiet day. Casualties - Nil	2.R.B.
YPRES	24th March		Situation normal. Quiet day. Casualties - Nil	T.R.B.
YPRES	25th March		Enemy shelled SANCTUARY WOOD in neighbourhood of BIRDER DUGOUT from 1.20 o'clock until 4.0 o'clock in the afternoon. LAHORE Divisional artillery attached to 5th Canadian Division retaliated with good effect. Guns of M.G.C. in SANCTUARY WOOD took return by EATON Battery and 7th Canadian Bty. Guns in SANCTUARY WOOD relieved by guns of EATON Battery and	

Army Form C. 2118.

WAR DIARY
or
INTELLIGENCE SUMMARY.
(Erase heading not required.)

Place	Date	Hour	Summary of Events and Information	Remarks and references to Appendices
YPRES	25th March		2 guns in MAPLE Copse by guns of 7th Canadian Brigade. Guns in Left Sector, HOOGE, relieved by guns of 5th CH Battery & 1/E.I.M.M.M.Ry POST CULVERT & BRAFTON ST and J.F.Ry. 10 guns of M.G.Coy relieved on night of 25/26th. Relief very late and teams did not get back to billets at POPERINGHE before 6.30 am. All the Company and half personnel of 4th Bn M.G.Coy in billets at POPERINGHE	SEE S
POPERINGHE	26th March		Company at rest.	SEE S
POPERINGHE	27th March		Transport proceeded by road to new rest area at GODDESWSOE in morning. Company half personnel of F. Company and 4th B.M.G.C. attached T.H.B. went by train in afternoon and half personnel by train to GODDESWSIDE. Company arrived for night at GODDESWSOE	SEE S
GODDESWSIDE POPERINGHE	28th March		Company at rest. O.C. Company proceeded to new lines which was to be taken over, PLOEGSTEERT — WYTSCHAETE.	SEE S

T2134. Wt. W708–776. 500000. 4/15. Sir J. C. & S.

Army Form C. 2118.

WAR DIARY
or
INTELLIGENCE SUMMARY.
(Erase heading not required.)

Instructions regarding War Diaries and Intelligence Summaries are contained in F. S. Regs., Part II. and the Staff Manual respectively. Title pages will be prepared in manuscript.

Place	Date	Hour	Summary of Events and Information	Remarks and references to Appendices
GODDAESWELDE POPERINGHE 1914	29 Mch		Half personnel, transport and 10 guns left GODDAESWELDE at 8.45 am and proceeded to new area and billet at PETIT PONT, rf T 22 b 18.1 Route FLETRE, METEREN, BAILEUL,	TCR
			This half company, Capt Buck, Lieut Gorrie & 2/Lieut Harriman at billet, occupied by 2nd Canadian B.M.G.C. at 2.30 pm - front road line that night. Trenches in front line held by Divisn 128 - 136 both inclusive	
PETIT PONT 30th Mch			8 guns and teams relieved 2nd Canadian B.M.G.C. into following letters RIGHT SECTOR - LA HUTTE rf. V. 14. C. 13. 4½. 2 guns & 2 teams LOCALITY "A" 1 gun and 1 team, Locality "O" 1 gun & 1 team. LEFT SECTOR, ROSSIGNOL -	RCB
			2 guns v 2 teams, DEAD COW FM. 1 gun v 1 team, WINTER TRENCH 1 gun & team. 2 officers in dugouts at LA HUTTE viz Lieut Goodie & 2/Lieut Harriman. Remainder of personnel & 6 guns arrived at billet at 6 am in afternoon, officers 2/Lieut Sandy & 2/Lieut Hancock. 2 guns sent to SWKB v 12 - 2.F. 6 guns in billet v. 6 teams.	

WAR DIARY
or
INTELLIGENCE SUMMARY.
(Erase heading not required.)

Army Form C. 2118.

Instructions regarding War Diaries and Intelligence Summaries are contained in F. S. Regs., Part II. and the Staff Manual respectively. Title pages will be prepared in manuscript.

Place	Date	Hour	Summary of Events and Information	Remarks and references to Appendices
PETIT PONT	31/5/16		Situation normal. Weather dry. Half company in field carrying on with training. Rest of line at night and reinforcing and to/from bivouac at LA HUTE CHATEAU.	ACC

17th Brigade.
24th Division.

17th MACHINE GUN COMPANY.

April 1916.
(31.3.16 - 30.4.16)

CONFIDENTIAL

(24)

D.A.G.
3rd Echelon

Herewith War Diary of

17th Brigade Machine Gun Company

from 31st April 1916
to
31st May 1916.

(Volume 4)

H.Q.
17th Bde. M.G.C.

E.R. Birch Capt.
O.C. 17th Bde. M.G.C.

Army Form C. 2118.

WAR DIARY
or
INTELLIGENCE SUMMARY.
(Erase heading not required.)

Instructions regarding War Diaries and Intelligence Summaries are contained in F. S. Regs., Part II. and the Staff Manual respectively. Title pages will be prepared in manuscript.

Place	Date	Hour	Summary of Events and Information	Remarks and references to Appendices
PETIT PONT	31/3/16		Situation normal. Weather dry. Half company in fields carrying on with training. Rifles in at night and "working parties" out of "P"/Coot trenches at LA HUTE CHATEAU.	SRB
PETIT PONT	1/4/16		Situation normal. Weather warm and dry. 2/Lieut Hancock & 2/Lieut Kafka at LA HUTE CHATEAU. Rifle grds proceeded in bus on 2/4/16. Instruct for carried out from CHATEAU at V.14.c.15 during night on to MESSINES RD running through enemy's lines from U.9.B.10 to V.9.C.1. Casualties : Nil.	SRB
PETIT PONT	2/4/16		Situation normal. Weather warm and dry. Lieut Wright returned from leave and resumed his killed instructing. Casualties: 1 man who was wounded on 18th March in YPRES was died at ETAPLES.	SRB
PETIT PONT	3/4/16		Situation normal. Enemy's artillery active in aft. 73rd Bde , brigade area. Enemy shelled DEAD COW FARM, nf, V.13.b.4.5. 1½, in afternoon. No damage	

Army Form C. 2118.

WAR DIARY
or
INTELLIGENCE SUMMARY.
(Erase heading not required.)

Instructions regarding War Diaries and Intelligence Summaries are contained in F. S. Regs., Part II. and the Staff Manual respectively. Title pages will be prepared in manuscript.

Place	Date	Hour	Summary of Events and Information	Remarks and references to Appendices
PETIT POMT	3/4/16		Orders to leave N.Yprs. Upon end of leave moved to ADVANCED ESTAMINET, at V13.a.6.5. From this position plansing pn. is attached to the right mulding Bns. ASH ROAD.	3Bns
			Casualties: Nil	
PETIT POMT	4/4/16		Situation Normal. Attended a Brigade conference at H.Q. 1st R.F. (GRANDE MUNQUE FERM). 8 men from the following battalions in the brigade reported in afternoon to 1st R.F, 3rd R.B, 8th Buffs, 12th R.F. These men to be instructed with a view to formation of new M.G. Companies, in the Vickers gun. Commenced instruction the next day.	2 RB
			Casualties: Nil	
PETIT POMT	5/4/16		Situation Normal. Instruction of 32 men attached commenced. Went round the LEFT SECTOR in the morning with Wright. Sergt Young reported that the enemy had fired much HE. About that afternoon along MESSINES RD had new ADVANCED EST. Major of 5/6 a battalion in relief but heavy in both right + left sector. 1st RF relieved 12th RF, 8th Buffs relieved 3rd RB at about 5 pm enemy's artillery	

T2134. Wt. W708-776. 500000. 4/15. Sir J. C. & S.

WAR DIARY
or
INTELLIGENCE SUMMARY.
(Erase heading not required.)

Army Form C. 2118.

Place	Date	Hour	Summary of Events and Information	Remarks and references to Appendices
PETIT PONT	5/4/16		Opened a heavy fire along MESSINES ROAD. H.E. shrapnel being mostly used. Relief (intended) was completed with few casualties but on left of the Brigade the enemy shelled heavily and casualties were more severe. It appeared that the enemy had knowledge of a relief taking place. Casualties (of Coy) :- Nil	S.K.B.
PETIT PONT COURTE DREVE FARM (M.X.I.d.3.3.)	6/4/16		14th I.B. HQ and Y3rd I.B. HQ changed over their billets and rations to furnish reported by each other. The Company changed over with the Y3rd B.M.G.C. and at 11 am occupied COURTE DREVE FARM, the Transport lines remained as before, ref. T.27.b.3.5. Brigade HQ occupied LA PETITE MUNQUE, ref X.17.C.3.3. Right teams of Company relieved 8 teams in the line 6 guns were relieved the 2 guns in LA HUTTE CHATEAU remaining. Lieut Searby relieved Lieut Monson in charge of LEFT SECTOR. Casualties :- Nil	S.R.B.

Army Form C. 2118.

WAR DIARY
or
INTELLIGENCE SUMMARY.
(Erase heading not required.)

Instructions regarding War Diaries and Intelligence Summaries are contained in F. S. Regs., Part II. and the Staff Manual respectively. Title pages will be prepared in manuscript.

Place	Date	Hour	Summary of Events and Information	Remarks and references to Appendices
COURTE DREVE	7/4/16		Enemy Artillery Active. Enemy shelled narrow ridge of M.1 & 63 and HYDE PARK CORNER during afternoon. An artillery retaliation effectively. During day enemy shelled LA HUTTE CHATEAU with 4.2 and Whizzbangs. Casualties: Nil	S.R.B.
COURTE DREVE	8/4/16		Enemy artillery active round ASH ROAD and locality "A". ADM BACK EST up 21.14.a.6½. shelled at noon and M.G. Emplacement in building damaged; fortunately no gun was in the building. DEAD COW FM also shelled during afternoon. In the evening Jacomie ROSSIGNOL A16 and proceed to LAC Cryptol Longtans Casualties: Nil	S.R.B.
COURTE DREVE	9/4/16	2.30am	In conjunction with Lt Baff's Lewis gun no of enemy guns at LA HUTTE fired at intervals up the MESSINES ROAD. Last round LEFT SECTOR in the evening with St Quinn. 2/Lieut Hancock was relieved at LA HUTTE CHATEAU in the afternoon by 2nd Lieut Wright who took over LEFT SECTOR. 2/Lieut Hancock proceeded on leave a 10th at night. 13 reinforcements arrived from Base. These include 1 Corporal. Physique of new arrivals good. Casualties: Nil	S.R.B.

WAR DIARY or INTELLIGENCE SUMMARY

Army Form C. 2118.

Place	Date	Hour	Summary of Events and Information	Remarks and references to Appendices
COURTE DREVE	10/4/16		Quiet day on whole. Went up to LA HUTE CHATEAU in the evening and round the LEFT SECTOR with Lieut Wright. Decided to move the gun from FORWARD BACK EST and place it in emplacement of V.14.A.9.1½. This gun fire NORTH covering ground from M. V.14.B.4.9½ to M.V.8.A.9½.3 and also has a loophole firing SOUTH across PROWSE PT. ROAD.	
		9 pm	One 18 Pounder Battery fire 50 rounds at point V.2.D.4.¢3. to V.2.D.5.7. One of our M.G.'s fired in this work a few evenings later from near ANTON'S FARM and from LA HUTE CHATEAU onto the German gun pits nth MESSINES RD WEST of the work. Casualties Nil	SR8
COURTE DREVE	11/4/16		Situation Normal. Quiet day on whole but enemy's artillery in "C" LOCALITY and shells fell round this locality most of the day. making things unpleasant for Cpl. Marriage's team, went up to LA HUTE CHATEAU with provisions in the evening. Moved gun from ROSSIGNAL 15.A. into HAYSTACK POSITION. REF. V.14.A.½.7. Casualties 1 man wounded Cpl Marriage (team)	SR8

T2134. Wt. W708—776. 500000. 4/16. Sir J. C. & S.

Army Form C. 2118.

WAR DIARY
or
INTELLIGENCE SUMMARY.
(Erase heading not required.)

Instructions regarding War Diaries and Intelligence Summaries are contained in F. S. Regs., Part II. and the Staff Manual respectively. Title pages will be prepared in manuscript.

Place	Date	Hour	Summary of Events and Information	Remarks and references to Appendices
COURTE DREVE	12/4/16		Situation normal. Went round LEFT SECTOR with Lieut Wright in evening. Casualties:- nil	SRB
COURTE DREVE	13/4/16		Situation normal. Company relief at night. 8 teams relieved as formerly, and 6 guns, 2 guns in ROSSIGNOL. POSITIONS not relieved. Casualties:- nil	SRB
COURTE DREVE	14/4/16		Situation normal. Our guns did not fire during night 13/14. Enemy during went right across with but fainter. Casualties:- nil	JWS
Court Dreve	15/4/16		A few whizzbangs & a few heavy shells fired at Rossignol. Our guns did some indirect fire. Casualties:- nil	JWS
COURT DREVE	16/4/16		Situation normal. Chateau shelled with whizzbangs and H.E. Casualties:- nil	JWS

WAR DIARY
or
INTELLIGENCE SUMMARY.
(Erase heading not required.)

Instructions regarding War Diaries and Intelligence Summaries are contained in F. S. Regs., Part II. and the Staff Manual respectively. Title pages will be prepared in manuscript.

Place	Date	Hour	Summary of Events and Information	Remarks and references to Appendices
COURT DREVE	17/4/16		Some whizbangs at Rosignol, "C" locality shelled. Casualties - nil.	
COURT DREVE	18/4/16		Chateau & "C" locality shelled with H.E. & whizbangs. Mr Hancock arrived back from leave night of 17/18/4/16. In evening, Mr Wright & Mr Hancock went over our front, and decided on places for two new gun positions, exact sights to be chosen later. Casualties - nil.	
COURT DREVE	19/4/16		Mr Hancock relieved Mr Morrison our 8 teams returned. Our 8 teams in the line. "C" locality very heavily shelled, got permission from the Brigade to move gun to another part, on conditions that we had the same field of fire. Chateau whizbanged & also a few H.E's came over. Casualties — nil	
COURT DREVE	20/4/16		8 teams relieved our sight of our teams in the line, Mr Hancock relieved Mr Morrison "C" locality gun changed to U.14.a.5.8½. Casualties - nil.	

INTELLIGENCE SUMMARY.

(Erase heading not required.)

Instructions regarding War Diaries and Intelligence Summaries are contained in F. S. Regs., Part II. and the Staff Manual respectively. Title pages will be prepared in manuscript.

Place	Date	Hour	Summary of Events and Information	Remarks and references to Appendices
COURT DREVE	21/4/16		Too wet for satisfactory working parties, scratched the men. Situation normal - Casualties - nil.	JWS
COURT DREVE	22/4/16		WINTER TRENCH was wheyhanged 8 to 8.30am and 132 8.30 to 9.30am. Very wet day and night interfered with work. Quite quiet on whole. First brig'de relieved Rgt Gardie in RIGHT SECTOR last night. All available men at work at night. Casualties - Nil	JWS
COURT DREVE	23/4/16		Some artillery activity. Enemy shelled 128 & 129 at 8.30 & 9am. SEAFORTH FARM, 131 & close farm, shelled 1-15am to 2am. HEATH TRENCH whey hanged 8 to 8.30am. DEAD COW shelled about 2.30pm. All available N.C.O.S and men sent up to West bridge at night to work on M.G. Emplacements and digging drains. Casualties Nil.	JWS
COURT DREVE	24/4/16		Went round "A" locality with 1st Bn & 26th Bde troops. 20.15 Pde decided to have a gun in N.14.a.B.S.	

WAR DIARY
or
INTELLIGENCE SUMMARY.
(Erase heading not required.)

Army Form C. 2118.

Instructions regarding War Diaries and Intelligence Summaries are contained in F. S. Regs., Part II. and the Staff Manual respectively. Title pages will be prepared in manuscript.

Place	Date	Hour	Summary of Events and Information	Remarks and references to Appendices
COURT DREVE	24/4/18	7.35am	A German aeroplane was brought down by our Lewis m/c guns S. of PETITE MUNQUE at T.23.d.8.9. Our artillery was active in front of left sector during the day with good effect. The enemy retaliated by firing from 10 noon to 12 pm at LA HUTTE CHATEAU U.14.c.3.6. Enemy machine guns active during the night, firing in RATION FM. wooded area near Hill 63 at U.14.c.3.6 (WEST RISE) to THATCHED COTTAGE all available N.C.O.'s and men of Battalion working on emplacements at night under Lieut Wright after returning out from Hammock. Casualties — nil	SEG
COURT DREVE	25/4/18	9.44am 2.15pm	ROSSIGNOL was slightly shelled. Our artillery reduced MESSINES CHURCH TOWER by 40 FT. at 2.15pm. Working parties up during evening & not harassing or implements thrown etc. Casualties nil	JWB

WAR DIARY
or
INTELLIGENCE SUMMARY.
(Erase heading not required.)

Place	Date	Hour	Summary of Events and Information	Remarks and references to Appendices
COURT DREVE	26/4/16		Constant but desultory fire in ROSSIGNOL area during 48 hrs also on WOOD S of 63 and CREST of HILL from LAHUTTE to FORT RUSSOT. Enemy M.G. active in LOCALITY A and 128 firing from FACTORY PAPEM. M.G. in PETITE DOVE fire along ROSSIGNOL RD and sweep circuit. 1 working party in no mans land covering wounded by 2/Lt. gun near ROSSIGNOL ZEPPELIN Junction MESS RDS at same. Work proceeded on emplacements & drains etc. at night. New officers 2/Lieut Doughty arrived from Base. Casualties— 1 man wounded.	TRB
COURT DREVE	27/4/16		Relief of guns and 6 guns at night. Guns in position in Brigade front as follows:— RIGHT SECTOR: LA HUTTE CHATEAU 2 guns. A (LOCALITY) 1 gun. ONLY WAY 1 gun. LEFT SECTOR – U.14.A.1.7. and 2 m. O'CLOCK TH HAYSTACK POSITION U.14.A.3.8. 1L ROSSIGNOL U.13.b ¾ ? 1 gun. WINTER TRENCH 1 gun. Officers – RIGHT SECTOR — 2/Lieut Harrison and 2/Lieut Doughty. LEFT SECTOR: 2/Lieut Hancock. ONLY WAY gun 16.0/11 was shelled at 6.30 p.m. 2 D.R. Reinforcements arrived from Base. Casualties. NIL	SRB

WAR DIARY
or
INTELLIGENCE SUMMARY.
(Erase heading not required.)

Instructions regarding War Diaries and Intelligence Summaries are contained in F. S. Regs., Part II. and the Staff Manual respectively. Title pages will be prepared in manuscript.

Place	Date	Hour	Summary of Events and Information	Remarks and references to Appendices
COURT DREVE	28/4/16		Slight shelling at CHATEAU & ROSIGNOL areas. Half company in fields working on new emplacement and dug out. No alarm during night. Casualties - nil	JW
COURT DREVE	29/4/16		Shelling at CHATEAU and a few whizbangs near ROSIGNOL positions. Work continued on new dug out emplacements at U.14.a.5.9. also on dugout at U.14.a.8.1. & improvements at CHATEAU coach house cellars. Casualties nil.	JW
COURT DREVE	30/4/16		GAS on front of Brigade on left. Some shelling between Louis 1am & 3am night 29/30th. Our working parties got back safely. Work in progress on dugout at U.14.a.8.1. and at U.14.a.5.9. A few shells near CHATEAU. Casualties - nil	JW

17th Brigade.
24th Division.

17th MACHINE GUN COMPANY.

May. 1916

Army Form C. 2118.

WAR DIARY
or
INTELLIGENCE SUMMARY.
(Erase heading not required.)

Instructions regarding War Diaries and Intelligence Summaries are contained in F.S. Regs., Part II. and the Staff Manual respectively. Title pages will be prepared in manuscript.

Place	Date	Hour	Summary of Events and Information	Remarks and references to Appendices
COURT DREVE	1st May/16		Work in progress, the position at U.14.a.2.9., and FORWARD ESTAMINET, the half company in billets went into the line & work on above from dusk to midnight. One of our guns at the CHATEAU fired on the MESSINES ROAD between hours 12 midnight (1st/2nd) and 1 a.m. Casualties – nil	M.G.7
COURTE DREVE	2/6/16		Work progressing a position U 14 a. & 9 and FORWARD EST. working parties at night sent up from billets. Casualties – nil	E.G.8
COURTE DREVE	3/6/16		LE ROSSIGNOL shelled intermittently from 11.30 am to 12.50 pm with H.E. between 12.5 am & 1 am. Machine guns at PETITE DOUVE ray action on North 135 & North 734 at 9.45 pm Usual working parties from billets working at U.14.a.2.9. and FORWARD EST. work nearly completed. Casualties – nil	E.G.8

T2134. Wt. W708–776. 500000. 4/15. Sir J.C. & S.

Army Form C. 2118.

WAR DIARY
or
INTELLIGENCE SUMMARY.
(Erase heading not required.)

Instructions regarding War Diaries and Intelligence Summaries are contained in F. S. Regs., Part II. and the Staff Manual respectively. Title pages will be prepared in manuscript.

Place	Date	Hour	Summary of Events and Information	Remarks and references to Appendices
COURTE DREVE	4/6/16		Situation normal. Enemy machine guns very active at "Stand To" in the morning. Enemy aircraft active during the day. One of our planes was attacked by 4 hostile planes who however behind the enemy lines. Company relief at night. Lieut Grindle and 4 teams relieved Lieut Moulden in RIGHT SECTOR. Lieut Fancourt remained in LEFT SECTOR and teams were relieved. Teams which were relieved in LEFT SECTOR remained behind to work on shafts and stood at U.14.a & q. Trench requires incessant revetting, otherwise dugouts and listening-posts fall in. Casualties:- Nil	SRB
COURTE DREVE	5/6/16		Situation normal. Working party employed on trench & dug-out at U.14.a.t.q. Casualties Nil	SRB.

WAR DIARY
or
INTELLIGENCE SUMMARY.
(Erase heading not required.)

Army Form C. 2118.

Place	Date	Hour	Summary of Events and Information	Remarks and references to Appendices
COURTE DREVE	6/5/16		Stables of LA HUTTE CHRV were shelled with a few 6" shells. Enemy M.G. fired on the CHATEAU most of the night from its position of LA PETITE DOUVE U.8.A.9.2.5. and from about U.9.C.2.3. This probably in retaliation for our gun firing on MESSINES 20. Working Party from billets working on tank & dug out at V.14.9.2.9. Casualties - Nil.	GRS
COURT DREVE	7/5/16		A few shells near ROSIGNOL position, & STABLES of LA HUTTE. A few 5.9's and whizz-bangs. One of our guns at CHATEAU fired on MESSINES ROAD. Work proceeding in billets on large dugout for gun stores. Casualties - nil.	GWS
COURT DREVE	8/5/16		2nd LIEUT. E. W. WALLACE joined from M.G. Corps. LA HUTTE STABLES lightly shelled with 5.9's throughout our guns firing again on MESSINES ROAD. Live enemy M.G. fire Work proceeding in billets - Casualties - Nil	GWS

WAR DIARY or INTELLIGENCE SUMMARY

Army Form C. 2118.

Place	Date	Hour	Summary of Events and Information	Remarks and references to Appendices
COURT DREVE	9/5/16		CHATEAU STABLES (LA HUTTE) shelled slightly. Work proceeded on dugout in hillside. A carrying party working overtime to gather for new emplacement. Casualties – nil	NWD
COURT DREVE	10/5/16		CHATEAU (LA HUTTE) had one or two whizzbangs, also positions near a locality to only way. Our artillery fired some rounds in many trenches in PETITE DOUVE vicinity. We fired on the approaches to PETITE DOUVE to catch & retain parties during the following night (15/11 N) All communications nil. Casualties – nil	NW
COURT DREVE	11/5/16		CHATEAU grounds shelled slightly. Working party on carrying to new emplacement. Casualties – nil.	
COURT DREVE	12/5/16		CHATEAU grounds shelled. Dugout at CHATEAU & STABLES worked on & considered strong enough to stop a S.9. Emplacement completed in front of towards ESTAMINET on ASH ROAD – Casualties – 1 wounded.	

Army Form C. 2118.

WAR DIARY
or
INTELLIGENCE SUMMARY.
(Erase heading not required.)

Instructions regarding War Diaries and Intelligence Summaries are contained in F. S. Regs., Part II. and the Staff Manual respectively. Title pages will be prepared in manuscript.

Place	Date	Hour	Summary of Events and Information	Remarks and references to Appendices
COURT DREVE	13/5/16		Situation Normal. Casualties - nil.	JW
COURT DREVE	14/5/16		CHATEAU grounds shelled. Casualties - nil	JW
COURT DREVE	15/5/16		CHATEAU + grounds hit a few times. troops. Casualties - nil	JW
COURT DREVE	16/5/16		Situation normal. Germans in trenches relieved - no shelling party. Casualties - nil.	JW
COURT DREVE	17/5/16		A few shells near ROSIGNOL - also near CHATEAU + STABLES & LA HUTTE. Work proceeding on New emplacement near ROSIGNOL U.13.B.1.5. CASUALTIES - nil.	JW
COURT DREVE	18/5/16		Situation normal - emplacement at U.13.B.1.5 completed. Sir Willis & Major reports to artillery. Casualties - nil	JW

WAR DIARY
or
INTELLIGENCE SUMMARY.
(Erase heading not required.)

Army Form C. 2118.

Place	Date	Hour	Summary of Events and Information	Remarks and references to Appendices
COURTE DREVE	19/5/16		Hill 68 and LA HUTTE shelled intermittently during early afternoon. Enemy M.G. less active. "Casualties": Nil	S.R.B.
COURTE DREVE	20/5/16		Situation normal. "Casualties": Nil	S.R.B.
COURTE DREVE	21/5/16		Enemy shelled approach road, 15Pr. battery close to Lieut. Miller with H.E. shrapnel at 4.7 from 7am till 5pm. STRAFED GREY FM. O.9.B.5.0. 9 pm S.S.E of Hut with 3 guns for about half which 9 and 10 at night, enemy shell not retaliate. "Casualties": Nil	S.R.B. / S.R.B.
COURTE DREVE	22/5/16		Situation Normal. A few whizzbangs fell near ROSSIGNOL area 2.6/150km. "Casualties": Nil	

Army Form C. 2118.

WAR DIARY
or
INTELLIGENCE SUMMARY.
(Erase heading not required.)

Instructions regarding War Diaries and Intelligence Summaries are contained in F. S. Regs., Part II. and the Staff Manual respectively. Title pages will be prepared in manuscript.

Place	Date	Hour	Summary of Events and Information	Remarks and references to Appendices
COURTE DREVE	23/5/16		Situation Normal. LA HUTE CH^U shelled in morning with about 10 4.2". Casualties nil	
COURTE DREVE	24/5/16		Situation Normal. Company relief at night. Extra gun put in FORWARD EST V.14.A.6.1.4 and 1 gun put in new position at V.14.A.9.2.8.5. Gun manned by Coy. Guns in new position 9a. Casualties - Nil	T.R.B.
COURTE DREVE	25/5/16		Situation Normal. Carrying parties at night to CHATEAU FORWARD EST work started on strafing position at V.13.D.6.7 and dug out in ONLY WAY POSITION. Casualties - Nil	T.R.B.
COURTE DREVE	26/5/16		Enemy's artillery active in front and entrenching line Dug out in ONLY WAY POSITION completed and strafing position continued. Casualties: Nil	T.R.B.

Army Form C. 2118.

WAR DIARY
or
INTELLIGENCE SUMMARY.
(Erase heading not required.)

Instructions regarding War Diaries and Intelligence Summaries are contained in F. S. Regs., Part II. and the Staff Manual respectively. Title pages will be prepared in manuscript.

Place	Date	Hour	Summary of Events and Information	Remarks and references to Appendices
COURTE DREVE	24/5/16		ROSSIGNOL shelled with whizzbangs and 4.2 between 6.30 am and 11 am at longish intervals. M.G. emplacement started near HYDE PARK CORNER (I.19.B.2.6.) Casualties :- Nil	JBB.
COURTE DREVE	26/5/16		Situation normal. 2/Lieut Jones was thrown from his horse in the afternoon and fractured his hip. T8in; he was admitted to the Cavalry clearing station. Casualties :- Nil	JBB.
COURTE DREVE	29/5/16		Situation normal. Took half the Company out at next into the open country and did a General scheme supporting advance over infantry etc; then regain much practice in tactical handling and use of cover. HYDE PARK CORNER Emplacement progressing. Casualties: Nil	JBB.
COURTE DREVE	30/5/16		Enemy's artillery active on front line & on SUBSIDIARY LINE E. of ROSSIGNOL and ROSSIGNOL during the day. An M.G. started 'MESSINES road & LOOP E. of Road & ASH ROAD. Work continuing in Emplacement S. of HYDE PARK CORNER & near CHATEAU LA HUTTE Casualties : Nil	JBB.

T2134. Wt. W708—776. 500000. 4/15. Sir J. C. & S.

Army Form C. 2118.

WAR DIARY
or
INTELLIGENCE SUMMARY.

(Erase heading not required.)

Place	Date	Hour	Summary of Events and Information	Remarks and references to Appendices
COURTE DREVE	31/5/16		Situation Normal. Our M.G. stationed as usual MESSINES road, GREY FARM, V.9.B.6.0. and vicinity has also fired upon from the gun at LA HUTE CHATEAU. Lots happening in the HYDE PARK CORNER Gun Placement & Emplacement near LA HUTE CAB". Casualties Nil	SK5.

17th Brigade.
24th Division.

17th MACHINE GUN COMPANY.

June 1916

11 Bde M G Coy

WAR DIARY or INTELLIGENCE SUMMARY

Army Form C. 2118.

(Erase heading not required.)

Place	Date	Hour	Summary of Events and Information	Remarks and references to Appendices
COURTE DREVE	Feb 1/6/16		Company relief. Officers in RIGHT SECTOR:- Lieut Goudie & 2/Lieut Phillips. LEFT SECTOR:- 2/Lieut Morrison & 2/Lieut Wallace. Two working parties sent up at night.	22B
COURTE DREVE	2/6/16		Situation normal. Working parties sent up from Hdqrs. Also working parties to work on CHATEAU STRAFING POSITION and emplacement near HYDE PARK CORNER behind firing trenches not far from the CHATEAU STABLES in the MESSINES ROAD and from LE ROSSIGNOL to BLACK SHED V.15. a. 5. 8. and on GREY FARM vicinity of TILLEUL FARM and trench ref:- P.9.8.6.0.	22B
COURTE DREVE	3/6/16		ONLY WAY, ADVANCED EST. and CHATEAU STABLES were shelled during today. Work proceeded with the STRAFING POSITION near CHATEAU & in HYDE PARK CORNER POSITION. 2nd Lieut Stevens & Cpl Fry received [illegible] extinguishing it. Cpl Fry killed before reaching it.	8BB
COURTE DREVE	4/6/16	12.30am	72nd Bde on left of Div. front carried out a raid on enemy's line entering an artillery 22B opened strongly & had place the hyperbole. Enemy retaliated with trench mortars. Casualties:- 1 man killed (WINTER TRENCH)	

WAR DIARY or INTELLIGENCE SUMMARY

Army Form C. 2118.

Place	Date	Hour	Summary of Events and Information	Remarks and references to Appendices
COURTE DREVE	5/6/16		Situation normal. Working party sent up at night from Villa took down emplacement of HYDE PARK CORNER and erected a strafe behind of U.13.D.9.3.7. Casualties: Nil	SRB
COURTE DREVE	6/6/16		Quiet day. Usual working parties sent up at night. Casualties Nil	SRB
COURTE DREVE	7/6/16		LA HUTTE STABLES shelled as usual during the day. Dugout frame put in near "A" LOCALITY POSITION and STRAFING POSITION U.13.D.7.7 completed. Casualties: nil	SRB
COURTE DREVE	8/6/16		Situation normal but enemy's artillery fairly active along whole front on brigade front. Work carried on as usual in the line. Casualties: Nil	SRB

WAR DIARY or INTELLIGENCE SUMMARY

Army Form C. 2118.

Place	Date	Hour	Summary of Events and Information	Remarks and references to Appendices
COURTE DEULE	9/6/16		FORWARD ESTAMINET shelled during the day and "cook hole" is in ruins. Gun position just in rear intact. Company relief at night. 'A' Coy Gun relieving FORWARD ESTABLISHED and remainder of Cellars relieved from half Company in Lille "Visitor's" Lining & Framework took over RIGHT SECTOR & "Stile Hoven" took over LEFT SECTOR. Casualties: – Nil	
COURTE DEULE	10/6/16		Situation normal – but word "LEFT SECTOR at night-which sent tonight. Casualties :- Nil	
COURT DEULE	10/6/16		Sgt. Naugh recommended for continuous & devotion to duty during attack in Craters at ST. ELOI – 30th – 31st October 1915, and also for gallant good work. Sgt. Whitley recommended for the skilful handling of his team during attack on VERMELLES – 17th – 18th March 1916 & general good work. Sgt. Ridley & Sgt. Greenwood for vigilance & ability & Cpl. & L.Cpl W.G.S. recommended for M. Gr.	

T2134. Wt. W708–776. 500000. 4/15. Sir J. C. & S.

Army Form C. 2118.

WAR DIARY
or
INTELLIGENCE SUMMARY.
(Erase heading not required.)

Place	Date	Hour	Summary of Events and Information	Remarks and references to Appendices
COURTE DREVE	11/6/16		Situation normal. Casualties - nil	(MW)
COURTE DREVE	12/6/16		Work interrupted owing to rain. Situation normal. Casualties - nil	MW
COURTE DREVE	13/6/16		Work interrupted owing to rain. Situation normal. Casualties - nil	MW
COURTE DREVE	14/6/16		No night work in line owing to rain. Situation normal. Casualties - nil	MW
COURTE DREVE	15/6/16		Gun emplacement covering ground around Hyde Park Corner completed. Situation normal. Casualties - nil	MW
COURTE DREVE	16/6/16		Weather has cleared up. Work proceeding on dugouts in "A" locality. New emplacement being put in on same place. Work was interrupted during the night 16/17 by shelling and gas. Troops in COURT DREVE having to stand to for some time. Some of the horses were affected by the gas but otherwise the Company did not suffer much inconvenience.	MW

WAR DIARY
or
INTELLIGENCE SUMMARY.
(Erase heading not required.)

Army Form C. 2118.

Hour, Date, Place	Summary of Events and Information	Remarks and References to Appendices
COURTE DREVE 16/6/16	The [?] men behaved splendidly, staying near entrance & a ready response to orders. Casualties during the night (16/17) one slightly wounded + two slightly gassed	(MD)
COURTE DREVE 17/6/16	Slight shelling of trenches of COURT DREVE. 2nd Lt Walker and teams relieved 2nd Lt Morrison + teams on left sector. 2nd Lt Gordon & 2nd Lt Miller and teams relieved 2nd Lt Irving & Handcock & teams in right sector. Casualties - nil	(MD)
COURTE DREVE 18/6/16	2nd Lt [?] transferred to-day. 2nd & Lt. Irving has received promotion in the Regt. and is now Lt. During night 18/19 9th Manch. relieved but none came over. Situation normal Casualties - nil	(MD)

WAR DIARY
or
INTELLIGENCE SUMMARY.
(Erase heading not required.)

Army Form C. 2118.

Hour, Date, Place	Summary of Events and Information	Remarks and References to Appendices
COURTE DREVE 19/6/16.	Situation Normal. Work on a dugout in "A" locality proceeding. Casualties - nil.	MWD
COURTE DREVE 20/6/16.	Situation Normal. Work on a dugout in "A" locality proceeding. Casualties - nil.	MWD
COURTE DREVE 21/6/16.	Went round the night sector with O/c 2nd Australian Brigade M.G.C. showing him all the gun positions. Situation - Normal.	MWD
COURTE DREVE 22/6/16.	Slight shelling in vicinity of Billets in the early morning & rather heavier eastward later. 2nd Lt Wallace was relieved by Lt Doran & one Australian Officer and Lt Gill was relieved by an Australian Officer. This to allow the 2nd Australians to get an idea of the line. Casualties - One wounded.	MWD

Army Form C. 2118.

WAR DIARY
or
INTELLIGENCE SUMMARY.
(Erase heading not required.)

Instructions regarding War Diaries and Intelligence Summaries are contained in F.S. Regs., Part II. and the Staff Manual respectively. Title pages will be prepared in manuscript.

Hour, Date, Place	Summary of Events and Information	Remarks and references to Appendices
COURT DREVE 23/6/16	Slight shelling in vicinity of billets. Weather warm. Other time with the 2nd Australian M.G.C. situation normal. Casualties – nil.	[initials]
COURT DREVE 24/6/16	Relief by 2nd Australian M.G.C. proceeded during the day and nights 24/25. 2nd finish up without hitch. Casualties – nil.	[initials]
X.S.C.3.S. 25/6/16 Belg. + France sheet 28.	Brigade party arrived here after march through Bailleul from our billets. No work was done owing to late of men during night 24/25. Casualties – nil.	[initials]
X.S.C.3.S. 26/6/16	Drawing & stores proceeding. Nothing unusual to state. Casualties – nil.	[initials]
X.S.C.3.S. 27/6/16	Drawing stores proceeding. Returned 7 men arranged for 6 M.G.C. men for further training on 28th (5 men not Casualties – nil.	[initials]
M.30.b.3.4 28/6/16 Bel. + France sheet 28	Moved from X.S.C.3.S. without incident or hitch. 8 ⇉ Reinforcements from base. Casualties – nil. [initials]	[initials]

Army Form C. 2118.

WAR DIARY
or
INTELLIGENCE SUMMARY.
(Erase heading not required.)

Instructions regarding War Diaries and Intelligence Summaries are contained in F. S. Regs, Part II. and the Staff Manual respectively. Title pages will be prepared in manuscript.

Hour, Date, Place	Summary of Events and Information	Remarks and References to Appendices
M. 30. b. 3. 4. 29/6/15	Training & drills proceeding with men. We had to "Stand to" during the night but nothing happened to alarm us. Casualties – nil.	MW.
M. 30. b. 3. 4. 30/6/15	Reconnoitred new line, gun positions left sector, and for line roughly N.33. 34. 35. 36. centres. In the left sector gun positions were non-existent, but there were a few dugouts. In the right sector gun positions were fair & the dugouts were strong. The whole sector offers positions for M.G. emplacements & the ground would easily be defended by M.G. Capt. Birch arrived back this evening from a further reinforcement of 1½ men arriving from Canada – Nil. I arrive in good health.	MW.

Forms/C. 2118/11.

17th Inf.Bde.
24th Div.

WAR DIARY

17th MACHINE GUN COMPANY.

J U L Y

1 9 1 6

WAR DIARY or INTELLIGENCE SUMMARY.

(Erase heading not required.)

Army Form 2118.

17 M.G Coy July

Hour, Date, Place	Summary of Events and Information	Remarks and references to Appendices
1/7/16 M.30 & 34	Company business carried out during day. Sent knight and self reconnoitred part of LEFT BDE SECTOR (N 25.D.9.5 – N.29.D.8.4) with a view to taking over from the 93rd Bde M.G.C. Casualties - Nil	Telephone (V.1) IRB.
2/7/16 N 31 B 3.5	Took over milletry from 72nd Bn M.G.C. (N 31.B.3.5) took over Bn Sector (N 36.A.6.2 – N.29.D.9.3.6.2) LEFT SECTOR 6 guns & teams. 2/Lieuts Horworth & Miller. RIGHT SECTOR 4 guns & teams under 2/Lieut Morrison Casualties - nil.	IRB (important boars) (Ref S.5. B.3.5)
3/7/16 N.31 B 3.5	Situation normal. Went round both sections during day. Gun in front line (N0 5 section) relieved by gun of 15th R.F. 9 guns of the company now in the line. Casualties - Nil	IRB.

Army Form C. 2118.

WAR DIARY
or
INTELLIGENCE SUMMARY.
(Erase heading not required.)

Instructions regarding War Diaries and Intelligence Summaries are contained in F.S. Regs., Part II. and the Staff Manual respectively. Title pages will be prepared in manuscript.

Hour, Date, Place	Summary of Events and Information	Remarks and references to Appendices
4/9/16 N31.B.5.5.	Situation normal. Quiet bright morning & in the line of communication trenches. 2nd Lieut Goodchild relieved 2nd Lieut Miller in LEFT SECTOR. 2nd Lieut Miller returned to Wilts. Company training, firing on range &c. Carried out during day. Very heavy rain at night. Casualties – Nil.	I.R.B.
5/9/16 N31.B.5.5.	In LEFT SECTOR about 50 minenwerfer were fired on F.5 retaliation was given by 60 kilo howitzer F.6. Company training carried out in billets & firing on the ranges. Casualties – Nil.	I.R.B.
6/9/16 N31.B.5.5.	Artillery put up a Barrage between R.E. FARM & KINGSWAY on our place on night of 5/6th and shrapnelled front line trench ; the barrage itself was of heavy shell (5.9)	

Forms/C. 2118/11

Army Form C. 2118.

WAR DIARY
or
INTELLIGENCE SUMMARY.
(Erase heading not required.)

Hour, Date, Place	Summary of Events and Information	Remarks and references to Appendices
6/9/16 N31.B½.5	M.G. action during night. 2/Lieut Wallace left for HAZEBROUCK for 2 weeks rest, having suffered through shell shock. Casualties. Nil	JRB.
7/9/16 N31.B½.5	Situation normal. Lieut Laming left for 150th Bde. M.G. Coy, having been transferred. Lieut Knight and self went from 2nd Army Lieut Knight and self went round right sector in evening, managed into O.C. 3rd R.B. (M.R. Laws gun to 4 place in bow) Autumn SHELL FM nr SP7 (M29.B.9.2). 2/Lieut Morrison came out of line to take over No. 4 Section during Company retirement this hollow. Casualties. Nil	JRB.

WAR DIARY or INTELLIGENCE SUMMARY

Army Form C. 2118.

(Erase heading not required.)

Instructions regarding War Diaries and Intelligence Summaries are contained in F.S. Regs., Part II. and the Staff Manual respectively. Title pages will be prepared in manuscript.

Hour, Date, Place	Summary of Events and Information	Remarks and references to Appendices
6/7/16. N.31.B.½.5.	Lieut Wright and self went up to line in morning to reconnoitre ground on left of 15th sects. Received orders to place two guns behind batteries on right of our Brigade which are at 26th Australian Bn. 12th R.F. relieved this Bn at night and our two guns were placed in PORT PINKIE MT.5.B.8.6. One gun without team, but to 12th R.F. Three batteries of the 19th R.M. now in the line from right to left as follows: 12th R.F. 3rd R.B. 1st R.F. Line held by Bde. from T.6.6.8 to N.24.B.0.5. Lieut Miller with half section in PORT PINKIE. Casualties Nil.	SRB.
6/7/16. N.31.B.½.5.	During afternoon enemy shelled from N.32.B.2.5. N.32.B.1.5. E of the [A.Q. with 4.2 and 6 inch, the shear dropped HE shrapnel in this vicinity. Lieut Wright and self went up to [illegible] in evening	

WAR DIARY
or
INTELLIGENCE SUMMARY.
(Erase heading not required.)

Army Form C. 2118.

Instructions regarding War Diaries and Intelligence Summaries are contained in F. S. Regs., Part II. and the Staff Manual respectively. Title pages will be prepared in manuscript.

Hour, Date, Place	Summary of Events and Information	Remarks and references to Appendices
9/7/16. N.31.B.½.5.	2nd visited FORT PINKIE T.5.B.9½.5". Casualties - Nil	T.R.B.
10/7/16. N.31.B.½.5.	3rd Rifle Brigade carried out a raid at night on enemy's front line in front of BULL RING (N.36.a.5.0) Lieut Wright in charge. Two guns kept up a flanking fire on the right & left of raid whilst it took place. 4 officers and 11 of the enemy were killed. Casualties in B Company during raid were 3 Lieut Patten killed. Men — Casualties in company — Nil	T.R.B.
11/7/16. N.31.B.½.5.	Wind Mills & Guns in FORT PINKIE relieved by 7.5th M.G.C. Also SHELL FARM line relieved Casualties: Nil	T.R.B.

WAR DIARY
or
INTELLIGENCE SUMMARY.
(Erase heading not required.)

Army Form C. 2118.

Hour, Date, Place	Summary of Events and Information	Remarks and references to Appendices
12/7/16. N.31.B.½.5.	Situation normal. Received orders to take over FORT REGINA (ref N.28.8½.4½) and S.P.10 (ref N.29.A.6.4½). Sent Mission to hire teams & guns, took over their positions at night. Sent guns now in the line of destination, 2 and half of 4. DRANOUTRE SHELLED. Casualties:- Nil in enemy with 11.6-9 between 6.30 & 8.45 pm.	JRB.
13/7/16 N.31 B.½ 5.	Situation normal. 17th R.F. relieved 13th R.F. in LEFT BDE sector. Casualties:- Nil	JRB.
14/7/16 N.31.B.½ 5.	Situation normal. Section 3 (Lewis Smith) relieved Section 1 (Lieut Grylls) in RIGHT SECTOR and 1 gun of No 2 Section (Lieut Murdoch) in S.P.8 (LEFT SECTOR) & 1 gun in FRENCHMANS Fm half of N0.4 Section (Lt Manning) relieved remaining half section of N0.1 Section Casualties:- nil	JRB.

WAR DIARY or INTELLIGENCE SUMMARY

Army Form C. 2118.

(Erase heading not required.)

Hour, Date, Place	Summary of Events and Information	Remarks and references to Appendices
15/7/16 N.31.B.3.5	Situation normal. Much work being done on the line in dug-outs & emplacements. Enemy bright in charge of work in north sector. Our artillery active all the day cutting German wire. Casualties Nil.	SKB
16/7/16 N.31.B.3.5	Enemy bright lately responded to the fire a whistle firing a gun at enemy's front line in front of sector held by 12th R.F. (night 16/17th July) Our artillery active during day cutting enemy's wire. Casualties: Evis 1 bright wounded.	2RB
17/7/16 N.31.B.3.5	Enemy Morrison badly wounded in left arm by shrapnel in front line shell by 12th D.F. Seven graphi bits over right sector & little change of guns. In the evening which fired before & after the bombardment of R.F.C. raided enemy's trenches. Raid was successful to 14 of the enemy were reported killed. 17th R.F. had our officer wounded & missing, one officer wounded & 5 other casualties.	

WAR DIARY
or
INTELLIGENCE SUMMARY.
(Erase heading not required.)

Army Form C. 2118.

Hour, Date, Place	Summary of Events and Information	Remarks and references to Appendices
18/7/16 N.31.B.5.6	2/Lieut Morrison had his left arm amputated at No 2. C.C.S BILLEUL. M.O. reports satisfactory progress of this officer. Company now 5 officers under strength. Mines trenched & self heat round line in afternoon & evening; found work progressing favourably. Casualties 1 - 2nd	J.R.B.
19/7/16 N.31.B.5	About 1 p.m. received sudden orders that the Bde was to be relieved by the 151 Bde (1st Canadian). Captain Grieve O.C. 151 Bde. M.G.C. came round to discuss relief. Relief completed 19th 20th July. Casualties - Nil	J.R.B.
20/7/16 N.31.B.5	Brigade and Company moved to vicinity of ST JEAN CAPPEL. Conditions. Nil	J.R.B.
21/7/16. ST JEAN	In billet camp; with Kemmey. 2/Lieut Pouting from 73rd M.G.C. reported for duty & posted to No. 4 Sect.	J.R.B.

WAR DIARY
or
INTELLIGENCE SUMMARY.

(Erase heading not required.)

Army Form C. 2118.

Instructions regarding War Diaries and Intelligence Summaries are contained in F. S. Regs., Part II. and the Staff Manual respectively. Title pages will be prepared in manuscript.

Hour, Date, Place	Summary of Events and Information	Remarks and references to Appendices
22/7/16. ST JEAN CAPPEL.	Change billets & move about 4 kilometres S.E. G.O.C. visited company and passed and informed me that he had given instructions for more officers to be posted to the company when attached men.	7K8.
23/7/16. MEUT BOOM.	Lieut. J. Baker from 89th M.G.C. reported for duty with company, posted to Command No 4 section. 2nd Lieut Peacock performing duties of 2nd in Command. Section leaving practice in attack etc.	7K8.
24/7/16. RIENCOURT	Entrain at 6 am at BAILLEUL for AMIENS. Arrived at LONGEAU at 6 pm. After two hours rest march to RIENCOURT a distance of 16 miles. First Hancock 2/Point Portugal O.M.S. when in advance to find billets. Company marched well one man at REST CORPL at about 4.30 am on 25/7/16.	7K8.

Army Form C. 2118.

WAR DIARY
or
INTELLIGENCE SUMMARY.
(Erase heading not required.)

Instructions regarding War Diaries and Intelligence Summaries are contained in F. S. Regs., Part II. and the Staff Manual respectively. Title pages will be prepared in manuscript.

Hour, Date, Place	Summary of Events and Information	Remarks and references to Appendices
25/7/16 RIENCOURT	Bn. HQ & Battalions in vicinity of RIENCOURT. Training carried on with	SPB
26/7/16 RIENCOURT	Lieut H.A. Smith from M.G.C. Base Depôt reported for duty with Company & placed in command of No 2 Section	SPB.
27/7/16 RIENCOURT	Training	SPB
28/7/16 RIENCOURT	Training	SPB.
29/7/16 RIENCOURT	32 men from the 4 Bns in the Bde attached to the company about 10 trained men amongst them who were reported to sections remainder unattached	SPB.

Army Form C. 2118.

WAR DIARY
or
INTELLIGENCE SUMMARY.
(Erase heading not required.)

Instructions regarding War Diaries and Intelligence Summaries are contained in F. S. Regs., Part II. and the Staff Manual respectively. Title pages will be prepared in manuscript.

Hour, Date, Place	Summary of Events and Information	Remarks and references to Appendices
30/7/16 RIENCOURT	2/Lieut. Jones reported for duty from M.G.C. Base Depôt. Transport returned to horse lines last night & under Bn. Transport Officer marched at 8 pm for BOIS DES TAILLES. 2/Lieut Jacks attached to us from 1st D.L.I. ordered to rejoin unit officers number 9.	SRB
31/7/16 BOIS DES TAILLES (K 12. B SHEET. 62 b	Company marched to PICQUINY at 7am and at 7/10 am entrained for MERICOURT. Detrained at MERICOURT at 2.30 pm & marched to BOIS DES TAILLES. Rush finally hot & trying day & several men fell out on late of march. Lost men afterwards admitted to 2/W Ambulance. Reached BOIS DES TAILLES at about 6.30 pm. Informed that we to be prepared to be ready by 5 am SPLIT $\frac{1}{2}$ (E.18.D. Juckhut) 62 DWS	SRB

17th Brigade.
24th Division.

17th MACHINE GUN COMPANY.

August 1916

"A" Form.
MESSAGES AND SIGNALS.

Army Form C. 2121.

TO: DAG 3rd Echelon GHQ

Sender's Number: MG 49
Day of Month: 15/9

AAA

Herewith War diary for August 1st - 31st. Regret delay.

ORIGINAL COPY

From: 17th M.G. Coy.

Army Form C. 2118.

17 M G C

WAR DIARY
or
INTELLIGENCE SUMMARY.
(Erase heading not required.)

Hour, Date, Place	Summary of Events and Information	Remarks and references to Appendices
SAND PIT (E.18.D) 1st August 1916	Marched from BOIS DES TAILLES to SAND PIT. Company in tents & bivouacs. Cpl Buckley evacuated to hospital.	SKS
SAND PIT (E.18.D) 2nd August	Brigade at rest. Company training carried out	SRB
SAND PIT (E.18.D) 3rd August	Brigade at rest.	SRB
SAND PIT (E.18.D) 4th August — 7th August	Brigade at rest. 7th August went up to line for maneuvers ground with a view to relieving 6th Bde M.G.C. 24th Division	SRB
SAND PIT	to hold the line from S. of DELVILLE WOOD (S.18.B.00) to N. half of TROVES WOOD (S.24.C.4.2.) Lieuts Baker & Grooke ?/Lieut Stanwich went up to line. 14 guns to be relieved by Brigade Kitchen C? Bde R/Batt. 2nd Division on night of 8/9 Aug	SKS

Army Form C. 2118.

WAR DIARY
or
INTELLIGENCE SUMMARY.
(Erase heading not required.)

Instructions regarding War Diaries and Intelligence Summaries are contained in F. S. Regs., Part II. and the Staff Manual respectively. Title pages will be prepared in manuscript.

Hour, Date, Place	Summary of Events and Information	Remarks and references to Appendices
Carnoy 8th Aug. 1916	Marched to old German 1st & trenches at Carnoy, in readiness to relieve 1/R.B. at 7½	J.P.
Carnoy 9th Aug. 1916	Relieved 6th M. Reg. in line 8 of Riddle Rd. to 1 half of Loaves 101 with eleven guns 1½ Bates + 1½ Lewis, + three guns in reserve at Bomyfay 101. Lt. Smith Capt. Murray. Pte. Thompson accidentally injured Pte. Thompson.	J.P.
10th Aug 1916 Carnoy	+ am. Got it the guns in the line, + have positions strengthened. Pte. Moore wounded in face	J.P.
11th Aug 1916 Carnoy	Consolidated positions. Pte Barker Gould + two reinforcements from Base Depôt	J.P.

Army Form C. 2118.

WAR DIARY
or
INTELLIGENCE SUMMARY.
(Erase heading not required.)

Hour, Date, Place	Summary of Events and Information	Remarks and references to Appendices
12th Aug 1916 Carnoy	Inspect gun position in morning. Teams relieved at night, 2/Lt Mellor 2/Lt Pountney & 2/Lt Jones 2/Lt Jones, ear drums perforated by bursting shell Casualties Station wounded 8 Fire Pte Mulhearn — Crook	
13 Aug 1916 Carnoy	Inspect guns & positions in morning. One gun badly damaged by shell fire The rest have been heavily shelled Gun ditto nil	
14th August CARNOY	Examined gun position in morning. Lieut Thomas position near WATERLOT FARM (S.18.S.24 central) heavily shelled during day and some have been hit. Gun never of ANGLE TRENCH (S.18.C.7.5) gun is being moved to newly dug trench in front of WATERLOT FARM.	

Army Form C. 2118.

WAR DIARY
or
INTELLIGENCE SUMMARY.
(Erase heading not required.)

Instructions regarding War Diaries and Intelligence Summaries are contained in F.S. Regs., Part II. and the Staff Manual respectively. Title pages will be prepared in manuscript.

Hour, Date, Place	Summary of Events and Information	Remarks and references to Appendices
1916 CARNOY 14th August (continued)	Unit suffered from shell shock admitted to field ambulance (Capt Roman Ean.)	T.R.B.
CARNOY 15th August	Go round the line at 9 a.m. fuel our position knocked in, all positions have been heavily shelled, no guns damaged. Casualties:- Pte. S. Humphreys - found wounded 8 Fusl. Pte. Barlow killed S.F. Reinforcement:- Pte. Hope - S/C Haddow	⚫
Camoy 16 Aug	Our positions wounded Reinforcements Pte. Oakley	Casualties Pte. Haynes	⚫

WAR DIARY
or
INTELLIGENCE SUMMARY.
(Erase heading not required.)

Army Form C. 2118.

Hour, Date, Place	Summary of Events and Information	Remarks and References to Appendices
1916		
CARNOY. 19th August.	Preparation for the attack under, machine gun rations the carried up to the line. Guns in line as follows:— RIGHT SECTOR, under O.C. 8th R.B. 6 guns. Officer Lieut Gardiner. LEFT SECTOR 6 guns under O.C. 8th Buffs, Officer Lieut Hancock & Lieut Baker. Reserve guns. BERNAFAY WOOD - 2 under Lieut Pomeroy. 2 guns back at CRATERS under 2/Lt Wills. Cemetery Nil.	R.B.
2nd R&R CARNOY. 18th August. BERNAFAY WOOD. 2.45 pm— (Coy H.Q.)	1st & 8th B. attacked 8th Buffs on left, 8th R.B. 1 Company 1st R.B. on right. Lieut Gardiner with his section went forward and established position near GUILLEMONT STATION. The Enemy's barrage attended ally & guns great support to the infantry. Lieut A. M. Gardiner was killed while doing very gallant work when badly wounded & under heavy shellfire directing the placing of his gun. Lieut Pomeroy took his place & behaved with great coolness and did good work until wounded on the 21st August after a second attack	R.B.

Army Form C. 2118.

WAR DIARY
or
INTELLIGENCE SUMMARY.
(Erase heading not required.)

Hour, Date, Place	Summary of Events and Information	Remarks and References to Appendices
BERNAFAY WOOD 1916 18th August (Continued)	During afternoon 1 gun & team under Sgt Brown were moved up to SHERWOOD TR. near 3rd R.B. H.Q. Sgt. Brown on both charge of 3 guns & did excellent work. Sergts Marsh & Allen, Cpls Ranger & Brown did splendid work & their teams were also splendid. An LEFT SECTOR 8th Buffs attacked a trench between DELVILLE WOOD & GUILLEMONT. Lieut Baker & 3 guns went forward immediately behind & was taken & took up positions & consolidated, & a gun went up immediately afterwards & / Lieut Honeywood was in charge of all guns in Buffs sector and did very splendid work & was congratulated & recommended by Lt. Lucas O.C. 8th Buffs. Lieut Baker soon after the attack was wounded & / Lieut Miller took his place & did excellent work & showed great coolness & all his actions made him fit. Sgt Whiting was badly wounded during the attack. Sgt Mann, Cpl Townsend Hopkins & Ptes. Boyd, Harris Cannock, Frickers & Knight Gaskell did splendid work.	

WAR DIARY
or
INTELLIGENCE SUMMARY

Army Form C. 2118.

(Erase heading not required.)

Place	Date	Hour	Summary of Events and Information	Remarks and references to Appendices
BERNAFAY WOOD	1916 18th August (contd)		Casualties during day's operations:- Officers killed, Lieut A. M. Gordon. Numerous Lieut. J. Baker. O.R. Killed - 5, Wounded - 12	SRS
Bernafay Wood	19th Aug		Strengthen our new positions, which have been heavily shelled. Casualties, C/S. Oakeville, Pte. Wills, Pte. Wright, Pte. Walker wounded. Pte. W. Rite, Bunc. Reinforcements:-	⚡
Bernafay Wood	20th Aug		One Lyon in action against enemy, who we shelled out of their dug-outs near Guillemont. Casualties:- Pte Crane W. Belam, Mitchell, Oakley Wright, wounded.	⚡
Bernafay Wood	21st Aug		Battalion in our night attack, & we assist with flushing fire from two guns, causing casualties among enemy's reinforcements, coming from two end of Guillemont. Casualties:- 2Lt. Pountenay wounded, Pte Taylor Brown, Warren wounded. Reinforcements:- Cliffe, Foreman, Brown, Coatledge, Storey, Joyce, 2Lt. Wintringham, 2Lt. Hudson, 2Lt. Smith	⚡

WAR DIARY
or
INTELLIGENCE SUMMARY

(Erase heading not required.)

Army Form C. 2118.

Instructions regarding War Diaries and Intelligence Summaries are contained in F. S. Regs., Part II. and the Staff Manual respectively. Title Pages will be prepared in manuscript.

Place	Date	Hour	Summary of Events and Information	Remarks and references to Appendices
Bernafay Wood	22nd Aug 1916		We are relieved at night by 61st Cnj. & move to camp at Happy Valley. Reinforcements :- 2/Lt Gilbert	
Happy Valley	23rd Aug		Inspection of guns & equipment. Reinforcements :- Pte Norman	
Happy Valley	24th Aug		Reinforcements :- L.Cpl Dilley. Pte's Chamlen, Crownshaw, Curd, Cunliffe, Deighton, Dawson, Baylish, Dickinson, Purser, Pickett, Emmett, Foster.	
Nr. Albert D.12.C	25th Aug		We march to camping ground near Albert (D.12.C) & bivouac	
Nr. Albert D.12.C	26 Aug		Reinforcements from Base Dept :- Pte's Jaques, Johnson, McTaggart, Smith, Rogers, Reft, Andrews, Parsons. 2/Lt TD Rite. Rejoined, after being wounded, Pte McAlenny	

2449 Wt. W14957/M90 750,000 1/16 J.B.C. & A. Forms/C.2118/12.

Army Form C. 2118.

WAR DIARY
or
INTELLIGENCE SUMMARY
(Erase heading not required.)

Instructions regarding War Diaries and Intelligence Summaries are contained in F. S. Regs., Part II. and the Staff Manual respectively. Title Pages will be prepared in manuscript.

Place	Date	Hour	Summary of Events and Information	Remarks and references to Appendices
D.13.C. Albert	27th Aug.		Training, Refitting. Sent to Base Depôt, Pte's Mason, Sweeney	✗
D.12.C.	28th Aug		Training. Sent to Base Depôt, Pte Browne, Elliott. Reinforcements :— Ptes Wells, Willett, Wales R. Wilkinson W.2nd	✗ ✗
D.12.C	29th Aug		Training.	
D.12.C	30th Aug		March to Camp near Fricourt, Brigade in reserve, Reinforcements :— Pte's Dooley, Munby, Camberley Smith	✗
Fricourt	31st Aug		In Reserve. Pte Gibson accidentally injured	✗

24th Divn.
G. 320

17th Infantry Brigade.
72nd Infantry Brigade.
73rd Infantry Brigade.

Will you please direct your Brigade Machine Gun Company Commander to write a short account so far as Machine-Guns are concerned of any operations in which your Brigade is engaged.

Special points on which information should be given are :-

Covering fire, protection of flanks, ammunition supply, Long range fire.

This information is required in order that instruction at Machine Gun Schools may be kept up to date.

Please forward any accounts to this Office.

24th Division.
9th August, 1916.   Lieut-Colonel, G.S.,

To Headquarters,
   17th Infantry Brigade.

With reference to the attached, the following notes are submitted of points observed of <u>Machine Guns in the Attack</u>:-

1. <u>The Advance</u> of the Machine Guns of the Company was made as soon as our Infantry had cleared the enemy's trenches, & few casualties occurred in the actual advance as the teams extended in skirmishing order.

2. Objectives were reached without difficulty, as Officers had clearly pointed these out to their teams beforehand.

3. <u>Covering Fire</u> was little used, as the ground was unsuitable.

4. <u>Protection of Flanks</u>. Assistance was given on our left flank by another Brigade, and this Company was able to assist the Brigade on its right, and on one occasion put out of action, from a flank, an enemy machine gun, which was impeding the attack of the infantry on our right.

5. <u>Long Range Fire</u> was not on this occasion brought to bear owing to the nature of the ground.

6. It was found that it is difficult to send back for ammunition, owing to the enemy's barrage, & it is advisable to take over as many belt boxes as possible by the ammunition carriers.

7. <u>Ammunition Carriers</u> should have a knowledge of the Gun, in case of heavy casualties amongst gunners.

8. <u>Liason Officer</u>. It would be advisable to leave an Officer in the jumping off trench, this officer to go round the guns as soon as possible, to collect reports and advise as to the situation.

9. <u>Trained N.C.O's</u> are essential, as in the case of this Company, owing to casualties amongst Officers, some N.C.O's had as many as four guns under their control, with no junior N.C.O's to assist

them, and difficult ground to work over.
10. General Employment of Machine Guns.
It was noticed during the recent operations that Battalion Commanders used Vickers guns freely in advanced trenches, where the work could have been done equally as well by Lewis Guns; the reserve of Vickers Guns was considerably weakened in this way.

E. R. Birch Captain.
O.C. 17th M.G.Co.

August 27th 1916.

Headquarters
24th Division.

In forwarding the attached remarks by O.C. 17th M.G, Company no new points seem to be brought out. I do not however agree with the remarks in para. 10. For securing ground won in an attack against counter-attack a gun capable of more sustained fire than the Lewis is required, and this seems to be essentially the role of the Vickers Guns of the Machine Gun Company.

The idea seems to be becoming too prevalent in Machine Gun Companies that their guns should only be used in back positions.

28/8/16   Brig. General.
                          Commanding 17th Infantry Brigade.

17th Brigade.
24th Division.

17th. MACHINE GUN COMPANY.

September 1916

"A" Form.
MESSAGES AND SIGNALS.
Army Form C. 2121.

TO	D.A.G.	3rd ECHELON		

Sender's Number.	Day of Month	In reply to Number		A A A
*M.G 1/0	30/9/16			

Herewith Original WAR DIARY of the
17th. Machine Gun Coy
From 1st - 30th September 1916

From 17th Machine Gun Coy

(Z) D. Shydd Lieut

Army Form C. 2118.

24/ 17. M.G. Coy

Vol 8

WAR DIARY
or
INTELLIGENCE SUMMARY
(Erase heading not required.)

Instructions regarding War Diaries and Intelligence Summaries are contained in F.S. Regs., Part II. and the Staff Manual respectively. Title Pages will be prepared in manuscript.

Place	Date	Hour	Summary of Events and Information	Remarks and references to Appendices
	1916			
MONTAUBAN	1st Sept		Company in reserve in orchards. 10 guns move into line, relieving 93rd M.G. Coy	
		6 A.M.	(No 3 Section - 2 guns ORCHARD TRENCH - 2 guns R.B. H.Q.) move first	
		5 P.M.	(No 4 Section - 1 gun in front of DELVILLE - 3 guns SAVOY TRENCH)	
		5 P.M.	(No 1 Section - 1 gun WORCESTER TRENCH - 1 gun POND STREET)	
			(No 2 Section and 2 guns No 1 Section in reserve at orchard MONTAUBAN) (6 guns)	JR
		CASUALTIES	No 20660 L/Corpl. MORRIS C. Wounded S/F	
			One horse killed, one horse wounded.	
			Lieut. D.L. Kyd and No 1794 Pte Donaldson J joined from 14th M.G. Coy	
MONTAUBAN	Sept 2	12 noon	Gun in WORCESTER shelled heavily	
		4 P.M.	1 Gun in SAVOY fired at enemy in groups retiring during afternoon RANGE 2000 X	
			2 Guns in SAVOY Afflied COVERING FIRE while 8th BUFFS retired	
		7.15 P.M.	Two guns in ORCHARD TRENCH relieved by 2 guns at R.B.H.Q.	
			CASUALTIES :- 2 Lieut H. SHACKELL wounded R/F	
			4 Other returned to MOBILE	
			Corpl FRY + Corpl ELLIS returned from Machine Gun School	JR

2449 Wt. W14957/M90 750,000 1/16 J.B.C. & A. Forms/C.2118/12.

Army Form C. 2118.

WAR DIARY
or
INTELLIGENCE SUMMARY
(Erase heading not required.)

Instructions regarding War Diaries and Intelligence Summaries are contained in F. S. Regs., Part II. and the Staff Manual respectively. Title Pages will be prepared in manuscript.

Place	Date 1916	Hour	Summary of Events and Information	Remarks and references to Appendices
MONTAUBAN	3rd Sept.	12.30pm	Guns in ORCHARD TRENCH applied COVERING FIRE to assist 8th BUFFS attacking S.P. junction of WORCESTER, PLUM, & TEA TRENCH. Same guns fired at extended line of enemy advancing, & about 15 minutes later, another extended line of enemy who fired at retiring. RANGE 400 X. Guns in SAVOY fired intermittently during night. CASUALTIES NIL. 2nd Lieut. G. WHITE & Sgt HOLLAND proceed to Machine Gun School.	JGR
MONTAUBAN	4th Sept		CALM DAY. Guns in WORCESTER shelled occasionally. CASUALTIES No 31842 Pte RELPH W. Killed " 20600 " FINLASS C. Killed " 24392 " PARSONS J. Wounded Sh	JGR
MONTAUBAN	5th Sept	5pm 9pm	Company relieved by No 165 M.G. Coy. Guns in support relieved Guns in front line relieved Quiet evening. Enemy aircraft active. Front line teams experienced great difficulty leaving trenches, owing to heavy rain, & enemy barrage. Teams rendezvous at ORCHARD MONTAUBAN, & on completion of relief marched to bivouac near FRICOURT.	JGR

2449 Wt. W14957/M90 750,000 1/16 J.B.C. & A. Forms/C.2118/12.

Army Form C. 2118.

WAR DIARY
or
INTELLIGENCE SUMMARY

(Erase heading not required.)

Instructions regarding War Diaries and Intelligence Summaries are contained in F. S. Regs., Part II. and the Staff Manual respectively. Title Pages will be prepared in manuscript.

Place	Date	Hour	Summary of Events and Information	Remarks and references to Appendices
NEAR FRICOURT	1916 6th Sept.	10 am	Company marches to Camp D.12.C. near ALBERT. REINFORCEMENTS:- No 33932 Corp¹ Cowan Q from Base Depot	J.G.F.
NEAR ALBERT. CAMP D.12.C.	7th Sept	11 am 2 pm 9 pm	Company marches to EDGE HILL station Company entrains Arrive LONGPRÉ. Detrain, march to billets in village of ERGNIES.	J.G.F.
ERGNIES	8th Sept	2 am	Arrive ERGNIES. REINFORCEMENTS:- Lieut S. MORRISON, 2/Lieut W.L. JESSOP and 4 other ranks from Base Depot.	J.G.F.
ERGNIES	9th Sept		General cleaning up of Guns & Equipment.	J.G.F.
ERGNIES	10th Sept		General cleaning up of Guns Equipment & Vehicles No 248795 A/Corp² Dalby Q returned to Base Depot (physically unfit) REINFORCEMENTS:- 2 other ranks from Base Depot.	J.G.F.

Army Form C. 2118.

WAR DIARY
or
INTELLIGENCE SUMMARY

(Erase heading not required.)

Instructions regarding War Diaries and Intelligence Summaries are contained in F.S. Regs., Part II. and the Staff Manual respectively. Title Pages will be prepared in manuscript.

Place	Date	Hour	Summary of Events and Information	Remarks and references to Appendices
ERGNIES	11 Sept.	10am	Parade for inspection by Brigadier General Commanding. 2nd Lieut. W.O. JONES & 2nd Lieut. E.W. WALLACE struck off strength of company.	
ERGNIES	12 Sept.		Training	
ERGNIES	13 Sept.		Training. Sgt. YOUNG G. & Pte. McTAGGART struck off strength of company. REINFORCEMENTS:- 10 other ranks from 53rd Machine Gun Coy. Base Depot. 1 " " " " " " "	
ERGNIES	14 Sept.		Training	
ERGNIES	15 Sept.		Training. No 20552 Corpl. MARRIAGE injured from Base Depot.	
ERGNIES	16 Sept.		Training. No 20588 Corpl. FRY J. leave to U.K.	
ERGNIES	17 Sept.		Captain. E.R. BIRCH admitted to Field Ambulance. REINFORCEMENTS:- Lieut. J.C. WILLIAMS from Base Depot.	

Army Form C. 2118.

WAR DIARY
or
INTELLIGENCE SUMMARY
(Erase heading not required.)

Instructions regarding War Diaries and Intelligence Summaries are contained in F. S. Regs., Part II. and the Staff Manual respectively. Title Pages will be prepared in manuscript.

Place	Date	Hour	Summary of Events and Information	Remarks and references to Appendices
	1916			
ERQUINGHEM	18 Sept		Training.— No.20688 Pte HOLDGATE R. to U.K. (one months leave). REINFORCEMENTS:- 1 other rank from Base Depot.	
ERQUINGHEM	19 Sept	6.30am	Parade marched to PONT REMY station	
		10am	Entrain at PONT REMY.	
		4pm	Arrive PERNES - en - ARTOIS. Detrain marched to billets and town. No.20570 Sgt CONDON J. leave to U.K.	
PERNES	20 Sept		General cleaning of Guns & Equipment.	
PERNES	21 Sept		Training —	
		8.30am	Lieut. S. MORRISON, 2/Lieut J. HANCOCK, 2/Lieut E.L. HUDSON, + 3 N.C.O's proceed to reconnoitre the line.	
PERNES	22 Sept		Training — 34 other ranks attached to company as "Carriers", report themselves	
PERNES	23 Sept	8am	March to RUITZ, where Brown Company billetted in village. 2/Lieut C. WHITE, Sgt. HOLLAND, + Pte. CONNOLLY report from Machine Gun School	

2449 Wt. W14957/Mgo 750,000 1/16 J.B.C. & A. Forms/C.2118/12.

Army Form C. 2118.

WAR DIARY
or
INTELLIGENCE SUMMARY

(Erase heading not required.)

Instructions regarding War Diaries and Intelligence Summaries are contained in F.S. Regs., Part II and the Staff Manual respectively. Title Pages will be prepared in manuscript.

Place	Date 1916	Hour	Summary of Events and Information	Remarks and references to Appendices
RUITZ	24 Sept		2/Lieut W.S. MILLER leave to U.K. L/Corp.t KNIGHT. S. to Machine Gun School	
		4.15 am	March to CAMBLAIN L'ABBE	
		1 p.m.	Arrive CAMBLAIN L'ABBE, take over temporary billets from 98th M.G. Coy. Six L.D. horses drawn.	
CAMBLAIN L'ABBE	25 Sept		Coy relieves 27th M.G. Coy in the line during morning & afternoon. Distribution of Guns:- No 1 Section - Lt S. MORRISON, 2/Lieut. C. WHITE 2 guns ZOUAVE VALLEY (SUP) - 1 gun SOMBART TRENCH (FL) - 1gun ROYAL AVENUE (FL) No 2 Section - 2/Lieut. E.L. HUDSON & Lieut. J.C. WILLIAMS 3 guns INTERNATIONAL AVENUE RIGHT (FL) No 3 Section:- 2/Lieut. W.L. JESSOPP 3 guns COLISEUM TRENCH (SUP) No 4 Section:- 2/Lieut. C.D.C. GILBERT 2 guns ALHAMBRA (SUP) 1 gun GRANBY (FL) 1 gun GOBRON (FL) RESERVE:- 2 guns at Coy. H.Q.	
CAMBLAIN L'ABBE	26 Sept	10 am	Coy H.Q. and details march to VILLERS au BOIS taking over billets from 27th M.G. Coy. Coy TRANSPORT remains at CAMBLAIN L'ABBE	

Army Form C. 2118.

WAR DIARY
or
INTELLIGENCE SUMMARY

(Erase heading not required.)

Instructions regarding War Diaries and Intelligence Summaries are contained in F. S. Regs., Part II and the Staff Manual respectively. Title Pages will be prepared in manuscript.

Place	Date 1916	Hour	Summary of Events and Information	Remarks and references to Appendices
VILLERS BOIS	23rd Sept.		Quiet day. APPOINTMENTS:– Lieut. (Temp'y Capt) E.R. BIRCH to be temporary Major dated 14.9.16	D.R.O 1504
			HONOURS & AWARDS:– 2/Lieut. J.A. HANCOCK – THE MILITARY CROSS	D.R.O 1505
			No 30559 Pte. R.L. BOUGHTFLOWER – THE D.C.M.	D.R.O. 1505
			" 30608 " P. RYAN – THE D.C.M.	30/34.9.16
VILLERS BOIS	24th Sept.		Quiet day. L/Corp SAIGEMAN C. Leave to U.K.	
VILLERS BOIS	25th Sept.		Quiet day. No 30554 Corp'l KNUBLEY J. returned from Base Depot.	
VILLERS BOIS	26th Sept.		Quiet day.	

J E Kyd Lt.
for O.C. 17th M.G. Cy.

24th Division
17th Brigade.

17th MACHINE GUN COMPANY.

October 1916.

WAR DIARY
or
INTELLIGENCE SUMMARY

(Erase heading not required.)

Army Form C. 2118.

Vol 9
17.M.G.C.

Place	Date 1916	Hour	Summary of Events and Information	Remarks and references to Appendices
VILLERS BOIS	Oct 1.		No 20398 L/Corpl. DEMPSEY R. proceeds to ABBEVILLE for course of Transport duty	P2B
VILLERS BOIS	Oct 2.		2/Lieut E.L. HUDSON & 2/Lieut C. WHITE withdrawn to Coy HQrs from the line. REINFORCEMENTS:- No 30289 Pte PEIRCE S. joined from Base Depot (signaller)	P2B
VILLERS BOIS	Oct 3.		Coy relieved by 72nd M.G. Coy in the line (except 3 guns of No 3 Section.)	P2B
		9.30am	3 guns No 3 Section takes over BATAILLE SWITCH from 72nd M.G.Coy. Remaining one gun & team No 3 Section moves from Coy H.Q. to BATAILLE SWITCH	
		11am	Coy Hd Qrs & details march to CAMBLAIN L'ABBE, taking over billets from 72nd M.G. Coy.	
CAMBLAIN L'ABBE	Oct 4.		Coy (less No 3 Section) in Brigade Reserve. General cleaning up of guns & equipment. 2/Lieut. E.L. HUDSON, Sgt. MEIGH, & Pte ICOME proceed to Divisional School at MAISNIL BOUCHE for course of Infantry Training.	P2B
CAMBLAIN L'ABBE	Oct 5.		Cleaning up. Training.	P2B

Army Form C. 2118.

WAR DIARY
or
INTELLIGENCE SUMMARY

(Erase heading not required.)

Instructions regarding War Diaries and Intelligence Summaries are contained in F. S. Regs., Part II. and the Staff Manual respectively. Title Pages will be prepared in manuscript.

Place	Date	Hour	Summary of Events and Information	Remarks and references to Appendices
CAMBLAIN L'ABBÉ	Oct.6		Training. Major BIRCH E.R. granted leave to U.K. from ROUEN.	926
CAMBLAIN L'ABBÉ	Oct.7		Training.	926
CAMBLAIN L'ABBÉ	Oct.8		Training. 2nd Lieut MILLER W.S. reported from leave to U.K.	926
CAMBLAIN L'ABBÉ	Oct.9		Training	926
CAMBLAIN L'ABBÉ	Oct.10		Training	926
CAMBLAIN L'ABBÉ	Oct.11		Coy relieves 93rd M.G. Coy in the line. Disposition of Guns:- No.1 Section (less 1 team) takes over positions No 8. 10. 6. No 2 Section takes over positions No 11. 3. 2. 5. No 3 " at BATOLLE SWITCH is relieved by 3 guns of No 4 Section. No 3 Section moves to new Coy/Bn Qrs at VILLERS BOIS.	926

2449 Wt. W14957/M90 750,000 1/16 J.B.C. & A. Forms/C.2118/12.

WAR DIARY
or
INTELLIGENCE SUMMARY

Army Form C. 2118.

(Erase heading not required.)

Place	Date	Hour	Summary of Events and Information	Remarks and references to Appendices
CAMBLAIN L'ABBÉ	Oct 11 (continued)		No. 4 Section relieved one gun of No. 1 Section takes over positions BAJOLLE SWITCH (3 guns) BAJOLLE LINE (2 guns) Coy. Hd Qrs & No. 3 Section moved to VILLERS BOIS taking over camp from 43rd M.G. Coy. Transport remains at CAMBLAIN L'ABBÉ. No. 19541 Cpl. PRUE W. reported from Base Depot. 2/Lieut G.M. DOUGHTY granted leave to U.K.	J.R.B.
VILLERS BOIS	Oct 12		No. 3 Section General cleaning up of guns & equipment. 2/Lieut C. WHITE takes over duties of Transport Officer during absence of 2/Lieut G.M. DOUGHTY. No. 13653 Pte DWYER G. evacuated sick to No. 23 C.C.S.	J.R.B.
VILLERS BOIS	Oct 13		Situation on line NORMAL. No. 3 Section training.	J.R.B.
VILLERS BOIS	Oct 14		Situation NORMAL. No. 3 Section training.	J.R.B.
VILLERS BOIS	Oct 15		Situation CALM. No. 3 Section training.	J.R.B.
VILLERS BOIS	Oct 16		No. 3 Section training	J.R.B.
VILLERS BOIS	Oct 17		No. 3 Section training	J.R.B.
VILLERS BOIS	Oct 18		Enemy T.M's more active. No. 3 Section training	J.R.B.

Army Form C. 2118.

WAR DIARY
or
INTELLIGENCE SUMMARY
(Erase heading not required.)

Instructions regarding War Diaries and Intelligence Summaries are contained in F. S. Regs., Part II. and the Staff Manual respectively. Title Pages will be prepared in manuscript.

Place	Date	Hour	Summary of Events and Information	Remarks and references to Appendices
VILLERS BOIS	Oct 19		No 3 Section training. No 20645 Sgt MEIGH T, No 20046 Sgt WHITNEY F, and No 20615 Sgt BISHOP H awarded MILITARY MEDAL vide D.R.O. 1642.	2218
VILLERS BOIS	Oct 20		No 3 Section training. 2 Lieut E.L. HUDSON, & Sgt MEIGH rejoin by from 24th Divn School.	2R3
VILLERS BOIS	Oct 21		Situation NORMAL. No 3 Section training. 2 Lieut J. HANCOCK transferred to M.G.T.C. GRANTHAM. 2 Lieut A.G. WIDDICOMBE joined from Base Depot (Reinforcement)	2R4
VILLERS BOIS	Oct 22		Situation NORMAL. No 3 Section employed improving camp. Lieut D.G. KYDD transferred to M.G.T.C. GRANTHAM.	2R5
VILLERS BOIS	Oct 23		2 Lieut G.M. DOUGHTY reported from leave to U.K. 2 Lieut W.S. MILLER and Sgt STEVENS proceed by bus to reconnoitre rear line (LOOS area)	2R6
VILLERS BOIS	Oct 24		Situation NORMAL. Lieut C.F. BEYTS reported from ENGLAND for temporary command 1st Canadian M.G. Coy reconnoitre are positions in the line.	2R7

Army Form C. 2118.

WAR DIARY
or
INTELLIGENCE SUMMARY

(Erase heading not required.)

Instructions regarding War Diaries and Intelligence Summaries are contained in F. S. Regs., Part II. and the Staff Manual respectively. Title Pages will be prepared in manuscript.

Place	Date	Hour	Summary of Events and Information	Remarks and references to Appendices
VILLERS BOIS	Oct 25		Coy relieved by 1st Canadian M.G. Coy.	
		2 noon	Coy. H.Q. & No 3 Sections move to billets at GOUY SERVINS	A.B.
		10 pm	Relief complete. Teams from trenches move to billets at GOUY SERVINS.	
GOUY SERVINS	Oct 26	9 am	Coy marches to MAZINGARBE. Transport from CAMBLAIN L'ABBE joins Coy enroute.	A.B.
		12 noon	Arrive, take over billets in MAZINGARBE.	
		6 pm	Coy paraded, marched to trenches relieving 121st M.G. Coy. (16 guns)	
			Dispositions: No 1 Section took over positions R.40, R.41, R.42, R.43	
			No. 2 " " " R.36, R.37, R.38, R.39	
			No. 3 " " " R.33, R.34, R.35 and CRAISSIER.	
			No. 4 " " " 2 guns LENS REDOUBT, 1 gun "C" KEEP	
			2 guns LENS DEFENCES, 1 gun DEEP LENS DEFENCES	
			LOOS DEFENCES, 1 gun Commandant LOOS DEFENCES	
			The 2 guns in C & D KEEPS under charge of Commandant LOOS DEFENCES	
MAZINGARBE	Oct 27		Situation NORMAL	A.B.
			MAJOR E.R. BIRCH reported from leave to U.K.	
MAZINGARBE	Oct 28		Situation NORMAL	A.B.
			2 Lieut A.G. WIDDICOMBE withdrawn to Coy. Hd. Qrs. from the line	

Army Form C. 2118.

WAR DIARY
or
INTELLIGENCE SUMMARY

(Erase heading not required.)

Instructions regarding War Diaries and Intelligence Summaries are contained in F. S. Regs., Part II. and the Staff Manual respectively. Title Pages will be prepared in manuscript.

Place	Date	Hour	Summary of Events and Information	Remarks and references to Appendices
MAZINGARBE	Oct 29	10am	Had Coy march to LES BREBIS, & take over billets from 131st M.G. Coy	
LES BREBIS	Oct 30		Situation NORMAL. Indirect fire carried out by 9 guns. 2/Lieut. A.G. WIDDICOMBE proceeds to Base Depot.	
LES BREBIS	Oct 31		Situation NORMAL. Indirect fire carried out by 9 guns	

F R Birch Major.
O.C. 14th Machine Gun Coy.

24th Division
17th Brigade.

17th MACHINE GUN COMPANY.

November. 1916.

Prefix... Code... m.	Words	Charge	This message is on a/c of:	Recd. at... m.
Office of Origin and Service Instructions.				Date...
...	Sent		...Service.	From...
...	At... m. To... By...		(Signature of "Franking Officer.")	By...

TO { D.A.C. 3rd Echelon

Sender's Number.	Day of Month.	In reply to Number.	AAA
* M.G	2/12		

Herewith Original Copy WAR DIARY 1st to 30th November 1916. of 17th Machine Gun Company.

From 17th Machine Gun Coy
Place
Time

The above may be forwarded as now corrected. (Z) E R Birch Major

Censor. Signature of Addressor or person authorised to telegraph in his name.

* This line should be erased if not required.

Army Form C. 2118.

17 M G Coy

Appx 10

WAR DIARY
or
INTELLIGENCE SUMMARY

(Erase heading not required.)

Place	Date	Hour	Summary of Events and Information	Remarks and references to Appendices
LES BREBIS	1916 Nov.1		8 men 3rd Batt. The Rifle Bgde. attached pending transfer to M.G.C.	JRB
		5 " 1st Batt. Roy. Fus.	
		6 " 12th Batt. Roy. Fus.	
		6 " 8th Batt. The Buffs.	
		Situation NORMAL. Indirect fire carried out by 10 guns.	
LES BREBIS	Nov.2		" " " " " 10 guns.	JRB
		Enemy aeroplane dropped 3 bombs behind trench between HUGO LANE and CHALK PIT ALLEY, but none of them exploded. Enemy M.G's quiet. Snipers active.	
		Indirect fire carried out by 9 guns.	
LES BREBIS	Nov 3		Situation NORMAL. Indirect fire carried out by 7 guns.	JRB
		1 gun 12th Batt. Roy. Fus. attached pending transfer.	
LES BREBIS	Nov 4		Situation NORMAL. Indirect fire carried out by 10 guns.	JRB
		2/Lieut. W.L.JESSOPP and L/Cpl. R.G.BOUGHTFLOWER rejoined from Vickers Gun Course CAMIERS.	
		2/Lieut C.WHITE and 2/Lieut C.G.G.GILBERT withdrawn to Coy Hd.Qrs.	
		2/Lieut C. WHITE takes over duties of Transport Officer temporarily.	
		2/Lieut G.W. DOUGHTY takes command of No.4. SECTION temporarily in the line.	
		LIEUT. C.F. BEYTS leaves to take command of 23rd M.G. Coy. Auth. AM/826 D.A.G. 2/11/16	

2449 Wt. W14957/M90 750,000 1/16 J.B.C. & A. Forms/C.2118/12.

WAR DIARY
or
INTELLIGENCE SUMMARY

(Erase heading not required.)

Army Form C. 2118.

Place	Date	Hour	Summary of Events and Information	Remarks and references to Appendices
LES BREBIS	1916 Nov.5		SITUATION - NORMAL. Indirect fire carried out by 7 guns. Nos 36 & 41 guns and teams withdrawn to Coy Hd.Qrs. 2/Lieut. W.L.JESSOPP relieves Lieut. S. MORRISON, & takes over temporary command of No.1. Section. Lieut. S. MORRISON takes over temporary command of No.3 Section from 2/Lieut. C.G.G.GILBERT. 2/Lieut. C.G.G.GILBERT withdraws to Coy. Hd.Qrs. on relief. No. 16628 Pte LLOYD R.O. evacuated to C.C.S. Situation - NORMAL. Indirect fire carried out by 6 guns.	RB
LES BREBIS	Nov.6		REINFORCEMENT. - No.37621 Pte. CLYNE K (Signaller) joined from BASE DEPOT. 8 Men returned to BASE DEPOT. Auth. G.H.Q. O.B/121 d/13-10-16. No.9237 Pte. ADAMS W, No.10577 Pte. ALEXANDER G, No.28663 Pte.CARD H. No.8323 Pte. CROWNSHAW F, No.12373 Pte. DAWSON D, No.3561 Pte. FEENNEY A, No.35416 Pte. JOYCE W, No.28199 Pte. PARKER G. Situation - NORMAL. Indirect fire carried out by 4 guns.	RB
LES BREBIS	Nov.7		CASUALTIES - CRASSIER POSITION No. 22121 Pte WILLETT J. and No. 12721 Pte DELICATE A., KILLED by our own Trench Mortar, gun out of action. Situation - NORMAL. Indirect fire carried out by 5 guns.	RB
LES BREBIS	Nov.8			RB

Army Form C. 2118.

WAR DIARY
or
INTELLIGENCE SUMMARY

(Erase heading not required.)

Instructions regarding War Diaries and Intelligence Summaries are contained in F. S. Regs., Part II and the Staff Manual respectively. Title Pages will be prepared in manuscript.

Place	Date	Hour	Summary of Events and Information	Remarks and references to Appendices
	1916			
LES BREBIS	Nov. 9		Situation:- NORMAL. Indirect fire carried out by 6 guns. CASUALTY: Lieut. MORRISON, S. wounded (Trench Mortar). 2/Lieut. WHITE, C. proceeds to ABBEVILLE via BETHUNE to escort convoy of Horses & G.S. Limber.	JRB
LES BREBIS	Nov. 10		Situation: NORMAL. Indirect fire carried out by 7 guns. Enemy M.G.'s quiet. Sniper active. No. 3284 Pte. BELSCHER. C. 12th Batt. Roy. Ins. returned to Unit.	JRB
LES BREBIS	Nov. 11		Situation: NORMAL. Indirect fire carried out by 6 guns. 1.Q.R. from 12th Batt. Roy. Ins. attached pending transfer.	JRB
LES BREBIS	Nov. 12		Situation: NORMAL. Indirect fire carried out by 6 guns. No. 10631 Pte. HENRY, T. wounded slightly (Shell fire). No. 36299 Pte. JONES. L. (Driver) joined Coy. from A.S.C. ABBEVILLE. REINFORCEMENTS: Pte. BLYTH, J.T. (Driver) joined Coy. from A.S.C. ABBEVILLE. No. 22926 Pte. WILLIAMS, J.C. joined G.S. from ABBEVILLE. 1 Wagon, Limbered G.S. 2 Horses, Light draft. Lieut. HUDSON, E.L. in the line, relieves 2/Lieut. WILLIAMS. J.C. relieves 2/Lieut. HUDSON. E.L. in the line, & takes over command of No. 2. Section. 2/Lieut. GILBERT. C.G.G. relieves 2/Lieut. DOUGHTY. G.M. and takes over command of No. 4. SECTION. 2/Lieut. JESSOPP. W.L. remains in command of No. 1. SECTION.	JRB

Army Form C. 2118.

WAR DIARY
or
INTELLIGENCE SUMMARY

(Erase heading not required.)

Instructions regarding War Diaries and Intelligence Summaries are contained in F. S. Regs., Part II. and the Staff Manual respectively. Title Pages will be prepared in manuscript.

Place	Date	Hour	Summary of Events and Information	Remarks and references to Appendices
LES BREBIS	1916 Nov 13		Situation:- NORMAL. Indirect fire carried out by 8 guns. 2 O.R. of 6th Batt. The BUFFS. attached to Coy. pending transfer. No 20506 Corp. FRY. J. returned to BASE DEPÔT. Auth. A.58 dop/1/6.17/Adm	T.B.B.
LES BREBIS	Nov. 14		Situation:- NORMAL. Indirect fire carried out by 8 guns.	TBB
LES BREBIS	Nov 15		Situation: NORMAL. Indirect fire carried on by 7 guns.	SRB
LES BREBIS	Nov. 16		Situation: NORMAL. Indirect fire carried out by 7 guns. CASUALTY. No 26598. Pte. HOLDGATE. R.,- WOUNDED by Aeroplane Bomb or Shell, whilst dropped behind Coy. Billet.	TKB
LES BREBIS	Nov 17		Situation: NORMAL. Indirect fire carried out by 7 guns.	TKB
"	Nov 18		Situation: NORMAL. Indirect fire carried by 6 guns. 1. O.R. of 8th Batt. The BUFFS. attached pending transfer. No 6694 Pte. ROBERTS. D. Evacuated sick.	TRB
"	Nov 19		Situation:- NORMAL. Indirect fire carried out by 6 guns. REINFORCEMENT. No 31612. Pte. PHILLIPS, A. (Down) reported from ABBEVILLE.	TRB

Army Form C. 2118.

WAR DIARY
or
INTELLIGENCE SUMMARY
(Erase heading not required.)

Place	Date	Hour	Summary of Events and Information	Remarks and references to Appendices
LES BREBIS	1916 Nov.19 (cont.)		**RELIEF**	
			No.1. SECTION relieves No.4 SECTION in the RIGHT SECTOR.	JRB
			No.4 SECTION takes over positions in RESERVE LEFT.	
			No.2. SECTION relieves No.3 SECTION in LOOS DEFENCES & LENS REDOUBT	
			No.3 SECTION takes over positions in RESERVE CENTRE.	
			COMMAND.	
			Lieut. WILLIAMS, J.C. takes over temporary command of No.1. SECTION.	
			& the 2 Sections in LOOS DEFENCES.	
			2/Lieut. DOUGHTY, G.M. takes over temporary command of No.4 SECTION	JRB
			& the 2 Sections in LENS REDOUBT.	
			2/Lieut. HUDSON, E.L. takes over temporary command of No.3 SECTION.	
			WITHDRAWAL.	
			2/Lieut. GILBERT, C.G.G. & 2/Lieut. JESSOPP, W.L. withdrawn to Coy.	
			Hd.Qrs. on completion of relief.	
			Situation: NORMAL. Indirect fire carried out by 7 guns.	
LES BREBIS	Nov.20		Enemy fired 12 Rifle Grenades on L. CRASSIER about 2.30 A.M.	
			Situation: NORMAL. Indirect fire carried out by 8 guns.	
"	Nov.21		Situation: NORMAL. Indirect fire carried out by 7 guns.	
			REINFORCEMENTS. No.57577 Pte. CASTLE, E.H. No.17-16 Pte. CROSS, E.H.	JCB
			No.1765 Pte. JACKSON, W., No.9405 Pte. DELDERFIELD, F., No.1966 Pte.	
			CLARKE, T., No.1759 Pte. LIVESLEY, J., No.5321, Pte. HELSON, O.	
			The above joined Coy. from BASE DEPOT.	

WAR DIARY
or
INTELLIGENCE SUMMARY

Army Form C. 2118.

Place	Date	Hour	Summary of Events and Information	Remarks and references to Appendices
LES BREBIS	1916 Nov. 22		Situation NORMAL. Indirect fire carried out by 7 guns. REINFORCEMENT: The following officer reported from BASE DEPÔT. 2/Lieut. FELLS, H.W.	JRB
"	Nov 23		Situation NORMAL. Indirect fire carried out by 6 guns. No. 20090 Sgt. CONDON J. proceed to ABBEVILLE for TRANSPORT COURSE.	JRB
"	Nov 24		Situation NORMAL. Indirect fire carried out by 7 guns.	JRB
"	Nov 25		No. 20659 L/Cpl MAHONEY E. reported back from MACHINE GUN COURSE, CAMIERS. Situation NORMAL. Indirect fire carried out by 7 guns. 2 O.R. attached, returned to their 8th Batt. The BUFFS.	JRB
"	Nov 26		CASUALTIES: No. 21491. Pte. HOPE A. M.G.C. } KILLED No. 10203 Pte SCOTT, E. 8th Batt. The BUFFS (T.M.) 1 O.R. 12th Batt. Roy. Fus. attached, pending transfer. SITUATION - NORMAL. Indirect fire carried out by 3 guns. 1 O.R. 6th Batt. The BUFFS. attached pending transfer.	JRB
	(Cont^d)			

Army Form C. 2118.

WAR DIARY
or
INTELLIGENCE SUMMARY
(Erase heading not required.)

Instructions regarding War Diaries and Intelligence Summaries are contained in F. S. Regs., Part II. and the Staff Manual respectively. Title Pages will be prepared in manuscript.

Place	Date	Hour	Summary of Events and Information	Remarks and references to Appendices
LES BREBIS	1916 Nov.26 (Cont)		**RELIEF.** No.2 Section relieves No.1 in the RIGHT SECTOR, No.1 Section relieves No.2 Section in LOOS DEFENCES & LENS REDOUBT. The half section of No.3 & 4 at present at Coy. Hd. Qrs. relieve their own half sections in RESERVE CENTRE & RESERVE LEFT respectively. **COMMAND** 2/Lieut C.G.GILBERT takes over temporary command of No.2 Section and the two teams in LOOS DEFENCES. 2/Lieut W.L. JESSOPP takes over temporary command of No.4 Section and the two teams in LENS REDOUBT. 2/Lieut H.W. FELLS takes over temporary command of No.3 Section. **WITHDRAWAL.** Lieut J.C. WILLIAMS & 2/Lieut Q.M. DOUGHTY withdrawn to Coy Hd. Qrs.	TRB TRB
LES BREBIS	Nov.27		Situation:- NORMAL. Indirect fire carried out by 6 guns. 2/Lieut E.L. HUDSON, No.20627 Pte IVES.E & No.20766 Pte DUNNER & Pte INCOME proceed to CAMIERS for course on VICKERS GUN.	TRB
LES BREBIS	Nov.28		No.20619 Pte HOLDGATE.R. rejoined Coy. from REST STATION (1st CORPS) Situation:- NORMAL. Indirect fire carried out by 5 guns	TRB
LES BREBIS	Nov.29		**REINFORCEMENTS.** - No.10214 Pte AINSLEY E.J. & No.23944 Pte. HIGGINS, J. reported from TRANSPORT DEPÔT, ABBEVILLE.	TRB

WAR DIARY
or
INTELLIGENCE SUMMARY

(Erase heading not required.)

Army Form C. 2118.

Place	Date	Hour	Summary of Events and Information	Remarks and references to Appendices
LES BREBIS	1916 Nov 29		Situation:- NORMAL. Indirect fire carried out by 7 guns. APPOINTMENTS N° 20549 Coy. Q.M. Sgt, MUNNS, J. appointed Coy. Sergt. Major A.3. 27/11/16 auth. 17th Inf Bgde. A.3. 27/11/16. N° 20645 Sergt. MEIGH. T. appointed Acting C.Q.M. Sgt. vice Coy QMS MUNNS J. 29/11/16 auth A.9. N° M.G. 707 A.9. 29/11/16	ERB ERB
"	Nov 30		Situation:- NORMAL. Indirect fire carried out by 6 guns.	

F.R. Birch
Major
O/C 17th Machine Gun Coy.

30-11-1916

24th Division
17th Brigade.

17th MACHINE GUN COMPANY.

December, 1916.

"A" Form.
MESSAGES AND SIGNALS.

Army Form C.2121.
(in pads of 100).
No. of Message ....

Prefix .... Code .... m.	Words	Charge	This message is on a/c of:	Recd. at .... m.
Office of Origin and Service Instructions.				Date ....
	Sent		.... Service.	From ....
	At .... m.			
	To			
	By		(Signature of "Franking Officer.")	By ....

TO { Hd. Qrs. 12th I. Bde.

Sender's Number.	Day of Month.	In reply to Number.	
*M.G. 868	2/1/17		AAA

Herewith original copy WAR DIARY of 12th Machine Gun Company from 1st to 31st December 1916, please.

From 12th Machine Gun Coy.
Place
Time

The above may be forwarded as now corrected.
Censor. (Z) [signature] Major.
Signature of Addressor or person authorised to telegraph in his name.

* This line should be erased if not required.

17 M G Coy

Army Form C. 2118.

WAR DIARY
or
INTELLIGENCE SUMMARY.
(Erase heading not required.)

Place	Date	Hour	Summary of Events and Information	Remarks and references to Appendices
	1916			
LES BREBIS	Dec.1.		Situation NORMAL. Indirect Fire carried out by 6 guns.	TRB
LES BREBIS	Dec.2.		Situation CALM. Indirect Fire carried out by 7 guns.	TRB
LES BREBIS	Dec.3.		Situation NORMAL. Indirect Fire carried out by 5 guns.	TRB
			No. 20563 Pte. CRANE. A. evacuated sick to No.1 C.C.S.	TRB
			RELIEF.	
			No.1. Section relieves No.3 Section in RESERVE CENTRE.	
			No.2. Section relieves No.4 Section in RESERVE LEFT.	
			No.3. Section relieves No.2. Section in RIGHT SECTOR.	
			No.4 Section relieves No.1. Section in LOOS DEFENCES & LENS REDOUBT.	
			COMMAND	
			2/Lieut G.M.DOUGHTY takes over temporary command of No.3. Section in LOOS DEFENCES.	
			2/Lieut C.G.G.GILBERT takes over temporary command of No.2 Section & 2 Teams in LENS REDOUBT.	
			Lieut J.C.WILLIAMS takes over temporary command of No.1 Section	
			WITHDRAWAL	
			2/Lieut W.L.JESSOPP. & 2/Lieut H.W.FELLS withdraw to Coy. Hd. Qrs.	TRB

Army Form C. 2118.

WAR DIARY
or
INTELLIGENCE SUMMARY.
(Erase heading not required.)

Instructions regarding War Diaries and Intelligence Summaries are contained in F. S. Regs., Part II. and the Staff Manual respectively. Title pages will be prepared in manuscript.

Place	Date	Hour	Summary of Events and Information	Remarks and references to Appendices
	1916			
LES BREBIS	Dec 4.		Situation NORMAL. Indirect Fire carried out by 5 guns.	TRS
LES BREBIS	Dec 5.		Situation NORMAL. Indirect Fire carried out by 6 guns.	TRS
LES BREBIS	Dec 6.		Situation NORMAL. Indirect Fire carried out by 5 guns.	TRS
LES BREBIS	Dec 7.		Situation NORMAL. Indirect Fire carried out by 5 guns.	TRS
LES BREBIS	Dec 8.		Situation NORMAL. Indirect Fire carried out by 5 guns.	TRS
			No 11994 Pte DONALDSON. J.N. transferred to 14 Machine-Gun Coy.	TRS
LES BREBIS	Dec 9.		Situation NORMAL. Indirect Fire carried out by 5 guns.	TRS
LES BREBIS	Dec.10.		Situation NORMAL. Indirect Fire carried out by 3 guns.	TRS
			RELIEF.	
			No.3 Section relieves No 4 Section in LOOS DEFENCES & LENS REDOUBT.	
			No 4 Section relieves No 3 Section in the RIGHT SECTOR.	
			The half-sections of Nos 1 & 2 from "Coy. Hd. Qrs. relieve their own half-sections in RESERVE CENTRE & RESERVE LEFT respectively.	
			COMMAND	
			2/Lieut G.M.DOUGHTY takes over temporary command of No.1. Section in RESERVE CENTRE.	
			2/Lieut. W.L.JESSOPP takes over temporary command of No.4 Section in the RIGHT SECTOR & 2 Teams No 3 Section in LOOS DEFENCES.	

Army Form C. 2118.

WAR DIARY
or
INTELLIGENCE SUMMARY.
(Erase heading not required.)

Place	Date	Hour	Summary of Events and Information	Remarks and references to Appendices
	1916 (Continued)			
LES BREBIS	Dec 10		2/Lieut H.W.FELLS takes over temporary command of No 2 Section in RESERVE LEFT & 2 Teams of No 3 Section in LENS REDOUBT. WITHDRAWAL Lieut. J.C. WILLIAMS & 2/Lieut C.G.G.GILBERT withdrawn to "Coy. Hd. Qrs. No 33922 Corpl COWAN. A. proceeds to Divisional School for course of Infantry Training	R.S.
LES BREBIS	Dec 11		Situation NORMAL. Indirect Fire carried out by 3 guns.	R.S.
LES BREBIS	Dec 12		Situation NORMAL. Indirect Fire carried out by 5 guns.	R.S.
LES BREBIS	Dec 13		Situation NORMAL. Indirect Fire carried out by 6 guns. No 20599 Pte DONOVAN. J. evacuated sick to No 33 C.C.S.	R.S.
LES BREBIS	Dec 14		Situation NORMAL. Indirect Fire carried out by 5 guns	R.S.
LES BREBIS	Dec 15		Situation NORMAL. Indirect Fire carried out by 7 guns. 33. O.R. transferred from Infantry to MACHINE GUN CORPS & posted to 17th M.G. Coy. 30 with effect from 24·11·16 & 3 with effect from 15·12·16.	R.S.
LES BREBIS	Dec 16		Situation NORMAL. Indirect Fire carried out by 6 guns. 2/Lieut E.L HUDSON, Pte IVES, Pte DUMMER, & Pte ICOME rejoined from Vickers Course, CAMIERS.	R.S.

WAR DIARY
or
INTELLIGENCE SUMMARY.

(Erase heading not required.)

Army Form C. 2118.

Place	Date	Hour	Summary of Events and Information	Remarks and references to Appendices
	1916			
LES BREBIS	Dec 17		Situation NORMAL. Indirect Fire carried out by 6 guns.	
			Reinforcement. - Lieut G.H. WRIGHT. posted as 2nd in Command of Coy. from BASE DEPÔT.	
			RELIEF	
			No 3 Section relieves No 2 Section in RESERVE LEFT.	
			No 4 Section relieves No 1 Section in RESERVE CENTRE.	
			No 2 Section relieves No 4 Section in RIGHT SECTOR.	
			No 1 Section relieves No 3 Section in LOOS DEFENCES & LENS REDOUBT.	
			COMMAND	
			2/Lieut. C.G.G. GILBERT. takes over temporary command of No 2 Section & 2 Teams LOOS DEFENCES	
			2/Lieut W.L. JESSOPP takes over temporary command of No 4 Section.	
			2/Lieut E.L. HUDSON takes over temporary command of No 3 Section & 2 Teams LENS REDOUBT.	
			WITHDRAWAL	
			2/Lieut G.M. DOUGHTY. & 2/Lieut H.W. FELLS withdrawn to Coy. Hd. Qrs.	JRS
LES BREBIS	Dec 18.		Situation. NORMAL. Indirect Fire carried out by 5 guns.	
			RELIEF - 2/Lieut W.S. MILLER relieves 2/Lieut W.L. JESSOPP. in the line.	
			WITHDRAWAL - 2/Lieut W.L. JESSOPP withdraws to Coy. Hd. Qrs.	

Army Form C. 2118.

WAR DIARY
or
INTELLIGENCE SUMMARY.
(Erase heading not required.)

Place	Date	Hour	Summary of Events and Information	Remarks and references to Appendices
LES BREBIS	1916 Dec 18 continued		No 25784 Pte WHITLEY. J. evacuated sick to No 33. C.C.S.	NB
LES BREBIS	Dec 19		No 20590 Sergt CONDON.J returned from Transport Course. ABBEVILLE. Situation NORMAL. Indirect Fire carried out by 7 guns.	NB
LES BREBIS	Dec 20		Situation NORMAL. Indirect Fire carried out by 7 guns. No 20614 Sergt ALLEN. F. promoted Colour Sergt & appointed Coy Quarter Master Sergt of 69th M.G Coy. left for new duties.	NB
LES BREBIS	Dec 21		Situation NORMAL. Indirect Fire carried out by 8 guns. No 20645 Sergt MEIGH.T. promoted Colour Sergt & appointed Coy Quarter-Master Sergt of this Coy. Dating from 29-11-16. Situation CALM. Indirect Fire carried out by 8 guns.	NB
LES BREBIS	Dec 22		2/Lieut. JAMES. G.D. 2/Lieut COLLINSON-JONES. H.N.S. Sergt PLACE.J. & Sergt ATKINSON. H. of the 191st M.G.Coy proceed to reconnoitre the line accompanied by Lieut G.H.WRIGHT.	NB
LES BREBIS	Dec 23		Situation NORMAL. Indirect Fire carried out by 9 guns.	NB
LES BREBIS	Dec 24		Situation NORMAL. Indirect Fire carried out by 9 guns. RELIEF No 1 Section relieves No 2 Section in RIGHT SECTOR.	NB

WAR DIARY
or
INTELLIGENCE SUMMARY.
(Erase heading not required.)

Army Form C. 2118.

Place	Date	Hour	Summary of Events and Information	Remarks and references to Appendices
	1916 Continued			
LES BREBIS	Dec 24		No 2 Section relieves No 1 Section in LOOS DEFENCES & LENS REDOUBT. The half-sections of Nos 3 & 4 Sections at Coy H.Q. relieve their own half sections in RESERVE LEFT & RESERVE CENTRE respectively. COMMAND. 2/Lieut W.L.JESSOPP takes over temporary command of No 3 Section in RESERVE LEFT & 2 Teams LENS REDOUBT. 2/Lieut H.W.FELLS takes over temporary command of No 1 Section in RIGHT SECTOR. Lieut J.C.WILLIAMS takes over temporary command of No 4 Section in RESERVE CENTRE & 2 Teams LOOS DEFENCES. WITHDRAWAL 2/Lieut W.S.MILLER. 2/Lieut C.G.G.GILBERT & 2/Lieut E.L.HUDSON. withdraw to Coy. H.Q. 2/Lieut H.N.S.COLLINSON-JONES & 1 Section of 191st Coy proceed to the line. N.C.O's & men attached to our Teams for instructional purposes.	
LES BREBIS	Dec 25		Situation NORMAL. Indirect Fire carried out by 8 guns. M.G's co-operated with Artillery in addition	IKS
LES BREBIS	Dec 26		Situation NORMAL. Indirect Fire carried out by 4 guns.	IKS IKS

WAR DIARY or INTELLIGENCE SUMMARY

Army Form C. 2118.

Place	Date	Hour	Summary of Events and Information	Remarks and references to Appendices
	1916 Continued			
LES BREBIS	Dec 26		No. 22186 Sergt ANDREWS proceeds on Vickers Course. CAMIERS.	JRS
LES BREBIS	Dec 27		Situation CALM Indirect Fire carried out by 5 guns. MGs cooperated with Artillery during the afternoon. 2/Lieut E.L. HUDSON proceeds on leave to U.K.	JRS
LES BREBIS	Dec 28		Situation CALM Indirect Fire carried out by 6 guns	JRS
LES BREBIS	Dec 29		Situation CALM. Indirect Fire carried out by 5 guns. 2/Lieut H.N.S. COLLINSON-JONES + 1 Section of 191st M.G. Coy withdrew from the line. The 2 gun position in LOOS DEFENCES taken over by 191st M.G. Coy. One gun position in NORTHERN SAP REDOUBT & one gun position in 65 METRE REDOUBT taken over by 194th M.G. Coy. Teams relieved from LOOS DEFENCES	JRS
LES BREBIS	Dec 30		Situation NORMAL Indirect fire carried out by 3 guns.	JRS
LES BREBIS	Dec 31		Situation CALM Indirect Fire carried out by 3 guns. RELIEF. No.1. Section relieves No.4 Section in RESERVE CENTRE. No.2. Section relieves No.3 Section in RESERVE LEFT. No.3. Section relieves No.1 Section in RIGHT SECTOR.	JRS

WAR DIARY
or
INTELLIGENCE SUMMARY.

(Erase heading not required.)

Army Form C. 2118.

Place	Date	Hour	Summary of Events and Information	Remarks and references to Appendices
LES BREBIS	1916 Continued Dec 31		No 4 Section relieves No 2 Section in LENS REDOUBT. NORTHERN SAP REDOUBT & 65 METRE REDOUBT. COMMAND Lieut W.S. MILLER takes over temporary command of No 2 Section in RESERVE LEFT. 2/Lieut C.G.G. GILBERT takes over temporary command of No 1 Section in RESERVE CENTRE 2/Lieut G.M. DOUGHTY takes over temporary command of No 3 Section in RIGHT SECTOR. WITHDRAWAL Lieut. J.C. WILLIAMS, 2/Lieut W.L. JESSOPP & 2/Lieut H.W. FELLS withdrawn to Bouflo Qrs.	

31-12-16

S.R.Bird MAJOR.
O/C. 14th Machine Gun Company

Army Form C. 2118.

WAR DIARY
or
INTELLIGENCE SUMMARY.
(Erase heading not required.)

17 M.G.Coy

Place	Date	Hour	Summary of Events and Information	Remarks and references to Appendices
1917				
LES BREBIS	Jan 1		Situation NORMAL. Indirect fire carried out by 5 guns.	8/1/17
LES BREBIS	Jan 2		Situation NORMAL. Indirect Fire carried out by 7 guns. Lieut. S.H. DYER & 1 Section of No 1 Squadron M.G.C. (Cavalry) attached for instructional purposes, proceed to the line, & are distributed among 17th M.G. Coy teams.	8/1/17
LES BREBIS	Jan 3		Situation NORMAL. Indirect Fire carried out by 5 guns. No 20612 Pte WIDDES severely WOUNDED (a) Machine Gun fire in front line trench. REINFORCEMENTS No 63614 Pte SCOTT. A. M.G.C. from BASE DEPÔT. No 63626 Pte BURNETT. E. M.G.C. from BASE DEPÔT.	9/1/17
LES BREBIS	Jan 4		Situation NORMAL. Indirect fire carried out by 7 guns.	8/1/17
LES BREBIS	Jan 5		Situation NORMAL. Indirect Fire carried out by 5 guns. MAJOR. E.R BIRCH granted leave to U.K. for 1 month authority 1st ARMY B/10/22 of 17-12-16.	8/1/17
LES BREBIS	Jan 6		Situation NORMAL. Indirect Fire carried out by 5 guns. No 20561 Pte CAWLEY. C. WOUNDED, accidentally. Horses took fright during shelling and broken rein over Pte CAWLEY. C. No 47091 Pte JORDAN. F. 1st Cavalry M.G Squadron, attached 17th M.G. Coy. accidentally shot with revolver by No 11220 Pte POLLEY. J. 17th M.G.Coy. Pte JORDAN. F. died later in the day from effect of wound.	9/1/17

WAR DIARY
or
INTELLIGENCE SUMMARY.

(Erase heading not required.)

Army Form C. 2118.

Place	Date	Hour	Summary of Events and Information	Remarks and references to Appendices
LES BREBIS	Jan 7.		Situation NORMAL Indirect Fire carried out by 7 guns. In addition MG's co-operated with Artillery. No 9901 Pte FROGGAT T.G. KILLED (e) Shell fire. No 54408 Pte DELDERFIELD. F. WOUNDED (c) Shell fire.	K.W.7
LES BREBIS	Jan 8		Situation NORMAL. Indirect Fire carried out by 2 guns. RELIEF 4 Teams of No 1 Squadron M.G.C. relieves No 2 Section in LEFT SECTOR & 1 team No 1 Section in RESERVE CENTRE taking over positions R39, R40, R42, R43. No 4 Section 17th M.G.C. together with 2 teams from Coy H.Q. relieve No 3 in RIGHT SECTOR taking over positions CRASSIER, R33, R34, R35, R36. No 2 Section 17th M.G.C. together with 3 teams from Coy H.Q. relieve No 4 & 1 team No 1 taking over positions LENS REDOUBT (2 teams), 65 METRE REDOUBT, NORTHERN SAP REDOUBT, R38. All personnel No 1 & No 3 Sections withdrawn to Coy H.Q. COMMAND 2/Lieut H. W. FELLS takes over temporary command of No 4 Section, less R 36 gun. Lieut J.C. WILLIAMS takes over temporary command of No 2. Section, and R.36. gun.	K.W.7

Army Form C. 2118.

WAR DIARY
or
INTELLIGENCE SUMMARY.
(Erase heading not required.)

Place	Date	Hour	Summary of Events and Information	Remarks and references to Appendices
Continued				
LES BREBIS	Jan 8		2/Lieut W.L. JESSOPP takes over temporary command of learn in LENS REDOUBT.	
			REDOUBT + NORTHERN SAP REDOUBT.	
			WITHDRAWAL	
			2/Lieut C.G.G. GILBERT & 2/Lieut G.M. DOUGHTY withdraw to Coy HQ &s.	
			2/Lieut E.L. HUDSON returned from leave to U.K.	
LES BREBIS	Jan 9		Situation QUIET.	
			No 20650 L/Corpl BROOKS. W. evacuated sick to No 33 C.C.S.	
			Lieut. S.H. DYER 1st Cavalry M.G Squadron proceeds to the line + takes over temporary command of R39, R40, R42 & R43 positions.	
LES BREBIS	Jan 10		Situation NORMAL. Indirect Fire carried out by 2 guns.	
			191st Machine Gun Coy attached to 14th Machine Gun Coy for administration from this day.	
			2/Lieut G.M. DOUGHTY proceeds to the line to take command of working party.	
LES BREBIS	Jan 11		Situation NORMAL. Indirect Fire carried out by 7 guns.	
			No 25482 Pte MINNS. A.S. evacuated sick to No 23 C.C.S.	
			No 18651 Pte HENRY, J. evacuated sick to No 1 C.C.S.	
LES BREBIS	Jan 12		Situation NORMAL. Indirect Fire carried out by 7 guns.	

Army Form C. 2118.

WAR DIARY
or
INTELLIGENCE SUMMARY.
(Erase heading not required.)

Place	Date	Hour	Summary of Events and Information	Remarks and references to Appendices
LES BREBIS	Jan 13		Situation NORMAL. Indirect fire carried out by 9 guns.	Point Grid
LES BREBIS	Jan 14		Situation NORMAL. Indirect fire carried out by 8 guns.	
LES BREBIS	Jan 15		Situation CALM. Indirect fire carried out by 5 guns. No 20650 L/Cpl BROOKS. W. rejoined Coy after being struck off strength. Sgt ANDREWS. W returned from Vickers Course. CAMIERS 2/Lieut G.M. DOUGHTY. Cpl HILL & Pte BOWRON proceeded on Vickers Course, CAMIERS. No 20594 Pte CAVANAGH. T. proceeded on one months leave to U.K. having completed his first period of engagement. RELIEF The 4 teams of No1 Squadron MG Coy at Coy H.Q. relieve their own 4 teams in positions R39, R40, R41, R42. No1 Section relieves No4 Section in positions R32.A, R33.A, R34, R35, R36. No3 Section relieves No2 Section in LENS REDOUBT (2 teams) 65 METRE REDOUBT, NORTHERN SAP REDT on R38. COMMAND 2/Lieut C.G.GILBERT takes over temporary command of guns R36, R38, R39. 2/Lieut W.L.JESSOPP takes over temporary command of guns R32.A, R33.A, R34, R35.	GW7

Army Form C. 2118.

WAR DIARY
or
INTELLIGENCE SUMMARY.

(Erase heading not required.)

Instructions regarding War Diaries and Intelligence Summaries are contained in F. S. Regs., Part II. and the Staff Manual respectively. Title pages will be prepared in manuscript.

Place	Date	Hour	Summary of Events and Information	Remarks and references to Appendices
LES BREBIS	Jan 15		Continued 2/Lieut E.L. HUDSON takes over temporary command of guns R40. R42. R43	AWD
			WITHDRAWAL	
			Lieut. J.C. WILLIAMS, Lieut S.H. DYER, 2/Lieut H.W. FELLS & all personnel of Nos 2 & 4 Sections of No 1. Cavalry M.G. Squadron withdrawn to Coy. Hd. Qrs.	AWD
LES BREBIS	Jan 16		Situation NORMAL. Indirect fire carried out by 6 guns	AWD
LES BREBIS	Jan 17		Situation NORMAL. Indirect fire carried out by 5 guns.	AWD
			REINFORCEMENT	
LES BREBIS	Jan 18		No 66969 Pte RODWAY. W.F. joined Coy from BASE DEPÔT. Situation NORMAL. Indirect fire carried out by 5 guns.	AWD
LES BREBIS	Jan 19		Situation NORMAL. Indirect fire carried out by 6 guns.	AWD
LES BREBIS	Jan 20		Situation NORMAL. Indirect fire carried out by 7 guns. Guns fired on BACK AREAS assisting in raid by 73rd Brigade.	AWD
LES BREBIS	Jan 21		Situation NORMAL. Indirect fire carried out by 5 guns	AWD
LES BREBIS	Jan 22		Situation NORMAL. Indirect fire carried out by 6 guns.	AWD
			REINFORCEMENT.	
			No 63788 Pte MARTIN. J.W. joined Company from TRANSPORT DEPOT ABBEVILLE.	

WAR DIARY
or
INTELLIGENCE SUMMARY.

Army Form C. 2118.

Place	Date	Hour	Summary of Events and Information	Remarks and references to Appendices
LES BREBIS	*Continued* Jan 22		**RELIEF**	
			No 2 Section takes over positions R32.A R33.A R34 & R35.	
			No 4 Section takes over positions R36. R38 also providing men for Gas Guard.	
			The teams of No 1 Cavalry M.G Squadron at Coy Hed. Qrs relieve their own half-section in RESERVE LEFT, taking over positions R39. R41 & R42. R43.	
			The teams in LENS REDOUBT, NORTHERN SAP REDOUBT, 65 METRE REDOUBT, remain in positions.	RKW?
			COMMAND	
			Lieut. J.C. WILLIAMS. takes command of guns R32.A R33.A R34 & R35	
			Lieut. S.H DYER. takes command of guns R36, R38, R39	
			2/Lieut H.W. FELLS. takes command of guns R41 & R42. R43.	
			2/Lieut W.L JESSOPP takes command of guns in VILLAGE LINE.	
LES BREBIS	Jan 23		**WITHDRAWAL**	
			2/Lieut C.G.GILBERT 2/Lieut E.L HUDSON & 2/Lieut W.L JESSOPP withdrawn to Coy Hed. Qrs.	R/W/J?
			Situation NORMAL. Indirect fire carried out by 4 guns.	
			No 25793 Pte GOMM A. Wounded slightly Machine Gun fire, remained at duty.	

Army Form C. 2118.

WAR DIARY
or
INTELLIGENCE SUMMARY.
(Erase heading not required.)

Instructions regarding War Diaries and Intelligence Summaries are contained in F.S. Regs., Part II. and the Staff Manual respectively. Title pages will be prepared in manuscript.

Place	Date	Hour	Summary of Events and Information	Remarks and references to Appendices
LES BREBIS	Jan 24		Situation NORMAL. Indirect Fire carried out by 4 guns.	8/WD
LES BREBIS	Jan 25		Situation NORMAL. Indirect Fire carried out by 7 guns assisting in raid. No 63614 Pte SCOTT. A.E. evacuated sick to No 33 CCS.	7/WD
			REINFORCEMENTS. No 4502 Pte POUNTNEY. A. No 144470 KENNEDY. S. No 67366 Pte SHEARS. H. M.G.C. Joined Coy from BASE DEPÔT.	
LES BREBIS	Jan 26		Situation NORMAL. Indirect Fire carried out by 4 guns. The following Officers, N.C.O.s men proceeded on course at Anti-Aircraft School:- Lieut J.C. WILLIAMS. Sgt MARRIAGE, Pte KEMPTON. J. Pte SMITH. H. Pte JACQUES. A. Pte ATTRILL. F. & Pte BROWN. L.	8/WD
LES BREBIS	Jan 27		Situation. NORMAL. Indirect Fire carried out by 6 guns.	8/WD
LES BREBIS	Jan 28		Situation NORMAL. Indirect Fire carried out by 5 guns.	8/WD
LES BREBIS	Jan 29		Situation NORMAL. Indirect Fire carried out by 2 guns.	8/WD
			RELIEF. 1st Cavalry M.G. Squadron relieved by teams of 17th M.G. Coy. Personnel of 17th M.G. Coy already attached to Cavalry team remain in position.	

WAR DIARY or INTELLIGENCE SUMMARY

Army Form C. 2118.

Place	Date	Hour	Summary of Events and Information	Remarks and references to Appendices
(Continued) LES BREBIS	Jan 29		The four teams in VILLAGE LINE are relieved by teams from Coy. Hd. Qrs. **COMMAND** 2/Lieut E.L. HUDSON takes over command of RIGHT SECTOR. 2/Lieut C.G.G. GILBERT takes over command of CENTRE SECTOR. 2/Lieut W.L. JESSOPP takes over command of LEFT SECTOR. 2/Lieut H.W. FELLS takes over command of the VILLAGE LINE. **WITHDRAWAL** 2/Lieut H.W. FELLS withdrawn to Coy. Hd. Qrs.	MWS
LES BREBIS	Jan 30		Situation NORMAL Indirect fire carried out by 5 guns. All personnel 1st Cavalry Machine Gun Squadron attached to 17th Machine Gun Corp. paraded at 2 p.m. to proceed to their own Hd Qrs NOEUX LE-MINES and cease to be attached to 17th M.G. Corp from this day.	MWS
LES BREBIS	Jan 31		Situation NORMAL Indirect fire carried out by 6 guns. No 31234 Gr. MILLINGTON.H evacuated sick to No 1 C.C.S	MWS
	31-1-17.			

M.W.Wright Capt P/M/o
17th Machine Gun Company

Army Form C. 2118.

WAR DIARY
or
INTELLIGENCE SUMMARY.
(Erase heading not required.)

17 M.G.Coy

Vol 3

Place	Date	Hour	Summary of Events and Information	Remarks and references to Appendices
LES BREBIS	Feb 1		Situation NORMAL. Indirect Fire carried out by 6 guns. No 27841 L/Cpl RIDLEY. D. evacuated sick to WEST RIDING C.C.S.	MW
LES BREBIS	Feb 2		Situation NORMAL. Indirect Fire carried out by 4 guns.	MW
LES BREBIS	Feb 3		Situation NORMAL. Indirect Fire carried out by 4 guns. No 25804 Pte LONG P.D. WOUNDED. Self-inflicted accidentally. Revolver shot in knee, slight.	MW
LES BREBIS	Feb 4		Situation NORMAL. Indirect Fire carried out by 6 guns. Machine Gun in position M.G.X damaged badly by Shell Fire, out of action. Major ER BIRCH. admitted sick to Hospital whilst on leave to U.K.	MW
LES BREBIS	Feb 5		Situation NORMAL. Indirect Fire carried out by 3 guns. Machine Gun fired at Enemy Aeroplane between 2 p.m & 3 p.m. No 20551 Sgt NORMAN promoted Colour. Sergt and appointed Coy, Qr. Mr. Sgt of the 108th M.G. Coy. Left for new duties. 2/Lieut G.M.DOUGHTY & Pte BOWRON returned from Vickers Gun Course, CAMIERS. RELIEF The Teams in M.G. Z, R36, R38 & R39 are relieved by Teams from Coy Hd Qrs.	

Army Form C. 2118.

WAR DIARY
or
INTELLIGENCE SUMMARY.
(Erase heading not required.)

Place	Date	Hour	Summary of Events and Information	Remarks and references to Appendices
LES BREBIS	CONTINUED Feb 5		COMMAND	
			2/Lieut H.W. FELLS takes over command of guns in R36. R38. R39.	
			Lieut. C.G.G. GILBERT takes over command of guns in the VILLAGE LINE	hw5
			WITHDRAWAL	
			Lieut C.G.G GILBERT withdraws 15 Coy Hd. Qrs.	
LES BREBIS	Feb 6		Situation NORMAL. Indirect Fire carried out by 6 guns	
			2/Lieut G.M. DOUGHTY relieves 2/Lieut W.L. JESSOPP. in the line.	
			Cpl HILL reported back from Vickers Gun Course CAMIERS.	
			No 25785 Pte CUNNINGHAM.G. evacuated sick to No 1. C.C.S.	hw5
LES BREBIS	Feb 7		Situation NORMAL Indirect Fire carried out by 6 guns.	
			RELIEF	
			The Teams in positions R40. R42. R43. & Gas Guard are relieved by teams from Coy H.Q.	hw17.
LES BREBIS	Feb 8		Situation NORMAL. Indirect Fire carried out by 6 guns.	hw5
LES BREBIS	Feb 9		Situation NORMAL. Indirect Fire carried out by 4 guns.	
			Lieut C.G.G.GILBERT granted leave to U.K.	hw7
LES BREBIS	Feb 10		Situation NORMAL Indirect Fire carried out by 4 guns	

Army Form C. 2118.

WAR DIARY
or
INTELLIGENCE SUMMARY.
(Erase heading not required.)

Instructions regarding War Diaries and Intelligence Summaries are contained in F. S. Regs, Part II. and the Staff Manual respectively. Title pages will be prepared in manuscript.

Place	Date	Hour	Summary of Events and Information	Remarks and references to Appendices
	CONTINUED		REINFORCEMENTS.	
LES BREBIS	Feb 10		No 5168 Pte WARNER. J. joined Coy from Transport Depôt ABBEVILLE. } M.G.C.	MWD
			No 6895 Pte STEWART. R.D. joined Coy from BASE DEPÔT.	MWD
LES BREBIS	Feb 11		Situation NORMAL. Indirect Fire carried out by 15 guns.	
LES BREBIS	Feb 12		The 14th Machine Gun Coy is relieved in the line by the 63rd Machine Gun Coy.	MWD
			Relief complete at 9 p.m. Teams of 14th M.G. Coy withdraw to Coy H.Q.	
LES BREBIS	Feb 13		Billeting Party consisting of Lieut W.S. MILLER & Coy Qr Mr Sgt NEIGH proceed to NOEUX-LES-MINES to arrange rest billets.	
			Coy proceed to new rest billets NOEUX LES MINES at 12 noon.	
			L/Cpl BROOKS & L/Cpl STEEL proceed on Vickers Gun Course at CAMIERS.	MWD
			No 20608 Pte RYAN. P. 14th M.G. Coy awarded the MEDAILLE MILITAIRE.	MWD
NOEUX-LES-MINES	Feb 14		Overhauling of Guns, Clothing, Equipment, etc.	MWD
NOEUX-LES-MINES	Feb 15		Overhauling of Guns, Clothing, Equipment, etc.	MWD
NOEUX-LES-MINES	Feb 16		Training.	
			The undermentioned returned to Base Depôt this day as not likely to become efficient gunners. No 25802 Pte BUDD. G. No 6631 Pte BOWERS. A.H.	

Army Form C. 2118.

WAR DIARY
or
INTELLIGENCE SUMMARY.
(Erase heading not required.)

Instructions regarding War Diaries and Intelligence Summaries are contained in F. S. Regs., Part II. and the Staff Manual respectively. Title pages will be prepared in manuscript.

Place	Date	Hour	Summary of Events and Information	Remarks and references to Appendices
	CONTINUED			
NŒUX-LES-MINES	Feb 16		No 28842 Pte FINN. T. No 5116 Pte HUDSON. J. No 71836 Pte MATTHIS. A.	MO77
			No 29391 Pte MAPLE. E.J. No 11016 Pte WINSOR. G.	
NŒUX-LES-MINES	Feb 17		Training.	
			Reinforcements	
			No 20595 Pte COUGHLAN. P & No 67751 Pte Mc NULTY. C. Machine Gun	MO77
			Corps joined Bay from BASE DEPÔT.	
NŒUX-LES-MINES	Feb 18		Training	
			2/Lieut. W.L. JESSOPP, L/Cpl IVES. E. & Pte FOSTER. G. proceed to Divisional	MO77
			School for Course of Instruction	
NŒUX-LES-MINES	Feb 19		Training	
			No 31245 Pte POPE. W. evacuated sick to WEST RIDING. C.C.S.	MO77
NŒUX-LES-MINES	Feb 20		Training	MO77
NŒUX-LES-MINES	Feb 21		Training	MO77
			No 35881 Pte EMMETT. P.J. evacuated sick to No 1. C.C.S.	MO77
NŒUX-LES-MINES	Feb 22		Training	MO77
NŒUX-LES-MINES	Feb 23		Training	MO77

Army Form C. 2118.

WAR DIARY
or
INTELLIGENCE SUMMARY.
(Erase heading not required.)

Place	Date	Hour	Summary of Events and Information	Remarks and references to Appendices
NOEUX-LES-MINES	Feb 23 continued		Reinforcement. No 15055 Pte BELL A. Machine Gun Corps joined Coy from BASE DEPÔT.	
NOEUX-LES-MINES	Feb 24		Training.	
NOEUX-LES-MINES	Feb 25		Training. Lieut C.G.G. GILBERT reported back from leave to U.K. L/Cpl BROOKS.W & L/Cpl STEEL G reported back from Vickers Gun Course CAMIERS. Sgt MARRIAGE S. Pte SMITH. H. Pte ATTRILL.F. Pte JACQUES.A. Pte BROWN L reported back from Course at Anti-Aircraft M.G. School.	
NOEUX-LES-MINES	Feb 26		Training. L/Cpl PUSEY. H proceeds on Vickers Gun Course. CAMIERS.	
NOEUX-LES-MINES	Feb 27		Training. Reinforcement:- The undermentioned men joined Company from BASE DEPÔT this day No 81923 Pte TWIST W.T.F. No 82484 Pte STOKES.F.W. 82242 Pte SMITH. J Nº 68253 " SMITH. J.W. Nº 82404 " SMITH. W. 82521 " SCOTT. L.S. Nº 68622 " SQUIRES. W. Nº 82532 " SALMOND. D. 82243 " SOWDEN. J.P.	

Army Form C. 2118.

WAR DIARY
or
INTELLIGENCE SUMMARY.
(Erase heading not required.)

Instructions regarding War Diaries and Intelligence Summaries are contained in F. S. Regs., Part II. and the Staff Manual respectively. Title pages will be prepared in manuscript.

Place	Date	Hour	Summary of Events and Information	Remarks and references to Appendices
NOEUX-LES-MINES	Feb 28		Training. Lieut W.S. MILLER, Lieut C.G.G. GILBERT, 2/Lieut E.L. HUDSON 2/Lieut H.W. FELLS, Sgt STEVENS & Sgt HOLLAND proceed to reconnoitre the line.	Inst
	28.2.17			

E.W.Knight Captain 4/0
17th Machine Gun Company

WAR DIARY or INTELLIGENCE SUMMARY

Army Form C. 2118.

17 M.G.C Vol 14

Place	Date	Hour	Summary of Events and Information	Remarks and references to Appendices
NOEUX-LES-MINES	March 1		**Training.** **Reinforcements:** Major J. Joyce joined Company from Henry Barrack M.G.C. appointed to Command unit. AG.S. Wire No DM/1104 of/26.2.17. No 1321 Pte PRINGLE H joined company from Heavy Branch M.G.C.(Bermers) No 5324, Pte HELTON O. No 37662 Pte JACKSON received orders to No 33 C.C.S.	
Do	2		Company went to mine there at FOSSE 10 & trenches near to mine there no less engaged. No 3301 Pte BRADFORD L carried on work to No 1. C.C.S. No 3, No 4 Gullies picnic. The other our positions in the dices front 2nd brigade Nocturne Rem. buy — 8 June. No 1, 2 sectors are reorganized previous to own own Nos 1, 2, 3rd Engineer M.C. cy on Bury-Grenay.	
BURY-GRENAY 4			Situation NORMAL Indirect fire carried out by 16 guns.	

Army Form C. 2118.

WAR DIARY
or
INTELLIGENCE SUMMARY.
(Erase heading not required.)

Instructions regarding War Diaries and Intelligence
Summaries are contained in F. S. Regs., Part II.
and the Staff Manual respectively. Title pages
will be prepared in manuscript.

Place	Date	Hour	Summary of Events and Information	Remarks and references to Appendices
Bury Camp	March 1917 5		Situation NORMAL	
			Suspect fire remained out. Avg 5° [illegible]	
do	6		Left 7. C. WILLIAMS and No 20659 Pte KELTON T. Wilkins for Chick Observers	
			Situation NORMAL	
			Ordinary fire remained out Avg 6° [illegible]	
do	7		Situation NORMAL	
			Suspect fire remained out Avg 6° [illegible]	
			500 rounds fired on enemy aeroplane	
			No 9931 L/C HOWARTH T injured BASE DEPOT	
			No 20669 Bpd SAIGEMAN C & No 10214 Pte GASTON W considered unfit. to No 23 CCS	
do	8		Situation NORMAL	
			Ordinary fire remained out Avg 5° [illegible]	
			No 63788 Pte MARTIN J W considered unfit to No 7 General Hospital	
			No 20520 Sergeant STEVENS E ⎫	
			No 20647 Corporal WATTS Gul ⎬ Proceed to BASE DEPOT and thence	
			No 20650 Sergeant BROOKS W ⎭ to England to join new Companies	

2353 Wt. W2544/1454 700,000 5/15 D, D. & L.   A.D.S.S./Forms/C. 2118.

Army Form C. 2118.

WAR DIARY
or
INTELLIGENCE SUMMARY.
(Erase heading not required.)

Instructions regarding War Diaries and Intelligence Summaries are contained in F. S. Regs., Part II. and the Staff Manual respectively. Title pages will be prepared in manuscript.

Place	Date 1917	Hour	Summary of Events and Information	Remarks and references to Appendices
Bully-Grenay	Nov. 9		Situation NORMAL. Indirect fire carried out by 5 guns.	
do	10		Situation NORMAL. Indirect fire carried out by 6 guns. No 1 Section relieved No 3 Section in the line. No 2 Section remains in at Bully-en-Bois.	
			REINFORCEMENTS: 2nd Lieut. C. H. TOLLEY joined unit from Base Depot (Auth. A.A./B/RANK/178 4/9/17)	
do	11		Situation NORMAL. Indirect fire carried out by 6 guns. 350 rounds fired on enemy aeroplanes.	
do	12		Situation NORMAL. Indirect fire carried out by 4 guns. 500 rounds fired at enemy aeroplanes.	
do	13		Situation NORMAL. Indirect fire carried out by 6 guns.	

2353 Wt. W2544/1454 700,000 5/15 L. D. & L. A.D.S.S./Forms/C. 2118.

Army Form C. 2118.

WAR DIARY
or
INTELLIGENCE SUMMARY.
(Erase heading not required.)

Instructions regarding War Diaries and Intelligence Summaries are contained in F. S. Regs., Part II. and the Staff Manual respectively. Title pages will be prepared in manuscript.

Place	Date 1917	Hour	Summary of Events and Information	Remarks and references to Appendices
Bucq-Grenay	March 14		Situation NORMAL. Guessed fire opened out by 7 guns	
Do	15		Situation NORMAL. Guessed fire opened out by 7 guns. 2nd Lieut W.L. Jessopp, 20027 Sppr 1 NE 3 E, 17988 L/c Foster 8.E returned from hospital at Beaumont school.	
Do	16		Situation NORMAL. Guessed fire opened out by 7 guns. 250 rounds fired at Enemy aeroplane.	
Do	17		Situation NORMAL. Guessed fire opened out by 7 guns. 300 rounds fired at Enemy aeroplane. No sign of Zeppelin. A Reference company from No. 1 Sta. Hospital.	
Do	18		Situation NORMAL. Guessed fire opened out by 5 guns. 500 rounds fired at Enemy aeroplane.	
			2nd Lieut C.H Tooly Transferred to discharge Dressing School on course	

Army Form C. 2118.

WAR DIARY
or
INTELLIGENCE SUMMARY.
(Erase heading not required.)

Instructions regarding War Diaries and Intelligence Summaries are contained in F. S. Regs., Part II. and the Staff Manual respectively. Title pages will be prepared in manuscript.

Place	Date 1917	Hour	Summary of Events and Information	Remarks and references to Appendices
Busnettes	March 19		Situation NORMAL. Quietest fire turned out to be at quick 3 rounds H.M. Fires Permission to snipers on listening posts	
Do	20		REINFORCEMENTS:- No 53211 Pte HELSON O. rejoined Company from S.B.D. Situation NORMAL. Intermittent fire opened out by 5 guns	
Do	21		Situation NORMAL. Intermittent fire opened out by 5 guns. Another gun mounted to bear Jackson boundary from Ensa Depot	
			REINFORCEMENTS:- No 26137 Pte CRUDD W. No 10947 SCRIVENER D. No 10910 GRAFTON J. " 3972 " POLL J. " 7504 " CARAHER J. " 13533 " BIRCHENSHAW J.H. " 2259 " JACKSON G. " 5397 " WHITTINGHAM W.G. " 14474 DAVIES H.T. " 1947 " KENDALL F.	
Do	22		Situation NORMAL. Quietest fire opened out by 7 guns	

Major OC 171 MG Coy

WAR DIARY or INTELLIGENCE SUMMARY

Army Form C. 2118.

Place	Date	Hour	Summary of Events and Information	Remarks and references to Appendices
Bonny Grenay	March 23rd 1917		Situation Normal. Quiet. Fire carried out by 3 guns	
Do	24		Situation Normal. Shooting fire carried out by 6 guns. 300 rounds from Gr. enemy trenches. No 1 Section from Bivot followed No 2 Section on the line. No 30626 Pte HUTCHINSON W evacuated to hospital.	
Do	25		Situation Normal. Quiet. Gun carried out by 6 guns. 1500 rounds fired on enemy occupancy. The enemy trenches between Bon Juin + Rue Lucien 2 am – 3am. Indirect fire carried out by 3½ guns.	
Do	26		Heavy enemy bombardment from 8.30 pm. to 10pm during which 6 O.Bus and gun Jones S.A.A.] putting barrage on enemy front line. 6 guns fired in cooperation with our aircraft 11 am.	

No 25310+ Pte LONG R.D. proceeded Roy. June to Biz.

Major
O.C. 17th M.G.C.

WAR DIARY or INTELLIGENCE SUMMARY

Army Form C. 2118.

(Erase heading not required.)

Place	Date 1917	Hour	Summary of Events and Information	Remarks and references to Appendices
Bully Grenay	March 27		Situation NORMAL. 2 guns fired in co-operation with Artillery bombardment.	
Do	28		2 guns fire raised on No.33 K.O.Ps. 18/23 pts TYMM M co-operated with Artillery in putting up Barrage during our Raid at dawn. 10 guns co-operation with Artillery in putting up Barrage during our Raid at dawn.	
Do	29		Harassing fire carried out by 2 guns. Situation NORMAL. Harassing fire carried out by 3 guns. 500 Rounds fired at Enemy Aeroplanes.	
Do	30		Situation NORMAL. Harassing fire carried out by 4 guns.	
Do	31		Situation NORMAL. Harassing fire carried out by 6 guns. 12 guns in the line. 3 Gun Barrage taken over from 73rd M/G Coy by our B.E.F. Section. M/Gun Coy. Pessop and 17 men withdrawn from the line to reserve.	

O/C 17th M.G.Coy.

Major
O/C 17th M.G.Coy.

1/4/17

17th BRIGADE MACHINE GUN COMPANY

24th DIVISION

APRIL 1917

WAR DIARY
or
INTELLIGENCE SUMMARY.
(Erase heading not required.)

Army Form C. 2118.

Place	Date	Hour	Summary of Events and Information	Remarks and references to Appendices
BULLY-GRENAY	April 5		Situation - NORMAL. Indirect fire carried out by 1 gun. 2/Lieut W.L. Jessopp & 24 N.C.O's. men from billets relieved 1/Lieut E.L. Hudson & 26 N.C.O's men in the line. The 8th Buffs made a raid on the enemy lines (Map LENS, 36c, S.W.b. 1:10,000 M.26.c.) 6 of our guns made a barrage on their flanks.	*Map 4 attached to Orig'n of W/D. AWS
	6		Indirect fire carried out by 3 guns.	AWS
	7		Situation NORMAL. Indirect fire carried out by 4 guns on enemy aeroplanes. 750 rds fired on enemy aeroplanes.	AWS
	8		Situation more quiet. Indirect fire carried out by 3 guns. 2/Lieut C. White proceeded on Special Leave to U.K. 8th to 18th April. Auth. 17th of J.B. L. 157. 4/5/4/17. (Continued)	AWS

Army Form C. 2118.

WAR DIARY
or
INTELLIGENCE SUMMARY.
(Erase heading not required.)

Instructions regarding War Diaries and Intelligence Summaries are contained in F. S. Regs., Part II. and the Staff Manual respectively. Title pages will be prepared in manuscript.

Place	Date	Hour	Summary of Events and Information	Remarks and references to Appendices
BULLY GRENAY	1917 April 8	Cont.	We received an Operation Order from 17th Infantry Brigade with reference to an attack by the 73rd Brigade on the Bois en Hache (G.O. & sketch Map of the Bois-en-Hache attached to Original of War Diary) We cooperated as ordered, & subsequent enquiries showed that the barrage was extremely successful some numbers of the enemy being found killed by M.G. fire. This minor operation coupled with the attack by the Canadians on the 'Pimple' led to a series of operations in which this Company was involved. A map is attached showing position of our guns in the line on this date, this map is an enlargement of LENS Trench Map 36 c. S.W.1. ed.5.a. All coordinates used in describing these operations refer to this map. (LENS. 36.c. S.W.1.)	Marked ① Marked ② (MW)

Army Form C. 2118.

WAR DIARY
or
INTELLIGENCE SUMMARY.
(Erase heading not required.)

Place	Date	Hour	Summary of Events and Information	Remarks and references to Appendices
BULLY GRENAY	1917 Apl.9.		Situation:- NORMAL. 1600 rounds fired at enemy aeroplanes. Indirect fire carried out by 4 guns. 2/Lt. C.W. Dolley returned to Field Ambulance from Divisional School whilst on Course of Instruction. 2/Lt. W.H. Fell rejoined from Vickers M.G. Corps Courses.	7WN5?
~	10th		Situation more lively. Indirect fire carried out by 3 guns. 1,000 rounds fired at Enemy aeroplanes.	7WN5?
~	11th		Situation. Shelling along our whole front, by the enemy. Indirect fire carried out by 2 guns.	8WN5
~	12th		Indirect fire carried out by 3 guns. 250 rounds fired at enemy aircraft. The Operation Order mentioned on the 8th was carried out at dawn (ZERO = 5.30.) in blinding snowstorm. The objective was attained at Snowview line. 8 guns fired 30,000 rounds in conjunction with attack by 73rd Inf. Bgde. #173. M.27.c. M.26.d. during nights 12/13, on the exit from Angres (Rollencourt. IV.33.a. Copy of orders in annex.	Map. (3) 8WN1

T134. Wt. W708—776. 500000. 4/15. Sir J.C. & 8.

Army Form C. 2118.

WAR DIARY
or
INTELLIGENCE SUMMARY.
(Erase heading not required.)

Instructions regarding War Diaries and Intelligence Summaries are contained in F.S. Regs., Part II. and the Staff Manual respectively. Title pages will be prepared in manuscript.

Place	Date	Hour	Summary of Events and Information	Remarks and references to Appendices
BULLY GRENAY	1917 Apl. 13		General Advance of our front commenced. Major J. Joyce & Lieut. R. Boughtflower & teams of one gun crossed the "No Man's Land" & established themselves in the Enemy's lines at about 5" in the afternoon. The Infantry, encouraged by their example, immediately followed up. The gun mentioned started from about M.20.C.2.6 and took up its final position at about 5 o'clock at M.21.C.V.2. It encountered a party of 9 of the enemy who fled after exchanging a few shots. A second gun of ours was brought into position at the same place shortly afterwards (say 5.30 pm). The rifle Battalion of the 72nd Brigade came into position at about the same time and entered Cité de Rollencourt on our left. Our Lefs. Batt", the R.M.L.1. (temporarily attached to the Brigade) took up position with their left at M.27.a.9.7, & other posts along the crest of Hill 70, facing S.E. Attached Map 1 has the North (and South	BWJ

Army Form C. 2118.

WAR DIARY
or
INTELLIGENCE SUMMARY.
(Erase heading not required.)

Instructions regarding War Diaries and Intelligence Summaries are contained in F.S. Regs., Part II. and the Staff Manual respectively. Title pages will be prepared in manuscript.

Place	Date	Hour	Summary of Events and Information	Remarks and references to Appendices
BULLY-GRENAY	1917 Sept 13 Cont'd		North and South of boundary of our Brigade line of advance marked in BLUE. (The Main Road for advance marked in RED.) From this it will be seen that the direction had been lost in the early stages of the advance. Our Right Battalion, The Buffs (8th Batt'n) were never down in getting forward, and only had a few patrols out before night. The 73rd Brigade on our Right were reported to be in ANGRES at 2 p.m. At about 3 p.m. two of our guns pushed forward from about M.26.d.7.7. and took up position in the QUARRIES at M.26.b.8.1. During the following night the situation was adjusted. All teams were brought up to full strength by the employed men from Coys. H/Q., & the remaining 12 guns were concentrated at points as follows:— 3 guns at M.32.a.5.4. ; 4 guns at M.25.d.8.6. 2 guns at M.19.d.9.2. ; 3 guns were kept in Reserve a short distance in the rear, in our original reserve line. All stores were dumped & arrangements made for trenching from	NN1

Army Form C. 2118.

WAR DIARY
or
INTELLIGENCE SUMMARY.
(Erase heading not required.)

17th Machine Gun Company

Place	Date	Hour	Summary of Events and Information	Remarks and references to Appendices
BULLY-GRENAY	April 1917 1st		Situation - NORMAL. Strength of Company:- 11 Officers, 170 O. Ranks. Indirect fire carried out by one gun. No. 30515 Pte Attrill J. evacuated to No.7 C.C.S sick (Epileptic)	A.W.S.I
"	2nd		Situation - NORMAL. Indirect fire carried out by 3 guns.	A.W.S.I
"	3rd		Situation NORMAL. Indirect fire carried out by 3 guns. 2,500 rounds fired at Enemy aeroplanes. Lieut. G.M. Doughty from Coy. H'Qrs. relieved Lieut. G.G. Gillam in Right Sector.	A.W.S.I
"	4th		Situation NORMAL. Indirect fire carried out by 4 guns. No.29712 Pte Hackworthy L. promoted to W/Cpl. vice G.G.G. No.2664 Cpl. Davies A.A. left on Special Leave to U.K. from Course at Div. Sch. A.W.S.I	

WAR DIARY
or
INTELLIGENCE SUMMARY.

Place	Date	Hour	Summary of Events and Information	Remarks and references to Appendices
BULLY GRENAY	1917 April 13	Cont	handing over to Salvage Company.	(initials)
LIÉVIN	14		During the night, as already stated the situation was adjusted. The 3rd Battn The Rifle Bde. had relieved the R.M.L.I. A Battalion of the Brigade on our Left had a strong post at M.21.d.4.7. The 3rd Rifle Bgde. had also a strong post at M.27.c.6.8. The 8th Buffs had a post at M.27.a.0.1. The 12th Roy. Fus. (temporarily attached to 73rd Brigade on our Right) held the S.W. side of ANGRES and had a patrol at M.27.c.6.5 (approx) The position of our guns had been altered during the night. One gun was moved from the S.W. of Cité de ROLLENCOURT to M.21.d.4.3. Two guns from the QUARRIES had been moved up to M.27.a.0.1. and M.27.c.9.9. The three guns from M.32.a.v.e. were	

WAR DIARY or INTELLIGENCE SUMMARY

Army Form C. 2118.

Place	Date	Hour	Summary of Events and Information	Remarks and references to Appendices
LIÉVIN	19th April	Cont.	were moved up to the S.W. of Cité de POLLENCOURT, making a strong point on Hill 70. All the remaining guns received orders to concentrate at Brigade H/Q. Eventually established in Gumboot Trench M.19.d. At about 6 a.m. the 3rd Batt. Rifle Bgde took over the Advance Guard & advanced through LIÉVIN on the whole Brigade front eventually coming into position & holding the enemy line & strong points extending from M.17.b.6.3 to the Chateau at M.23.d.5.7. The M.G.C. received no carrying party & their advance was considerably hampered. Four guns were put at the disposal of the Colonel of the 3rd R.B. & he kept them in reserve near his Headquarters at about M.23.a.1.8. Two guns were left in Reserve at GUMBOOT TRENCH. The remainder of the guns were kept in Brigade Reserve about M.28.a.7.8.	GWS

Army Form C. 2118.

WAR DIARY
or
INTELLIGENCE SUMMARY.
(Erase heading not required.)

Place	Date	Hour	Summary of Events and Information	Remarks and references to Appendices
LIÉVIN	1917 April 14th Cont.		During this advance the Artillery Activity was very slight on both sides.	army
	15th		On this day the enemy artillery livened up & towards evening some of our lighter guns also came into action. The advance was held up by enemy M.G's from Hill 65. (M.24.d.) & others on the front, positions not located. Two of our guns with the 3rd Rifle Bde were put in position, one at the Chateau M.23.d.5.6., the other at M.24.a.40.95. Both these guns were withdrawn later. The position of the former was taken by 2 guns of the 73rd M.G. Coy. Our Infantry patrols were pushed well forward & were on an approximate line North to South - M.18.d.8.1, M.24.b.5.8, M.24.d.4.7. A strong effort to advance was considered to be out of the question owing to the failure of the brigade on our Right & Left to get forward.	

WAR DIARY
or
INTELLIGENCE SUMMARY.

Army Form C. 2118.

Place	Date	Hour	Summary of Events and Information	Remarks and references to Appendices
LIÉVIN	1917 April 14th Cont?		During this day M.G. teams were employed in bringing up more ammunition. No fire of any kind was carried out.- Brigades deep dumps the consolidation of the objective. By this time the teams were very tired, having to carry up their own water, both for drinking & for guns, as well as ammunition. The 8th Batt. The Buffs relieved the 3rd Batt. The Rifle Bgde. in front line. The following alteration was made in the disposition of our guns:- Two of the four guns attached to the R.B.'s were kept at M.23.a.1.6., but were available as Brigade reserve; the remaining 2 guns were attached to the 8th Buffs, one of which was brought into position at about M.18.b.4.5. at the Railway Embankment,- the others at M.24.a.4.9.5. Two other guns were also put into the line with the 6th Buffs one in the strong point M.23.b., the other in an advanced	[illegible]

Place	Date	Hour	Summary of Events and Information	Remarks and references to Appendices
LIÉVIN	1917 Sept 15th	Coy Phone	in the Cité du Bois de LIÉVIN (about M.24.c.8.8.) direction of fire North, covering part of Battalion front.	MWS
	16th		The 6th Buffs were considerably troubled by enemy snipers & M.G's from Hill 65 M.7.d.d. There was also considerable shell fire, particularly in the vicinity of Cité de RIAUMONT. On this day the portion of the Infantry from Left to Right was as follows. - M.12.d.3.9. to M.13.c.5.6. Left Brigade from North M.12.a.3.9 to M.18.a.5.9. Our Brigade front from M.18.a.5.9. due South holding the enemy trench to the Chateau at M.23.d.5.6. The Brigade on our Right held the Eastern edge of the Bois de RIAUMONT. This was called the line of resistance. Our Brigade still held the outpost line already mentioned.	

Army Form C. 2118.

WAR DIARY
or
INTELLIGENCE SUMMARY.
(Erase heading not required.)

Place	Date	Hour	Summary of Events and Information	Remarks and references to Appendices
LIÉVIN	1917 Sept. 16	Cont.	The Brigade on our Right had no outposts on our Right flank. Four guns were sent up from Brigade Reserve to M.23.d.1. & another under Lieut. G.N.Waigh, three of which were pushed on to be put in position in houses at about M.23.c.9.5.05, to bring fire to bear on enemy lines & principally on Hill 65 to keep down sniping & M.G. fire. One gun fired short bursts during the night on the enemy lines at M.13.c.6.6. (approx). The third gun was got into position to let to stop sniping. An 3 am considerable artillery fire was brought to bear on our front, principally on the houses M.24.c. (North half square approx) at 5.30 - dawn, no enemy action followed & became quite brisk. Enemy snipers Two of the three guns brought up already were got into position in the attic of a house & the other in a front room, bringing fire to bear on Hill 65 & in a very short time	MM7 silencing
	17			

Army Form C. 2118.

WAR DIARY
or
INTELLIGENCE SUMMARY.
(Erase heading not required.)

Place	Date	Hour	Summary of Events and Information	Remarks and references to Appendices
LIÈVIN	1917 April 17th cont.		silencing the enemy sniping. Not more than 300 rounds in burst to be expended to produce this result. A further gun was sent up from H.Q. to Lieut. Wright and put into position at M.1.d.3.d.15.05. to cover the ground to its N.E. in case of attack. The remaining gun at this Officer's disposal was put into position at M.23.d.45.95. to cover the road to the East of the Avenue leading to the Chateau at M.23.d.5.6. These two guns covered our Indirect fire during the enemy's night on the approaches to the enemy front line.	MW1
"	18th		No change in the situation so far as M.G.'s were concerned. Artillery of both sides active.	
	19th		The 137th Company relieved our guns from dawn onwards, this Company having arrived in LIÈVIN and Dumpers the previous	

Army Form C. 2118.

WAR DIARY
or
INTELLIGENCE SUMMARY.
(Erase heading not required.)

Place	Date	Hour	Summary of Events and Information	Remarks and references to Appendices
LIÉVIN	1917 April 19	Cont?	the Previous evening as the roads were open for traffic. Relief was reported complete by 10 a.m. The 17 M.G.C. had arrived at BULLY GRENAY by midday.	MWJ

WAR DIARY
or
INTELLIGENCE SUMMARY.
(Erase heading not required.)

Army Form C. 2118.

Place	Date	Hour	Summary of Events and Information	Remarks and references to Appendices
LIÉVIN	April 1917, 19th		Some Notes on the foregoing Operations. During the foregoing Operations, Machine Guns were not called on to do much firing, as the Enemy fell back without much resistance, and when the Brigade was finally held up it was owing to the flanking Brigades failing to get forward. The only particular work assigned to the guns, i.e. keeping down fire from snipers was accomplished at the cost of a few belts of S.A.A. Some Indirect Fire was carried out but the result of this is unknown. The carrying to be done was particularly hard work in the front 1000 yds of the advance. The carrying party had to move over ground broken by trenches & shell fire, — some of the guns advanced at nights before reaching wheelbarrows. After the first 1000 yds, perambulators, wheelbarrows were found which, particularly the former, were of great assistance in getting the guns, belt boxes, rations & water forward quickly.	(MS)

Army Form C. 2118.

WAR DIARY
or
INTELLIGENCE SUMMARY.
(Erase heading not required.)

Place	Date	Hour	Summary of Events and Information	Remarks and references to Appendices
LIÉVIN	April 1917		Notes on Foregoing Operations. (Continued.)	
	19		(contd.) The teams were at times reduced owing to the number of messages to be sent in order to keep up proper communication. The roads were not completed through the original "No Man's Land" for about two days, & the 14th men of this thandent on the night acts as ration carriers. On the night of 15/16th the carrying party for rations was found by the Battalion in Brigade Reserve, after which date our line here were able to bring rations & water into LIÉVIN. The guns were pushed boldly forward, but as the enemy did not counter-attack, it is impossible to state if this action was justified or not. As these guns were pushed forward on particularly suitable ground it is probable that the enemy could not have attacked in daylight without very severe losses. By nighttime it would be conceded & in most cases the guns were unprotected by any, & the Infantry	5

Place	Date	Hour	Summary of Events and Information	Remarks and references to Appendices
LIEVIN	April 1917		Notes on Foregoing Operations (Cont'd) Infantry Company Officers were slow to press proper escort. The Company Casualties during these Operations were very light, 2 Officers wounded, 1 O. Rank killed & 2 Other Ranks wounded, - all by shell fire. This comparatively low percentage of casualties was due to the number of strong dugouts left by the Enemy & to the fact that his shell fire was not always accurate and could not be described as very heavy. Sniping, although brisk on the 13th, was not accurate,- the enemy appearing to be somewhat demoralised. About 8 of our men were unable to stand the strain & had to be sent sick; & men were useless for carrying after the first two days owing to sore feet, - some others went 'sick' in the ordinary way.	[signature]

Place	Date	Hour	Summary of Events and Information	Remarks and references to Appendices
LIÉVIN	1917 April 19		Note. In spite of the fact that we received no carrying party for ammunition, our men managed to keep up the necessary amount for fire (14 belt boxes). About the night of the 18th some of our men were very tired, though almost be described as exhausted. The N.C.O's knew behaved splendidly throughout. The following letter from the Brigadier General was received by Major Joyce, O/C Company. "Dear Joyce, I am most grateful to you for the assistance you have given me in this advance. I very much appreciate the able manner in which you have handled the guns in forward positions. I hope you will tell your Officers & Men how very well they have done. Yours sincerely, (signed) C. (Stone) Br. Genl. Cdg. 17 Inf. Bde.	JMS

Army Form C. 2118.

WAR DIARY
or
INTELLIGENCE SUMMARY.
(Erase heading not required.)

Instructions regarding War Diaries and Intelligence Summaries are contained in F. S. Regs., Part II. and the Staff Manual respectively. Title pages will be prepared in manuscript.

Place	Date	Hour	Summary of Events and Information	Remarks and references to Appendices
LIÉVIN	1917 April		A suitable reply was sent by Major J. Joyce.	
BULLY GRENAY	19th		Company paraded at 3 p.m. & marched to billets in NOEUX-LES-MINES.	
NOEUX-LES-MINES	20th		Billeting party of Lieut. W.S. Miller & 4 other ranks proceeded to Bully Grenay & at 8 a.m. proceeded from there by bus (motor) to ST HILAIRE & take over new billets for the Company. The Company left NOEUX-LES-MINES at 9.30 a.m. for ST HILAIRE, marching via MARLES-LES-MINES, LOZINGHEM, HAUTRIEUX & LILLERS, arriving at St Hilaire about 3 p.m. WS	

WAR DIARY
or
INTELLIGENCE SUMMARY.

Army Form C. 2118.

Place	Date	Hour	Summary of Events and Information	Remarks and references to Appendices
ST. HILAIRE	1917 April 21		Training at ST. HILAIRE.	AWS
	22		Do.	AWS
	23		D.	AWS
	24		Comp. % handed 9 am. travelled to GREUPPE near BOMY arriving at about 2 p.m.	AWS
GREUPPE	25		Training. The undermentioned Officers left on Special Leave to Paris from 25/4/17 to 29/4/17. Lieut. G.D. Murphy, Lieut. E.L. Hudson, Lieut. W.L. Joseph.	AWS
	26		Company paraded 2 p.m. travelled to LES PESSES near St. Hilaire arriving about 6 o 6 p.m.	AWS

Army Form C. 2118.

WAR DIARY
or
INTELLIGENCE SUMMARY.
(Erase heading not required.)

Instructions regarding War Diaries and Intelligence Summaries are contained in F.S. Regs., Part II. and the Staff Manual respectively. Title pages will be prepared in manuscript.

Place	Date	Hour	Summary of Events and Information	Remarks and references to Appendices
LES PESSES	1917 April 26		Major J. Joyce O/C. admitted to Hospital for Medical treatment (about 6 days).	
			No. 9241 Sgt. DUNSMORE H.Q. from 112th M.G.C. joined Coy for promotion to Col/Sgt for appointment to Coy Q.M. Sgt. vice No. 20645 Coy Q.M. Sgt. WEIGHT to report to 171st M.G.C. for promotion to Coy Sgt. Major (W/O. Class II)	fwd
"	27		Company paraded 2 pm forwarded to BETHUNE, arriving about 5 pm. Training.	8 NS?
BETHUNE	28		Do.	8 NS?
"	29		Do. Three Officers returned from leave in Paris	8 NS?
"	30		Do. The following Officers left on Special Leave to Paris — Oct 17-£90 (from 30/4/17 to 3/5/17). Lieut. E.G. Gillett, Lieut. J.G. Williams A25 4-22/4/1. Coy Q.M. Sgt. Weight D. left to take up new duties as Coy Sgt Major with 171st Coy M.G.C. Auth AG'S Nt. Auth M.G. 707/112 e 4/17/547	

WAR DIARY
or
INTELLIGENCE SUMMARY.
(Erase heading not required.)

Army Form C. 2118.

Place	Date	Hour	Summary of Events and Information	Remarks and references to Appendices
BETHUNE	1917 April 30		Strength April	
			Strength of Company on 1st April 11 Officers 178 Other Ranks	
			Reinforcements + 8	
			11 . 186	
			Battle Casualties	
			{ 2 Officers slightly wounded remained at duty }	
			Killed 1 O.R.	
			Wounded 2 O.R. — 3	
			Evacuated sick to C.C.S. — 1 — 19	
			Strength 30th April 10 Officers 16 & 6 Other Ranks	
			L.W.Vaughn Lieut O.C. 17th Machine Gun Coys.	

SECRET   17th I.Bde.
                                    O.O. 138/3   Copy ....

1. If the wind is favourable smoke will be discharged from Smoke
   Cases from the 17th Infantry Bde Front on the Night ZERO/ZERO
   plus 1, in order to assist the operations to be carried out
   by the 73rd Infantry Brigade.

   1 Officer 2 N.C.O's and 24 men 1st R.M.L.I. and 1 Officer 3
   N.C.O's and 60 men 8th Buffs will be required to discharge
   the smoke.

2. The O.C. 8th Buffs and 1st R.M.L.I. will detail the Officers &
   N.C.O's as above to report at Bn H.Qrs MECHANICS at 12 Noon
   to-morrow 9th April when they will be given instruction in the
   use of Smoke Cases by Lieut. DUFFEY, B Special Coy R.E.

3. At 9 p.m. 9th April parties as detailed in para 1 will report
   to Lieut. DUFFEY Special R.E. at Coy H.Qrs GUMBOOT TUNNEL.
   Lieut. DUFFEY will detail the parties to their posts on the
   smoke fronts according to table attached. They will draw the
   requisite number of smoke Cases and Fusees from GUMBOOT TUNNEL
   and move off to the smoke fronts, along which men, smoke cases
   and fusees will be distributed in posts in readiness for the
   discharge.
   Lieut. DUFFEY will detail as many N.C.O's as possible of "B" Special Coy R.E. to assist in supervision.

4. Lieut. DUFFEY will establish his Headquarters at Coy H.Qrs
   GUMBOOT TUNNEL and will wire Wind Decision to Brigade H.Qrs
   at 12 Midnight 9/10th April. If the wind is unfavourable then,
   but changes to a favourable direction between that hour and the
   time fixed for commencement of Operations, Lieut. DUFFEY will at
   once wire to Brigade H.Qrd his decision as to whether smoke
   can be discharged, and he will inform the Officers i/c Smoke
   Fronts accordingly.

   CODE WORDS. Smoke will not be discharged ......COFFEE.
               Smoke will be discharged ....TEA.

   8/4/17   Major.

                                   Brigade Major 17th Infantry Brigade.

   Copies No 1 & 2   O.C.8th Buffs.   Copy 3 & 4   O.C.1st R.M.L.I.
           5   3rd R.Bde   6   104th Coy R.E.
           7   173rd Tun. Coy.   8   H.Q.73rd I.Bde.
           9   H.Q.72nd I.Bde   10   "G" 24th Div.
          11   O.C.12th Sherwoods. 12   O.C."B" Special CoyR.E.
          13   17th M.G.Coy   14   17th T.M.Btty.
          15   Office

SMOKE OPERATIONS.

Detail.	South Front.	North Front.
Front.	Front Line from JEANROD SAP to DOUBLE SAP.	PYRENEES between SAP 16 - LEVER LANE.
Length.	100 yards.	600 yards.
No of Posts.	4	24
No of Smoke cases per Post.	35 Total required 150.	40 800
Boxes fuseos per Post.	5 Total required 20	5 Total required 120.
No of Candles to be discharged per 4 minutes.	6	6
No of Minutes per discharge.	20	20
No of men at each Post.	3	3
Total men for Front	12 (8th Buffs)	72 ** (24 R.M.L.I, 48 8thBuffs)
Time of commencement of discharge.	ZERO plus 1 Minute.	ZERO plus 1 minute.
Wind Limits.	N.W. to S.W.	N.W. to S.W.

H.Qrs of Officer in Charge ...Lieut DUFFEY, "B" Special Coy R.E
                                                  Coy. H.Qrs ...GUMBOOT.
  Telegraphic Address ....DUFFEY, AC 2.

** R.M.L.I. will man the 8 Northernmost Posts.
   8th Buffs " " " 16 Southern

SECRET

APPENDIX 1 (Issued with 17th Inf. Bde O.O. 138).

MACHINE GUN DISPOSITIONS.

17th MACHINE GUN COMPANY

Six Machine Guns will be employed in protecting the Left Flank of the 73rd Infantry Brigade, dispositions as follows :-

No.	Gun Position.	Objective.
1	R.30.c.70.20.	M.32.d.9.8.
2	R.30.c.75.30.	M.33.c.1.7.
3.	R.30.c.70.40.	M.32.d.40.95.
4.	M.25.b.05.15.	M.32.d.85.30.
5.	R.30.a.95.15.	M.32.d.85.30.
6.	R.30.a.95.30.	M.33.c.00.85

also 6 Guns on C.T's and F.T's in M.26.c and d and M.32.a and b.

All guns commencing at ZERO.

Issued to all recipients O.O.138.
8/4/17

SECRET   Copy No...... 6

17th INFANTRY BRIGADE OPERATION ORDER No 138.
Reference Trench Map 1/10,000

1. In conjunction with Operations on the VIMY RIDGE, the 73rd Infantry Brigade will on the night of ZERO/ZERO plus 1 attack and hold the enemy trenches in BOIS DE HACHE (S.2.b).
   The line of resistance to be held will be SEBASTOPOL SAP-M.32.d.15.25 - M.32.d.40.00- along trench running South to S.2.b.35.35 - thence back to our original front line.
   The line of Observation will be from about M.32.d.25.35- M.32.d.80.15 - thence South to S.2.b.70.62 - S.2.b.45.27.
   The position of troops in the line of Observation will be shown by day by White Triangular Notice Boards.

2. The 17th Infantry Brigade will co-operate as under :-
   8th Buffs will cut Gaps in our wire from ASH ROAD to SEBASTOPOL SAP after darkness on ZERO day - if possible all the wire should be removed - otherwise gaps of 8 yards cut at 25 yards intervals.
   These gaps will be marked by Boards, which are being supplied by 73rd Infantry Bde, in our trench and 8th Buffs will detail and an Officer to report to an Officer 9th Sussex Regt at junction of the STRAIGHT & BOCHE WALK(M.32.c.37.35) at Midnight ZERO/ZERO plus 1 who will then point out those places where gaps in our wire have been cut.
   These gaps must be completely cut by 12 Midnight.

3. RATION TRENCH will be closed to all traffic from 7 p.m. on ZERO day.

4. The following work will be carried out :-

   (a) RATION TRENCH to be put into and kept in good order throughout.
   (b) Front Trench between ASH ROAD and SEBASTOPOL SAP to be improved and sandbag steps made on the fire-steps and wooden fire-steps with upright poles placed in the intervals, care being taken that all men can get easily on to the fire-steps.
   (c) SEBASTOPOL ALLEY will be dug out and floor-boarded.
   (d) KELLETT LINE from ASH ROAD to SEBASTOPOL ALLEY to be improved and kept open throughout.

   Troops available for this work are as follows :-
   40 O.R......... 12th Sherwood Foresters.
   All available men of 2 Right Coys 8th Buffs(3rd Rifle Bde will work on this until relieved on Night 7/8th).
   3rd Rifle Brigade on night 8/9th.

5. On Night ZERO/ZERO plus 1 day ROTTEN ROW Locality will be held by 1 platoon which will be withdrawn on arrival of 9th Royal Sussex Regt under arrangements to be made by O.C. 8th Buffs.
   Coy H.Qrs in HEADQUARTER TRENCH at M.32.c.09.09 will be handed over to 9th Royal Sussex Regt as Battalion H.Qrs.
   BOCHE WALK & the STRAIGHT will be evacuated.
   The front line will be held lightly and remainder of troops kept under cover ready for counter-attack.

6. The consolidation of the Left Flank of the 73rd Infantry Bde will be covered by 1 platoon 8th Buffs(1 section and 1 L.G.Section at about M.32.d.0'7 and at about M.32.c.95.90). These will move out into NO MANS LAND when 73rd Brigade move to assembly.
   17th Bde M.G.Coy will cover the Left Flank of the 73rd Infantry Bde (See appendix 1 to follow).

7. Brigade Signal Officer will arrange to synchronise watches on ZERO day at 73rd Infantry Bde H.Qrs at 10 a.m., 2 p.m. and 6 p.m. and at 73rd Advanced Bde H.Qrs R.22.b.7.1. at Midnight ZERO/ZERO plus 1. and will synchronise with Battalions and M.G.Coy.

8. Acknowledge.

7th April 1917

Major.

Brigade Major 17th Infantry Brigade.

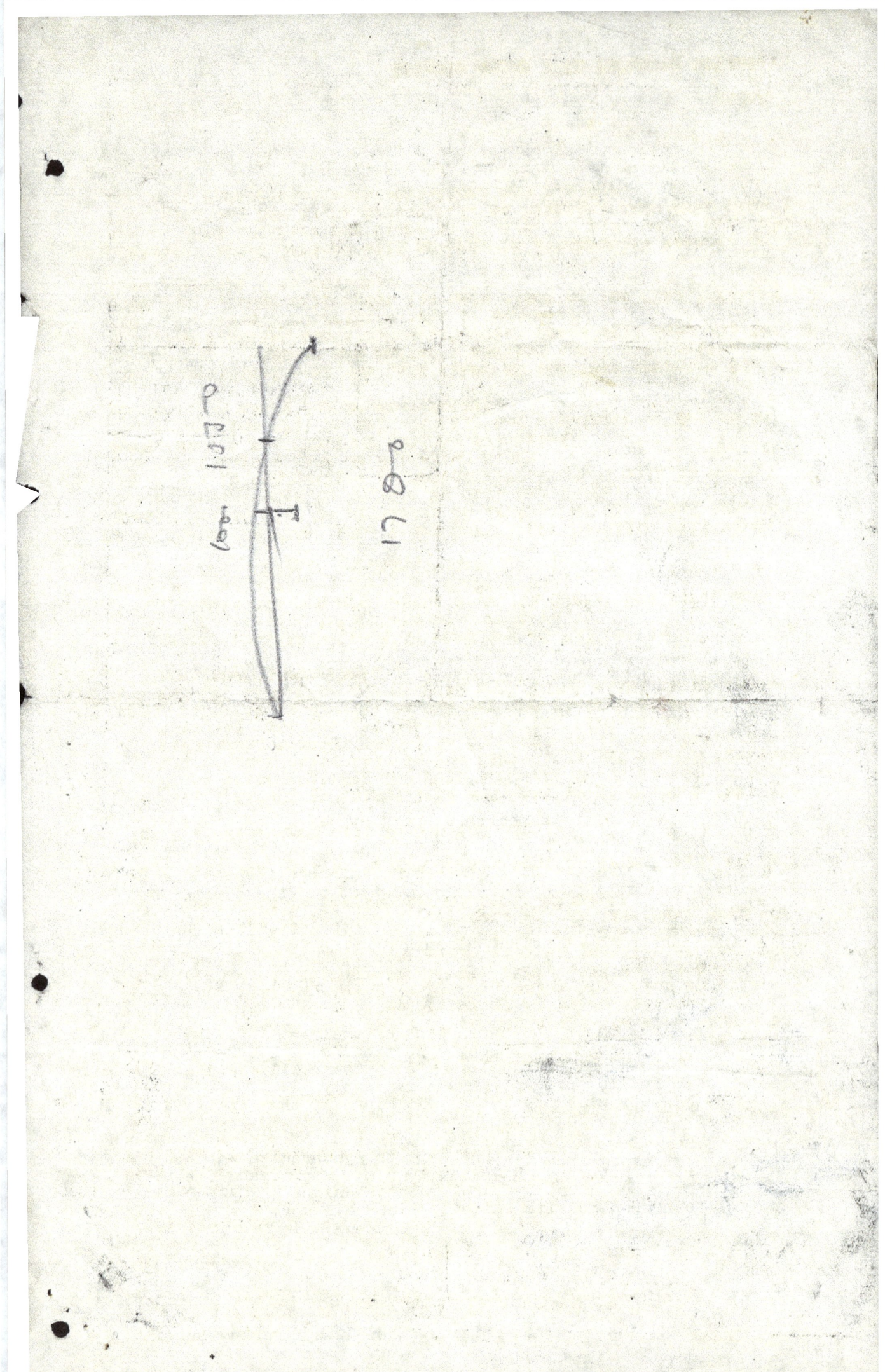

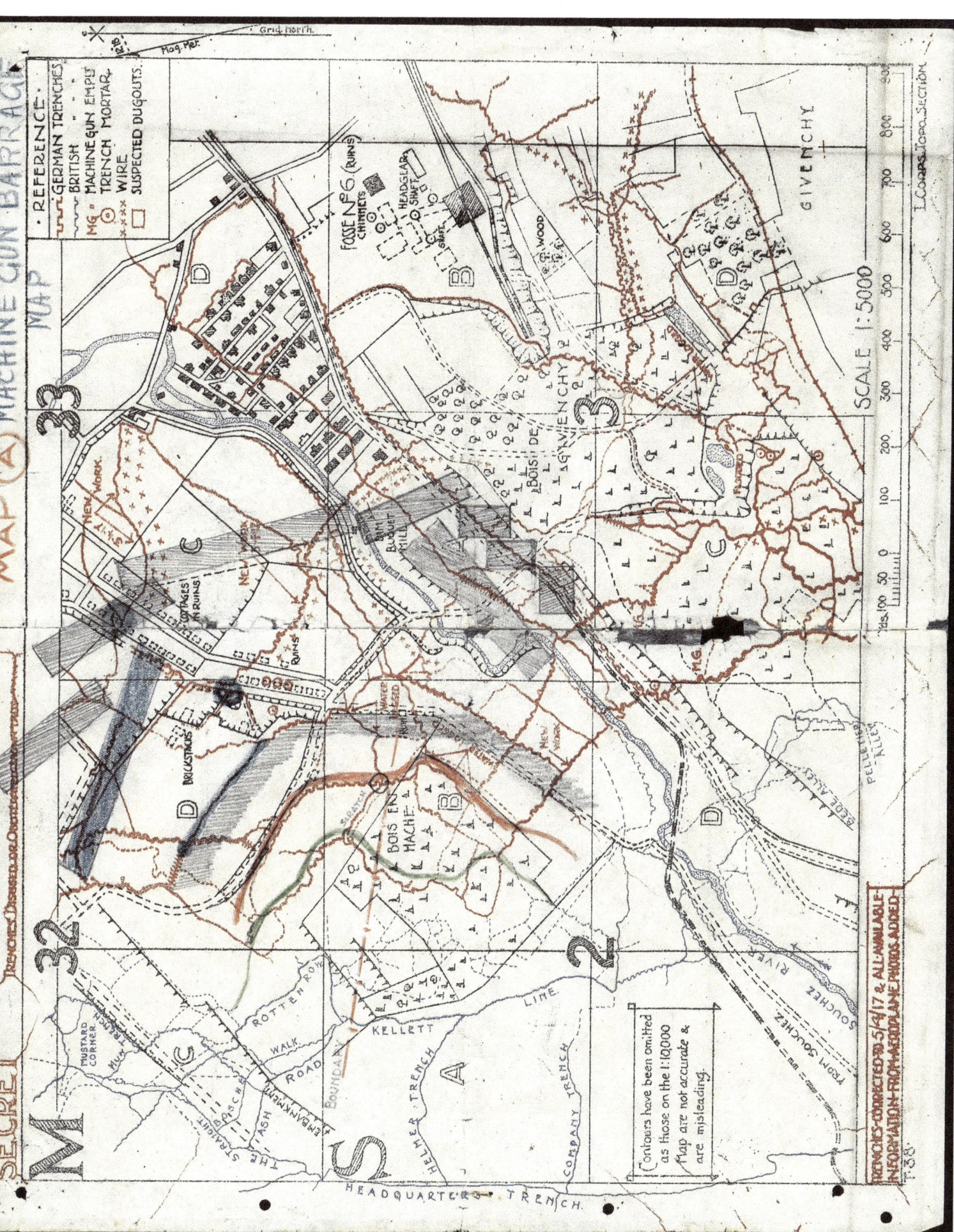

SECRET.   G.187

Officer Commdg.
  3/Buffs.
  3/Rifle Bde.
  7th Roy. M.L.Infy.
  17th M.G. Company. ✓

Herewith copy of Provisional
letter describing generally the
action to be taken in the
event of an enemy withdrawal
opposite the 17th Div. front.

                                   E.H. Iuarich
12/11/17
                        Brigade Major 17th Inf.Bde.
                                        Major

Secret.

In the event of a forward move, the role of the 24th Division will vary according to circumstances.

Our movement forward will be in conjunction with one by the troops on our right and left. It is obvious that we are on too great a front to undertake an offensive against an enemy in force in his present system of trenches.

Troops on our right and left will push forward pivoting on our flanks and as the result of their pressure the enemy in front of us will be in danger of being cut off. He may elect to stay where he is or to withdraw. In any case, unless reinforced, in which case our front would undoubtedly be narrowed, our role is the same viz., to follow him up closely, getting the earliest information of his movements, harassing him, cutting off small parties of machine guns and infantry left to cover his withdrawal, and by constant small attacks to delay him so as to enable other troops to surround him, or force him to withdraw quicker than he anticipated, and so upset his plans.

It is not the intention of the Divisional Commander to commit the Division to street fighting on a large scale in the numerous villages and towns in the immediate front, on the other hand he wishes to impress on all that patrols and supporting troops must press forward with the utmost boldness and vigour — holding on to all ground gained and sending back information at once to the unit behind.

Battalions in advance will move on a wide front. The Battn H.Q. will move forward at intervals establishing visual communication with fixed visual stations at or near Bde H.Q. Brigade & Divisional H.Q. will move in a similar manner.

The general principle being that ordinarily no H.Q. will move until it has established efficient means of communication backwards from its new H.Q. This does not mean that the Officer Comndg. should not himself go forward freely, on the contrary it is his duty to do so from time to time to ascertain by personal reconnaissance the situation at important points.

A main visual station will be established by the Division at FOSSE 11. de BETHUNE (M.8.b.1.2.) which can be called up by any formation unable to communicate otherwise.

10/4/17.

Action in the event of the Enemy withdrawal opposite the 24th Division Front.
―――――――

1. The first news that the enemy has withdrawn from his trenches should be obtained by fighting patrols.

   These patrols may very likely find the enemy front trench unoccupied since the enemy holds his front very lightly, and in places his front trench is abandoned altogether. Patrols must not be satisfied if they find the enemy front trench empty, but must penetrate to his support line, and, if that line is found to be unoccupied also, it may be taken as a fairly clear indication that the enemy has commenced to withdraw.

   In such a case the fighting patrols must remain out, sending back information to the Company Commander that the enemy trenches are not held.

2. The Company Commander, on receiving information from the patrols that the hostile trenches opposite his front are not held will at once move forward one or more platoons in support of his fighting patrol and in accordance with a general scheme for an advance which is explained in succeeding paras. of this letter.

   As soon as these platoons have moved forward and occupied the enemy trenches, the fighting patrols must be pushed further forward to ascertain whether or not the enemy is holding his next line, and so on.

3. Company Commanders before moving forward platoons in accordance with para. 2. will inform their Battn. Comdr. and also the companies on either flank that they are about to do so, and naming the trench which they are going to make the first objective of the platoons which are being sent forward.

   On receiving such information, commanders of companies on either flanks will, if they have not already done so, at once send forward fighting patrols and will follow these up with one or more complete platoons.

4. It must be expected that the enemy will leave behind certain posts and machine guns in his trenches, so that, although long lengths of his trenches may be found to be unoccupied, there will be certain points where resistance will be encountered. These posts must not be allowed to delay our whole advance and steps must be at once taken to deal with them. Good co-operation by units on the flanks of a unit which is temporarily held up will generally be the best way of dealing with such isolated hostile machine gun

5. Batt⁰ Comm⁰ʳˢ, directly they receive information from any of their Company Commanders that the enemy trenches have been found vacant will inform the Brigade and adjoining Batt⁰ⁿˢ. and the Brigade will inform the Division.

The Batt⁰ Comm⁰ʳ should himself go forward and direct the advance of his Companies, moving his support and reserve companies forward at first to our front system of trenches.

6. The system on which an advance will be carried out will be by a series of bounds from one tactical position to the next, each bound being preceded by strong reconnoitring patrols which should be closely followed by Lewis Guns.

Patrols will send back all information obtained; the patrol itself must remain out and must not withdraw from any position gained for the purpose of giving information. It was found during the recent advance of the British that patrols frequently came back to give information instead of sending it back by one or two men.

7. During the first night when it has been ascertained that an enemy withdrawal has taken place the advance will be made by the companies holding our front trenches. This will mean two Batt⁰ⁿˢ in each Brigade finding the foremost troops. But as soon as daylight comes it will be desirable to pass a Batt⁰ⁿ from Brigade Reserve through the two original leading Batt⁰ⁿˢ and, from then on, one battalion on each Brigade front will form the advanced guard to its brigade, moving as mentioned in para 6. above, by a series of bounds, each bound being preceded by a strong reconnoitring patrols.

8. To enable an advance on these lines to be carried out, it will be necessary to supply the leading troops with a large number of wire cutters. These wire cutters must be present with the unit at all times and not back in transport lines, Q.M. Stores, etc., B.G's. C will see that each unit is in possession of its full complement of wire-cutters in accordance with War Establishments and the C.R.E. will see that Field Co⁸ R.E. are similarly complete.

9. <u>MACHINE GUNS</u>. Machine Guns belonging to the Bde. M.G. Co⁸ must be prepared to move forward at

P.T.O.

9. but_d_ short notice. Forward positions in our own lines and positions in the enemy lines must have been reconnoitred or considered beforehand in order that some guns may be moved forward quickly to support the advancing Infantry. It may be desirable to place two or four Machine Guns under the command of the O.C. Advanced Guard (leading Battalion). In this case it is very necessary that the Batt^n Comd^r shall know how to use the guns given to him.

10. **REPORTS.** The necessity for sending back information quickly from the front and for communicating quickly with units on the flanks must be impressed on all. Unless this is done there will be delay in moving guns forward, strong points advance will be quickly dealt with by hostile machine guns which are temporarily holding up the artillery and, generally, the necessary artillery support will be lacking and the result of this must be that the advance will be delayed.

The advanced guard commander must receive frequent reports from his reconnoitring patrols, the gaining of each successive objective must be at once reported; the advanced guard commander must himself send back frequent reports as to the situation, and if there is no change in the situation he must send back information at least once every half hour. The fact that the situation has remained unchanged will not absolve him from the sending back of these half hourly reports.

The means of communication will be chiefly by runners and visual signalling. Runners have now been organized in all infantry units; but visual signalling has been allowed to lapse to a large extent; Batt^n Comd^r must see that their signalling equipment, especially flags and lamps, are complete and present with the units.

11. The boundaries of Brigades may be taken to be as follows:—
Right Boundary 73rd Inf Bde. The railway through S.3.a. M.34.c.50.75 thence the road to Cite de l' ABATTOIR thence the SOUCHEZ RIVER.
Boundary between 73rd Inf Bde and 17th Inf Bde. A line from M.30.a.90.80.— Northern boundary of ANGRES— Northern boundary of ROLLENCOURT— RED MILL — M.28.b.31.40 — ABSOLOM TRENCH (inclusive to 73rd I.B.).

(4)

<u>Boundary between 17th and 72nd Inf Bde</u> ABBEY TRENCH – ABRAHAM – CRANBERRY – CORSAIR – COWDEN – M.12.c.50.05. – railway to LENS (all inclusive to the 17th I.B.).

<u>Left Boundary 72nd Inf Bde</u> DOUBLE CRASSIER – railway towards CITE ST. AUGUSTE

12. The probable roads in the Brigade areas above which would be allotted to Brigades are given below. It will be one of the duties of the advanced guards to report on the condition of roads. There should not be great difficulty in repairing the roads as there will be plenty of debris from houses available. The 12th Sherwood Foresters (pioneers) will be under the orders of the C.R.E. and will be employed on repairing the roads, bridging obstacles etc.

<u>ROADS.</u> <u>73rd Inf. Bde.</u> M.31.b.90.55 – M.32.b.30.47 – M.26.d.80.20 – M.33.a.30.10. – M.33.d.87.30. – thence (a) through CITE de L'ABBATTOIR to S.E. corner of BOIS de RAIUMONT. or (b) via M.28.b.27.00 – M.28.b.87.77 – M.28.c.40.30. – M.23.d.40.57 – M.24.c.10.70.

<u>17th Inf Bde</u> GRENAY – CALONNE – CITE de ROLLENCOURT – M.27.d.60.95. – main road through LIEVIN towards LENS.

<u>73rd Inf Bde</u> FOSSE 11 – M.10.d.45.10 – thence by those roads which are in best condition through CITE ST. PIERRE to M.12.b.48.40 – thence main road to LENS.

13. The C.R.E. will consider schemes for repairing the above roads which may be expected to be really bad only in the neighbourhood of our and the enemy front lines.

14. The C.R.E. will consider schemes for the extension of our trench tram lines. It may be found possible to connect these with the enemy trench tram-lines, the tracks of which may not be much damaged although the rails may be found to have been removed. Until roads have been sufficiently repaired to stand heavy lorry traffic the supply of ammunition to heavy artillery will be best done by trench tramlines.

15. <u>ARTILLERY.</u> Vide appendix attached.

16. <u>ADVANCED GUARDS.</u> The advanced guards on each Brigade front will probably consist of :- one Battn., two sections R.E. The system on which the advanced guards will move is described in para: 6.

17. Brigade and Battalion Commanders will consider schemes on the above lines for an advance. Until the division on the right pivoting about on THE PIMPLE, has pushed well forward towards AVION and until the division on our left has occupied CITE ST. AUGUSTE the 24th Division will not make any forward move unless it is definitely ascertained that the enemy has withdrawn leaving only small detachments behind.

Whilst the divisions on our right and left are moving forward as above the flank brigades (73rd and 72nd) must ensure that proper touch is maintained with the troops on their outer flanks.

18. The administrative arrangements in connection with an advance have already been notified by "Q"

APPENDIX "A"
ARTILLERY

In the event of a withdrawal by the enemy from the 34th Divⁿ front, the following will be the procedure, in as far as can be foreseen.

Whilst the infantry are feeling their way forward through ANGRES, LIEVIN, and the houses in M.11 and M.12. each battery will send forward one section (2 guns) to a forward position. Left group (106th Brigade with D/38) to the valley N.W of CITE CALONNE. Right group (107th Brigade) to valley about M.31.b. and d. These advanced sections will select and occupy forward O.P's and arrange communications.

Upon receipt of definite information that our infantry have cleared ANGRES, LIEVIN, and the houses around M.11, and M.12. the remainder of the guns will be moved up to join the advanced sections, a battery at a time. Parties will then be sent out to reconnoitre routes of a further advance into enemy present lines and to fill in trenches, make roads etc., for the passage of the guns. Routes for the first move have already been reconnoitred and positions selected.

Every possible effort must be made to keep communication with this H.Q, probably the existing battⁿ lines and O.P. lines would be of use.

Owing to the numerous houses and villages, it is quite impossible to lay down any exact plan for the action of the Artillery whilst the Infantry are advancing, but it will probably take the form of barrages well in advance of the Infantry, and harassing fire down roads and communication trenches in rear.

Zones also cannot be allotted definitely but the guns, being in the open can be switched to wherever needed.

N. and S. groups will be directed as to their action by this H.Q.

Routes for 106th and 107th Brigades R.F.A;-

106th F.A.B.
1. BULLY GRENAY (R.11.a.8.8) via MAISON GABA R.12.c.0. to CALONNE (M.14.a.6.1).
2. GRENAY (M.1.a.b.3.) S.W. of Rly to CALONNE (M.14.a.6.1).
3. GRENAY (M.1.a.b.3.) N.E. of Rly to M.8.d.4.9.) thence S.W. into valley

107th F.A.B.
1. AIX NOULETTES (R.22.b.1.2) through NOULETTE to R.36.a.2.3. and thence Eastward into valley.
2. Main AIX NOULETTE — SOUCHEZ road.
3. AIX NOULETTE R.16.d.3.1 to M.25.d.

Army Form C. 2118.

Vol 16

17: Machine Gun Company

WAR DIARY
or
INTELLIGENCE SUMMARY.
(Erase heading not required.)

17: Machine Gun Company

Place	Date	Hour	Summary of Events and Information	Remarks and references to Appendices
BETHUNE	May 1917		Strength of Company. 10 officers 160 O. Ranks.	
	1st		Training.	
			2/Lieut A.W. Daugley promoted to T/Lieut - London Gazette 27.4.17.	
			2/Lieut W.L. Joseph promoted to T/Lieut - London Gazette 20.3.17.	
	2nd		Left Bethune 8hr. arr arrived at new billets FOUQUERIL 9.30 pm.	
	3rd		Training	
	4th		Training	
			Pte Thurlow G evacuated to C.C.S.	
FOUQUERIL	5th		Training	
"			No.36631 Sgt Brown G, No.36633 Pte Platt J. to 1st Army Rest Camp for 14 days.	
"			No.36680 Pte Douglas J evacuated to C.C.S.	

Army Form C. 2118.

WAR DIARY
or
INTELLIGENCE SUMMARY.
(Erase heading not required.)

Instructions regarding War Diaries and Intelligence Summaries are contained in F.S. Regs., Part II. and the Staff Manual respectively. Title pages will be prepared in manuscript.

Place	Date	Hour	Summary of Events and Information	Remarks and references to Appendices
FOUQUERIL	6th		Training	
"	7th		Training	
"	8th		Training	
			No. 3135 Pte Barnes W. evac. to No. 58 C.C.S.	
"	9th		Company left FOUQUERIL 9.30 am for ROBECQ arriving 1.30 pm.	
ROBECQ	10th		Inspection of Company by G.O.C.	
"	11th		Company left ROBECQ for HAZEBROUCK arriving at 1.30 pm.	
			No. 822243 Pte Sanders J.A. evac. to No. 58 C.C.S.	
HAZEBROUCK	12th		Company left HAZEBROUCK for near Licets nr. STEENVOORDE Kms 4.5 & at 2.7. arriving 11.45 am	
STEENVOORDE	13th		Training	
			No. 21791 Pte Roberts W. evac. to No. 17 C.C.S.	
"	14		Training	
			No. 21928 Pte Twist W.J. evac. to No. 17 C.C.S.	
"	15		Company left STEENVOORDE 6.30 am for near Little BRANDHOEK arriving 11[?] am	

WAR DIARY or INTELLIGENCE SUMMARY

Army Form C. 2118.

Place	Date	Hour	Summary of Events and Information	Remarks and references to Appendices
BRANDHOEK	16		Training	
"	17		12 OR joined Company from Base depot	
"	18		Training	
			Training	
			2/Lt D.S. Loughland joined for duty from Base depot. Authority A.G. No. AM/3265 2/15.5.17	
"	19		Training	
			Lieut W.J. Wills No.22630 Sgt Hemmens No 20582 Pte Lowsley G.R. Proceed to Calais on course of Vickers gun	
			Training	
"	20		No.20554 Sgt. Hurley, W. superceded from Sir Kers gun course Calais R.S.	
			Training	
"	21		No.26630 Cpl Wright E No.20639 Sener O.A. No 20861 L/Cpl Corbet D. to 2nd Army Rest Camp for 14 days	
			No.26159 PC Crump W. Garralia to No 20 C.C.S.	
"	"		No.20893 L/Cpl Murphy R goes on special leave to UK	

Army Form C. 2118.

WAR DIARY
or
INTELLIGENCE SUMMARY.
(Erase heading not required.)

Instructions regarding War Diaries and Intelligence Summaries are contained in F. S. Regs., Part II. and the Staff Manual respectively. Title pages will be prepared in manuscript.

Place	Date	Hour	Summary of Events and Information	Remarks and references to Appendices
BRANDHOEK	22		Training. Lieut. WOL Scott proceeded on 10 days leave to U.K.	
	23		Training.	
	24		3 OR. Return by from Base depot. Training	
	25		No. 20619 Sgt Hellard D. No. 20567 Sgt Ellis E.W. to BREE=L=S 4 days course of Map Reading. No. 20637 Sgt Brown G. & No. 20633 Pte Blunt J returned from Rest Camp. No. 20668 Pte Ward to Base & No. b 110/10 a.C.C.S	
	26		Training — No. Pte Moore H.H. to Base depot as P.A. (ADMS 21/22 21/5/17). No. 40884 Pte Bowen S. No. 18538 Pte Barter R. escorted to No 17 C.C.S. Training — Lieut ——— Wittmann J.P.M. on duty served at camp.	
	27		Left BRANDHOEK Bunks 1 area to No 2 x Corps C.C.S. No. 25036 Pte Bunks 1 area at C 20 c.4.4. at 6pm. arriving at new camp at C 20 c.4.4 S 28 NW	
	28		Left camp at C.20.c.4.4 at 7pm. 1.29 a. - 9.9 at 7pm. No. 3972 Pte. Poole Evacuated to No 20 C.C.S	R
C20c.4.4 + S28 NW				

WAR DIARY
or
INTELLIGENCE SUMMARY.
(Erase heading not required.)

Army Form C. 2118.

Place	Date	Hour	Summary of Events and Information	Remarks and references to Appendices
L.29.a.9.9.29.a. Sheet 28 NW	29		Training. No. 7049 Sgt. Ingrand D. No. 7056 L/Cpl. Ellis C.H. returned from top-sergeant course at REELS. No. 2218 Sgt. Andrews O. No. 20860 Pte. Breakspeare O. attached 25th Divisional Signalling for period of operations.	
	30		Training. Major J. Gage rejoined Bn. from Hospital. Lieut. von Sommerick No. 7619 Pte. Comp. N. 10 rejoined Coy. from No. 60 C.C.S.	
	31		Company left camp L.29.a.9.9 at 7.30 am and arrived at Siwah Kitchen K.15.D.4.3. at 1 pm.	6

Strength of Company 31st May 1917.

11 Officers   169 Other Ranks.

Major ....
OC 4 Machine Gun Coy.
31.5.17.

Army Form C. 2118.

WAR DIARY
or
INTELLIGENCE SUMMARY.
(Erase heading not required.)

War Diary June 1917

17th Machine Gun Company

1/14

(24th Division.)

Volume No XIV

WAR DIARY
or
INTELLIGENCE SUMMARY.

(Erase heading not required.)

Army Form C. 2118.

17th Machine Gun Coy (2nd Div)

Place	Date 1917	Hour	Summary of Events and Information	Remarks and references to Appendices
R.15.d.4.3	June 1		4 Officers and 82 men went 6 guns attached to and training with 3rd Rifle Brigade for coming attack. 1 Officer and 27 men with 6 guns attached to and training with 1st Royal Berks for coming attack.	
"	2nd		The above teams were engaged on a tactical scheme with 3rd R.B. & 1st R.B.	
			The remainder of the Company with 6 guns practised mounting guns on enemy & sleeping ground also advancing in the open.	
"	3rd		All teams including those attached to 3rd R.B. & 1st R.B. were engaged on tactical operations with the 72nd and 73rd Infantry Brigades — carrying out practice for coming operations.	
	4th		Company left billets at K.15.d.4.3 at 5 pm and arrived at camp M.36.c.15.25 at 9 pm.	

Army Form C. 2118.

WAR DIARY
or
INTELLIGENCE SUMMARY.
(Erase heading not required.)

Instructions regarding War Diaries and Intelligence Summaries are contained in F. S. Regs., Part II. and the Staff Manual respectively. Title pages will be prepared in manuscript.

Place	Date	Hour	Summary of Events and Information	Remarks and references to Appendices
M 36 c 15.25	8th		Company left camp. at 11.30 p.m. 9 arrived at Camp N.1 central at 1.30 a.m. 1 dgt & 32 O.R. attached to see from 12th R.I.R. & act as carriers to our teams.	
N 1 central	6th		2. of our teams attacked to the 8th A.ffs Yo. Forces of Operation. The 32 carriers from 12th R.I.R. were attached as follows:— At new took an the team occasion to 1st R.I. at " " " " " 2nd R. Innis at 12 " " " " " 5th R.I.R. The remainder (1 dgt & 12 men) returned as carriers to our own 6 teams (Brigade Reserve).	
			WYTCHAETE OPERATIONS.	
			Company left camp N.1 central at 10.30 p.m. for for H. assembly trenches arriving there at 1 a.m.	

Army Form C. 2118.

WAR DIARY
or
INTELLIGENCE SUMMARY.
(Erase heading not required.)

Instructions regarding War Diaries and Intelligence Summaries are contained in F. S. Regs., Part II. and the Staff Manual respectively. Title pages will be prepared in manuscript.

Place	Date	Hour	Summary of Events and Information	Remarks and references to Appendices
Nieuport	6th		Transport moved to ALBERTA CAMP.	
Assembly Trenches (VOORMEZELE)	7th	3/10 a.m.	Zero hour 3/10 a.m. Artillery opened and infantry advanced on first Objectives.	
VOORMEZELE SWITCH	7th	3/10 p.m.	New Zero hour. Our Brigade (17th) advanced on to GREEN LINE (final objective) 10 to 7 a.m. machine guns accompanied the infantry on the advance. The final objectives were taken without much resistance and our Machine-gun occupied positions so that they covers put up a defensive barrage in case of a counter-attack by the enemy. Enemy quiet.	
—	—		Our S.O.S. in front positions. Advanced by Major Coy advanced Brigade Hqrs at O9 c.2.8.	
O9c2.3	8th	7 p.m.	Received orders (Brigade Recce) move up to forward positions for the purpose of carrying the enemy on this line of communication.	

Army Form C. 2118.

WAR DIARY
or
INTELLIGENCE SUMMARY.

(Erase heading not required.)

Instructions regarding War Diaries and Intelligence Summaries are contained in F. S. Regs., Part II. and the Staff Manual respectively. Title pages will be prepared in manuscript.

Place	Date	Hour	Summary of Events and Information	Remarks and references to Appendices
Oge.2.8. (BAYM STRASSE)	8th	7.30 p.m.	The enemy put up a steady artillery barrage on our front and heavier line positions. Our artillery opened heavy fire which machine guns co-operated. During this artillery activity lots of our guns were observed by enemy shell fire our O.P. were common.	
		11 p.m.	Fire became normal.	
	9th		1st guns in position in forward line are - Intense fire being carried out on the enemy's communications.	
			Situation normal.	
	10th		During the night on our own guns were placed by the Company that this was carried out very good. As took the enemy's own our artillery were putting up a heavy barrage fire & OP observed by aeroplane.	

Army Form C. 2118.

WAR DIARY
or
INTELLIGENCE SUMMARY.
(Erase heading not required.)

Instructions regarding War Diaries and Intelligence Summaries are contained in F. S. Regs., Part II and the Staff Manual respectively. Title pages will be prepared in manuscript.

Place	Date	Hour	Summary of Events and Information	Remarks and references to Appendices
			Detailed account of the operations from the 7th to night 18/19 June 1917.	
			During operation the disposition of our Machine Guns were as follows.	
			6 guns with Brigade Reserve at O9c2.8	
			10 guns covered with the attacking infantry and were allotted as follows:—	
			6 guns with 3rd Rifle Brigade.	
			2 guns with 1st Royal Fusiliers	
			2 guns with 4th Y.B. Brigade.	
			The object of 6 guns being attached to the 3rd R.B. being the possibility of their making a right flank movement in case of opposition from OOSTAVERNE wood & village. This however did not materialize.	
			The team advance were very trying (carrying) owing to the intense heat and with the loads necessary for Machine Guns — gunners to carry	

A5834 Wt. W4973/M687 750,000 8/16 D. D. & L. Ltd. Forms/C.2118/13

Army Form C. 2118.

WAR DIARY
or
INTELLIGENCE SUMMARY.
(Erase heading not required.)

Place	Date	Hour	Summary of Events and Information	Remarks and references to Appendices
		(continued)	(The position carried not during evening, & machine gunners advancing with the infantry, were of the greatest value. The openings gained by this means assisted our advance in the action). In spite of this they kept up with the attacking waves. Owing to little opposition they were kept in Reserve and did not come into action until the Green line was taken. On taking up positions further of the enemy own pow were seen, prisoners being insufficient. One gun fired at a knack party and also by them surrendered to the gun team. The majority of the guns were concentrated in the area of Green Wood, from which parties were shown to be very strong, apparently endeavouring to prevent guns from being & possibly. I am aware enable attack to along defensive line was formed.	

WAR DIARY or INTELLIGENCE SUMMARY

Army Form C. 2118.

Instructions regarding War Diaries and Intelligence Summaries are contained in F. S. Regs., Part II. and the Staff Manual respectively. Title pages will be prepared in manuscript.

(Erase heading not required.)

Place	Date	Hour	Summary of Events and Information	Remarks and references to Appendices
		(Continued)	For this purpose the guns in Reserve occupied forward positions. On the night of the 8th a very heavy enemy Artillery barrage was put on our forward positions and our guns "Stood to" and kept up a strong machine gun barrage. On the enemy lines. This was maintained during the whole time that our S.O.S. signals appeared. During the barrage 2 of our guns were destroyed and 6 casualties occurred. The conduct of the teams during this trying time was remarkable, our guns maintaining a steady fire the whole time. On the night of the 10th whilst waiting to be relieved a repetition of the above occurred and our guns again put up a steady machine gun barrage fire.	

Place	Date	Hour	Summary of Events and Information	Remarks and references to Appendices
QUEBEC CAMP	11th		(Continued.) One gun was destroyed but was replaced by a salvaged Vickers gun. During the operations, from the time that the green line was taken, all our guns occupied positions in our advanced area, they constantly harassed the enemy by Machine Gun fire.	
DO	12th		All teams being relieved they proceed to QUEBEC CAMP arriving there 8 a.m. The remainder of the day was spent in cleaning up. The day was spent cleaning gun equipment and freeing hints. At 7 p.m. the Company left camp to participate in the moving operation in Hill 60 sector taking over from the Machine Gun Company Canadian Montgomery at S.P.9. Transport and Negro went to M.C.M.C Camp.	

WAR DIARY
or
INTELLIGENCE SUMMARY.

Army Form C. 2118.

Detailed Account of Hill 60 Section Operations 15.6.16 (?)

14 guns were used and were formed into sub sections under our Officers such as N.C.O.

The nature of the ground was highly suitable for handling machine guns locally in advanced positions and with this object in view guns were allotted to the attacking infantry, also placed in our advance, in or in forward positions on CANAL BANK in view of the enemy's positions - about 100 yards away - so that fire could be brought to bear on LOCK 6 and RAILWAY embankment.

Two guns (under 2/Lieut N.W.Jee) accompanied the left with the 13 R[oyal] F[usiliers], (coming up in a suitable position to fire across our Brigade front and the Brigade on our left ("73rd" Bde). The gun position being only 50 yards from the enemy Fire was not opened, but was used for observation purposes only. The right gun under No 20651 Sgt M.J. Green advanced along the Railway

WAR DIARY or INTELLIGENCE SUMMARY

Army Form C. 2118.

Place	Date	Hour	Summary of Events and Information	Remarks and references to Appendices
			(Continued)	

Barkakhurst passed through our own Artillery barrage & took up position at O.6.a.5.d., engaging the enemy retiring from Monnetle to Clarey Point. Two Hotchkiss were sent as a party of about 50 — cavalry being reported. The gun being on account of the infantry retiring — after the night R.2 company having had been fired — to a position 50 yards behind. On position was established there from which fire could be brought to bear along the whole of our front. Several parties of the enemy were engaged at this point, several casualties were inflicted, and a Corps killed at 250 yards. The total casualties of this team during these operations were three wounded. Two guns (under Lieut W.T. Jessopp) advanced with the 8th Bn. While firing heavy enemy change On time with the exception of one non concern of the gun became casualties.

WAR DIARY or INTELLIGENCE SUMMARY

Army Form C. 2118.

Place	Date	Hour	Summary of Events and Information	Remarks and references to Appendices
			(continued) annoyed with his gun but it was knocked over by heavy fire from the Ridge. The front then moved to the them on the Embankment, previously with them. The other gun got into position on the top of the SPOIL BANK, just at that point in the enemy going from aug-ent to the Railway, inflicting casualties. They also shot down over 50 enemy to the town. Two guns under Lieut G. M. Bayley were in an anxious position at Boom Bank at 0.5a.3.5. and with their fire the 8th Batt. being ones came along the Canal Bank + Jason's Farm to the array unit from which moving from aug-ant + but made hard by our M.G. fire had captured by the enemy infantry. The gun southern the RAILWAY EMBANKMENT, the LOCK and especially OAK HILL and OAT KEEP. From the beginning of operations they were heavily shelled by 5.9", 4.1" to the 6" the tops up a continuous fire while the northern our young teams, at the highest pitch+ practice 7,500 rounds were fired by Close Range	

Army Form C. 2118.

WAR DIARY
or
INTELLIGENCE SUMMARY.
(Erase heading not required.)

Instructions regarding War Diaries and Intelligence Summaries are contained in F. S. Regs., Part II and the Staff Manual respectively. Title pages will be prepared in manuscript.

Place	Date	Hour	Summary of Events and Information	Remarks and references to Appendices
			(Continued)	
	18		One gun was destroyed by direct hit and the crew had to evacuate. The remaining guns were in position to claim as effective. All guns were under a heavy shelling but a continuous Machine gun barrage was maintained on their forward objective. Guns fired during the night on lines & and at known pre-occupied enemy positions & over our positions as a counter-attack. Batteries were relieved by dawn of the 18th by the 73rd Company and proceeded to Micmac South camp, among them 1 crew.	
Micmac South	16		The remainder of the day was spent in resting, cleaning up, overhauling guns and cleaning guns and equipment, also washing & clothing.	
Do	17			

Army Form C. 2118.

WAR DIARY
or
INTELLIGENCE SUMMARY.
(Erase heading not required.)

Place	Date	Hour	Summary of Events and Information	Remarks and references to Appendices
MICMAC SOUTH.	18th		Lewis gun experiment in enemy lines held. Party preparing Gunnery for going into the line for 19th.	
Do.	19th		Company moved to a different part of the support line. Lewis gun Section with 8 guns proceeded to the line and took up positions from the 12th Machine Gun Company. Wire party went up and came under fire. Lieut. at 1.22 & at 75.30 (near ZILLEBEKE LAKE) and came under shell fire at 5 other momentarily occupied places. There was 1 OR. was hit and 5 others seriously wounded. Lewis gun Section remained at MIOMAG SOUTH during the following day, as the Cavalry Company Store also remained. 2 Lewis guns were established at tunnel in LARCH WOOD. Around them was established	
Do.	20th		No action. In the line were occupied in Lewis gun positions and heavy casualties imposing gun positions. Training at Camp. - Training.	
Do.	21st		Remainder of day. Training. Lewis gun employment made of gun fire from 4 100 Rounds fired at enemy aeroplane. 1500 rounds fired at the enemy lines of enemy communication.	

A 5834 Wt.W4973/M687 750,000 8/16 D.D.&L.Ltd. Forms/C.2118/13

WAR DIARY
or
INTELLIGENCE SUMMARY.

(Erase heading not required.)

Army Form C. 2118.

Instructions regarding War Diaries and Intelligence Summaries are contained in F.S. Regs., Part II and the Staff Manual respectively. Title pages will be prepared in manuscript.

Place	Date	Hour	Summary of Events and Information	Remarks and references to Appendices
MICMAC SOUTH	21st		The 2 sections at Camp engaged in overhauling ammunition & belts. No Registrations to be carried out owing to the 20th being Rested on their knowledge of the gun stoppages &c.	
Do	22nd		Reasons for ammunition made at gun positions twelve clear occur. Two new emplacements made. 200 rounds fired at enemy aeroplane. 500 rounds fired on the enemy's lines of communication.	
Do	23rd		The 2 sections in camp with 8 guns left at 11.30 p.m. to relieve the 2 sections in the trenches. During the night some of the gun positions were heavily shelled but no casualties occurred. 500 rounds fired at enemy aeroplanes.	
Do	24th		Situation Normal. O.C. machine guns gives on the enemy's lines also. Account of the night special attention being paid to Cross Roads at J.20.d.3.9. & J.20.C.9.1. Our Aeroplanes (Form 731 A.O.L. also bound for J.20.C.9.1. 250 rounds fired at enemy aeroplane.	

WAR DIARY
or
INTELLIGENCE SUMMARY.
(Erase heading not required.)

Army Form C. 2118.

Instructions regarding War Diaries and Intelligence
Summaries are contained in F. S. Regs., Part II.
and the Staff Manual respectively. Title pages
will be prepared in manuscript.

Place	Date	Hour	Summary of Events and Information	Remarks and references to Appendices
M/CM/AC Court	24 (6 our 4)		4 gun emplacements reconstructed & trenches cleared in vicinity of emplacements. The 2 sections in camp engaged cleaning overhauling gun equipment	
Do	25th		Our guns fired indirect on Kent John 588 & 8. x - Goossenberry Farm, 58, b.1.6 and Cross Roads 58, d 2.9. Our gun position was heavily shelled between the hours of 1 pm 8 pm. 10 pm to 11/30 pm and 2 am 6 3 am. Teams engaged repairing emplacements cleaning trenches when damaged by shell fire. The 2 sections in camp on belt filling, inspecting cleaning ammunition.	
Do	26.		Situation — Intense enemy shell fire on our our position - ... aug. out blown in. 2800 rounds fired at same objective As given on 25th. 1,250 rounds fired at enemy aeroplanes	

Army Form C. 2118.

WAR DIARY
or
INTELLIGENCE SUMMARY.
(Erase heading not required.)

Instructions regarding War Diaries and Intelligence Summaries are contained in F. S. Regs., Part II. and the Staff Manual respectively. Title pages will be prepared in manuscript.

Place	Date	Hour	Summary of Events and Information	Remarks and references to Appendices
MERYC SOUTH	27th		1000 rounds fired on Bosh posts 3.31 & 2.9. 250 yards fired at enemy aeroplane. No work carried out owing to the hearing down of firearm trench with the succeeding company. Coys in camp on route march.	
Do.	28th		The 2 C. Coys in the look were relieved by 2 & 40 at Company on night of 28/29. One team was put in before dawn of 29th. Owing to the preceding team not arriving before dawn and being able to get to our lines which was in a forward position. Transport came to decous. left camp at 10 am. In entraining piece (HODOUTRE SIDING) arriving there 1 pm the too horses which had been perfored in the lines arrived at 9h30 soon after.	
Do.	29th		Train left there by Motor lorry at 11am arriving at HODOUTRE SIDING at 12/noon. Transport and 2nd left HODOUTRE at 3/30 pm arriving at WIZERNES station 7h.	

Army Form C. 2118.

WAR DIARY
or
INTELLIGENCE SUMMARY.

(Erase heading not required.)

Instructions regarding War Diaries and Intelligence Summaries are contained in F. S. Regs., Part II. and the Staff Manual respectively. Title pages will be prepared in manuscript.

Place	Date	Hour	Summary of Events and Information	Remarks and references to Appendices
	9/7 (contd)		Company detrained at WISERNES Officers and Transport to the first camp at LUMBRES arriving 10 pm.	
LUMBRES	30		Company left camp at LUMBRES at 9.30 am and marched to billets at HABRINGHEN at 2.30 pm. Total Casualties of Offensive in Croisilles Reinforcements	

Killed 2
Died of wounds 5
Missing 1
Wounded 26
Evacuated C.C.S. sick 1
                        ___
                        35

Strength of Company on 30th June
90 + 11 Officers = 101 a.r.

J. Davis Major
O.C. 17. M.G. Coy

A5834 Wt.W4973/M687 750,000 8/16 D.D.&L.Ltd. Forms/C.2118/13.

"A" Form.
MESSAGES AND SIGNALS.

Army Form C.2121 (in pads of 100).

Disposition of Brigade Machine Guns during operations

	Position	Objective	
1	O.5.a.2.3	OAK ALLEY - CANAL BANKS	O.5.a & b
2	O.5.a.2.3	OAK KEEP TRENCH	
3	I.35.c.1.2		
4	I.35.c.1.2	Strong point I.36.d central	
5	I.35.c.2.1	Artillery dumps	
6	I.35.c.2.1	O.6.b.9.9 & aug road	
7	I.29.d.6.8	Railway from O.6.a to I.36.c	
8	I.29.d.6.8		
9	I.29.a.7.8	Artillery positions O.6.b.3.6	
10	I.29.d.7.8	to O.6.b.3.9	
11	with 7th Buffs to take up forward position		
12	O.5.b.6.8 & O.5.b.9.9		

"A" Form.
MESSAGES AND SIGNALS.
Army Form C.2
(in pads of 100).

Gun Position — Objective

Feb 13 — 9 uich 12th Royal Fusiliers to take up
14 — Gun position O6 a 4.9 (Railway) &
I 36 b 2.3 (KLEIN ZILLEBEKE ROAD)

Guns will open fire at Zero & clear to
meet Artillery barrage (where necessary)
ceasing fire on Zero plus 48'.

From 17th Machine Gun Company

Army Form C. 2118.

WAR DIARY
or
INTELLIGENCE SUMMARY.
(Erase heading not required.)

Vol 18

War Diary of the 17th Machine Gun Company.

July 1917.

Volume No 19

Army Form C. 2118.

WAR DIARY
or
INTELLIGENCE SUMMARY.
(Erase heading not required.)

Instructions regarding War Diaries and Intelligence Summaries are contained in F. S. Regs., Part II, and the Staff Manual respectively. Title pages will be prepared in manuscript.

Place	Date	Hour	Summary of Events and Information	Remarks and references to Appendices
NAERINGHEM	1917 July 1st		Company which left MOUNT SORRELL holds arrived here June 30th) The Company spent the day cleaning up & resting	
Do	2nd		Company parade for Kit inspection & re-equipping. The following appeared in DRO "26b d/ 3.7.17. N° 20681 Sgt BROWN G.J. awarded N° HR 24 d/27.7.17.) (authority 5th Corps N° "Distinguished Conduct Medal")	
Do	3rd		Cleaning of guns, guns equipment, ammunition belts.	
Do	4th		Training was carried out as follows:— 9 am to 12/30 p.m Physical training & Lewis drill 2 p.m to 4 p.m. Bombing parade 10 am. 6 p.m. Reinforcement commenced recruits training	

WAR DIARY
or
INTELLIGENCE SUMMARY.
(Erase heading not required.)

Army Form C. 2118.

Instructions regarding War Diaries and Intelligence Summaries are contained in F. S. Regs., Part II. and the Staff Manual respectively. Title pages will be prepared in manuscript.

Place	Date	Hour	Summary of Events and Information	Remarks and references to Appendices
NEUFCHEF	5th		Training carried out as follows.	
			6am to 12.30pm. - Firing on the range and musketry slippage.	
			2pm to 4pm - Bayonet fighting & visual training	
			Reinforcement - Elementary training continued	
Do	6th		Forenoon - Route March.	
			2pm to 4pm. - Practice in stripping of the gun.	
			2pm to 4pm. - Immediate action (stoppages)	
Do	7th		Firing on the range.	
Do	8th		Afternoon - Sports	
			Eleven a Side. Ground.	
Do	9th		At 6am. the Company with transport proceeds on line of march to ECAULT (a distance of about 16 miles) for training by the sea.	

(A7853) D. D. & L., London, E.C. Wt W8091/M1672 250,000 4/17 Sch 52a Forms/C/2118/4

WAR DIARY
or
INTELLIGENCE SUMMARY.

(Erase heading not required.)

Army Form C. 2118.

Place	Date	Hour	Summary of Events and Information	Remarks and references to Appendices
ECAULT	10		Training was carried out as usual:- Forenoon - Physical training & Gun Drill. Afternoon - Sea bathing	
Do	11		Morning - Apparatus Drill. Sea bathing	
Do	11		Afternoon - The Company marched back to NAERINGHEM leaving at 5/30 p.m., arriving at NAERINGHEM at 11.20 p.m. The brief sojourn by the sea was extremely beneficial to the men and a marked improvement in their health was seen as the result.	
NAERINGHEM	12		The day was spent in preparing for the march which to the line which was to commence on next day. Vide Appendix C.8.	

Lieut C.H. WRIGHT 2nd in command
145 C.M.G. Coy

Army Form C. 2118.

WAR DIARY
or
INTELLIGENCE SUMMARY.
(Erase heading not required.)

Instructions regarding War Diaries and Intelligence Summaries are contained in F. S. Regs., Part II. and the Staff Manual respectively. Title pages will be prepared in manuscript.

Place	Date	Hour	Summary of Events and Information	Remarks and references to Appendices
NAERINGHEM	July 13		The Company marched to Brigade sports which were held at a distance of about 6 miles from camp. A very interesting day of sport took place & was thoroughly enjoyed by the men.	
Do	14		Officers NCO's & N.1 gunners visited the Gunnery school at SENINGHEM. This model was a large scale one of the forthcoming operations & conveyed an excellent idea of the ground over which machine guns would operate. Remainder of Company training.	
NAERINGHEM	15th		Church Parade. The following award appeared in A.R.O. 213 of 13-7-17. "The 1st Field Marshal commanding in chief has awarded the Military Cross to Major T. Joyce 17 M.G. Coy."	Original

WAR DIARY
or
INTELLIGENCE SUMMARY

Army Form C. 2118.

Place	Date	Hour	Summary of Events and Information	Remarks and references to Appendices
NAERINGHEM	16		Lieut. J. M. Doughty and a Sub-Section attached to the 3rd Rifle Brigade for training for forthcoming Operations. It will [except a 2nd?] lift 100 yds. also detail will guard a each of the 1st and 12th Royal Fusiliers respectively. The remainder of the Company when not so engaged "Carry Parties" in forthcoming Operations practice Range Testing Operations practice storage work.	
NAERINGHEM	17th		The Company recommenced its march to the line leaving NAERINGHEM at 4.45 a.m. for WATTERDAL & arrived there at 9 a.m. Sect inspection by Section officer as soon as the Company was billeted in tilleuls. The Commander of the 2nd Corps visited the Headquarters of the Company & personally interviewed all officers. He was accompanied by the Divisional Brigr. General.	
WATTERDAL	18th		The Company left WATTERDAL at 7.30 a.m. for BOYENGHEM arriving there at 8.45 a.m.	

Army Form C. 2118.

WAR DIARY
or
INTELLIGENCE SUMMARY.
(Erase heading not required.)

Instructions regarding War Diaries and Intelligence Summaries are contained in F. S. Regs., Part II. and the Staff Manual respectively. Title pages will be prepared in manuscript.

Place	Date	Hour	Summary of Events and Information	Remarks and references to Appendices
WATTIKERKE	18	(seen 11)	Lieut E.M. TIBBITT from 73rd M.G. Coy. joined company and assumed 2nd in command of company. Vice Lieut. G.H. WRIGHT to 146th M.G. Coy. as L.O.	
BRYENGHEM	19		The company left for fields in RENISCURE area at 2.15 am arriving there at 9.50 am.	
		At 10:30 am felt inspection by Section Officer.		
RENISCURE	20	at 9am	Company left for billets in CAESTRE area arriving there at 9am.	
CAESTRE	21		Lieut. J.C. WILLIAMS with H gun teams proceeded RENINGHELST area at 5am and reported to the O.C. 73rd M.G. Coy. This section formed the second portion of "A" barrage battery in forthcoming operations. The company left at 8am for camp in STEENVOORDE area (Q.7.Z.1.2.) arriving there at 8.am am.	
STEENVOORDE	22		Company left at 6:30 am for camp in STEENVOORDE area arriving at 7.30 am.	

WAR DIARY
or
INTELLIGENCE SUMMARY.
(Erase heading not required.)

Army Form C. 2118.

Place	Date	Hour	Summary of Events and Information	Remarks and references to Appendices
STEENVOORDE (K 24 & 9)	23		Company inspected by the C.O. at 9.30 a.m. The remainder of the forenoon spent in practicing belt filling by the belt-filling machine.	
Do	24		The company paraded at 5.30 a.m. with guns & equipment & carried out a tactical scheme. Lieut. E.M. Wright & Lieut. C.G. Gilbert left coy. at 6 a.m. to reconnoitre the line. The company with coy. wits of No. 16 Brigade paraded at 12.40 p.m. for church parade and were addressed by the Archdeacon of York.	
Do	25		Company left at 2.30 a.m. for MICMAC CAMP (E) arriving there at 9 a.m. Gun inspection by section officers 12 noon.	

WAR DIARY or INTELLIGENCE SUMMARY

Army Form C. 2118.

Place	Date	Hour	Summary of Events and Information	Remarks and references to Appendices
MICMAC CAMP	26		Training was carried out as follows:—	
H31.A3.8			9 am to 9.45 am — Physical training.	
			10 am to 11 am — Bde. preparation order under Sub. Officers	
			2 pm to 4 pm — Inspection of guns, gun equipment.	
Do	27		Officers N.C.O's & section commanders left camp at 8.30 am for Busseboom to recce ground & general lie covered by in forthcoming operations.	
			Training was carried out as follows:—	
			Forenoon. Physical training & section drill.	
			2 pm to 4 pm. Company paraded in full battle order with guns, gun equipment &ct. and practised battery on the march, recceing the most suitable firing positions this practice was found extremely useful.	
Do	28		The company paraded in full battle order, equipped as for Ct. forthcoming Operations and was then inspected by the Brigadier General Mine D.S.O. commanding 17th Brigade. After closely inspecting the [signature]	

WAR DIARY
or
INTELLIGENCE SUMMARY.
(Erase heading not required.)

Army Form C. 2118.

Place	Date	Hour	Summary of Events and Information	Remarks and references to Appendices
Micmac Camp H31d4.8.	28		the equipment he allowed the men, congratulated them upon their past good work at LIEVIN, WYTSCHAETE RIDGE & BATTLE WOOD. He then drew their attention to the importance of machine guns in the coming operations and what was expected of them.	
Do	29		The company paraded at 9 am for C.O's inspection. Remainder of day spent in preparing guns & equipment & instructing M.G.O.'s & Barrage guns crews were given instructions regarding the operation. 3 Vickers under Lieut W.L. Jockett left camp with the Key 1st Royal Zuiches to take up position in the line.	
Do	30		The Barrage guns crews under Lieut E.H. Webb went by G.S. Wagon left camp at 10am & take up position in the line. Assembly point being HEDGE St trench at I24d 6.0. 3 team under 2Lt. N.O. Bells left camp at 9am went to 12th Royal Zuickein to take up position in the line hour/[?] hour left camp at 2 pm for Jn HEDGE St tunnel	J Dyer[?]

Army Form C. 2118.

WAR DIARY
or
INTELLIGENCE SUMMARY.
(Erase heading not required.)

Place	Date	Hour	Summary of Events and Information	Remarks and references to Appendices
HEDGE ST. Tunnel	August 30	6 p.m.	All teams arrived in the tunnel, with the exception	
	1/24	1.0	of 9 teams with the 3rd Rifle Brigade who is due to arrive	
			at midnight.	
			The tunnel are frightfully congested & unwholesome & the	
			Section commanders had the greatest difficulty in keeping	
			their teams together. The carrying parties who were attached	
			found great difficulty in relieving the tunnel owing to	
			their loads and it was found to be inexpedient to	
			order to with draw them packs. There has to be discarded.	
			ZERO hour was announced to be 3.50 am of the morning of the 31st	
HEDGE St. Tunnel	31		Disposition of guns for the attack was as follows:—	
			16 guns employed — (8) of which were to go forward with	
			the attacking infantry and 8 to form A battery of	
			Divisional machine gun barrage.	
			Distribution — 3 guns under Lieut Col Joseph to cooperate with	
			the 1st Royal Fusiliers who were attacking the BLUE LINE.	

WAR DIARY or INTELLIGENCE SUMMARY

Army Form C. 2118.

(Erase heading not required.)

Instructions regarding War Diaries and Intelligence Summaries are contained in F.S. Regs., Part II. and the Staff Manual respectively. Title pages will be prepared in manuscript.

Place	Date	Hour	Summary of Events and Information	Remarks and references to Appendices
HEDGE ST	31		for advance	REFERENCE MAP
			Our three guns were to precede and come up on the	ZILLEBEKE 1/10,000
			BLACK LINE - 3 guns under 2/Lt H.W. Zell were to advance	
			with the 12th Royal Fusiliers who were attacking the	
			BLACK LINE and there was to provide covering fire for the advance	
			on to the GREEN LINE - 2 guns were to advance	
			under Lieut R.M. Doughty with the 3rd Rifle Brigade who	
			were attacking the GREEN LINE (TOWER HAMLETS spur) these were	
			to be used as an offensive against the returning enemy	
			The final intention was to use 10 to 15 of our guns off R.	
			the GREEN & RED lines were taken to harass the enemy	
			around the GHELUVELT SPUR and down the valley towards	
			ZANDVOORDE. If the attack on the GREEN & RED lines was	
			successful the situation from a machine-gunners	
			point of view was the ideal.	

Army Form C. 2118.

WAR DIARY
or
INTELLIGENCE SUMMARY.
(Erase heading not required.)

Place	Date	Hour	Summary of Events and Information	Remarks and references to Appendices
HEDGE ST. Tunnel	7		The attack opened with a heavy now bombardment at 3.50 a.m. and our troops advanced with their proposition indications. The teams with the 1st Royal Fusiliers advanced with the battalion. Unfortunately at zero hour it was also dark that and teams lost touch. The section officer Lieut. Al Jagg was killed early in the advance and Sgt. G. L. Penn, the section Sgt. was also killed soon afterwards. Gt. Davies a.a. was also heard after he had [?] I placed his guns in position and engaged the enemy at J.25.d.4.4. One [?] team came with lost death a marker J25.a.40.50. Took up defensive position there. The other gun of this section was akways in the advance. 3 guns under Mr. two.O. Jess advanced with the 12th Royal Fus. They were less at by machine gun fire and from which one of Shrewsbury forest took with the teams. Very favorable work the advancing wave of the 3rd Rifle Brigade [?]	REFERENCE ZILLEBEKE 1/10,000.

Army Form C. 2118.

WAR DIARY
or
INTELLIGENCE SUMMARY.
(Erase heading not required.)

Instructions regarding War Diaries and Intelligence Summaries are contained in F. S. Regs., Part II. and the Staff Manual respectively. Title pages will be prepared in manuscript.

Place	Date	Hour	Summary of Events and Information	Remarks and references to Appendices
HEDGE ST Trenches	31		and took up position on their right flank engaging those parties of the enemy. Give casualties to their own. One of their causes under Sgt Hensley I took up a defensive position on London (the edge of CROMPER COPSE at about L 28 a 50.90 - Three guns fired on small parties of the enemy at long range on the TOWER HAMLETS spur also at enemy aeroplanes which were flying low at the time. This team suffered no casualties. Two guns under Lt. J. M. Doughty advanced with the 3rd Rifle Brigade leaving HEDGE ST trenches at 7.40 am. On of the guns became inaffective. Heavy casualties the gun was destroyed. Remaining gun with Lt. Doughty laboured under heavy fire of all our descriptions on they reached BODMIN COPSE & there got into position at L 19 d 45.48. They fired at a large party of enemy retreating to the scene of sheltering from JAVA DRIVE.	RE: MAP ZILLEBEKE 1/10000

WAR DIARY
or
INTELLIGENCE SUMMARY.
(Erase heading not required.)

Army Form C. 2118.

Instructions regarding War Diaries and Intelligence Summaries are contained in F. S. Regs., Part II. and the Staff Manual respectively. Title pages will be prepared in manuscript.

Place	Date	Hour	Summary of Events and Information	Remarks and references to Appendices
HEDGE ST Trench	31		engaged an enemy machine gun at J.35 b 98.78 also another which was killing up our advance on the right. They silenced the gun & inflicted casualties. Owing to the rollers/collar split pin being broken the nose of the first aid case carried by casualty up the gun was temporary out of action until the gunner used his tri-gun when this in turn became though he used the spirit gun. 2 a miss-spirits. After this repairing the gun & continuing it good work this team was subjected to reno-bant rifle and machine gun fire also very heavy shelling. Remain fell heavily during the evening causing greatly to this discomfort. At 5 pm 2 guns were sent up & gilbert advanced from George Farm trench in George Copse to our front line of J.35 b J.2.8. They went lead to this position by their guide through No. 206 + 9 Sgt D. Holland (Section 19th) On their way they passed through W.C. Lyn...	REF. MAP. ZILLEBEKE 1/10,000

WAR DIARY or INTELLIGENCE SUMMARY

Army Form C. 2118.

Place	Date	Hour	Summary of Events and Information	Remarks and references to Appendices
HEDGE ST TUNNELS	31		A heavy E.g. barrage. Sgt. Holland D leading was burned & on hearing he was being wounded in the right hand came to the knee. Sergeants Holloway & Holland gallantly led his team to their position & support to the opening. Afterwards reporting to advance Coy hqrs which had then been established at CLONMEL COPSE. At Zero barrage where had been arranged by the Brigadier 1 of our guns being deficient for this purpose. Theo guns went to take up position at Z-a Hd 95T Open fire at ZERO plus 1 hour 15 mins. Owing to the fact that the positions were in the enemy line no heavy emplacements, laying lines of fire & devising ammunition etc it was found impossible to carry out instructions. Guns moved forward into 1st Royal Fusiliers & eventually 1 gun opened fire	REF MAP ZILLEBEKE 1/10,000

(A7833) Wt W809/M1672 50,000 4/17 J. D. & L., London, E.C. Sch 58a Forms/C/2118/14

Army Form C. 2118.

WAR DIARY
or
INTELLIGENCE SUMMARY.
(Erase heading not required.)

Place	Date	Hour	Summary of Events and Information	Remarks and references to Appendices
HEDGE ST Tunnels	31		At Zero plus 2 hours 30' continued to Zero plus 7 plus 8 hours. One gun was destroyed & the crew suffered casualties. Average rounds per gun by the barrage guns 2 of this guns then took up barrage positions in CRONGE COPSE J25 a 30.80 & the remaining 3 guns refused. HEDGE ST tunnels at the following points J24 d 60.05. J30 & 45.90 J30 & 45.80. Our guns remained in these positions throughout the night. The casualties up this time has been 1 officer killed 1 sgt killed 2 sgts wounded 2 corporals wounded & 6 O.R. wounded. Throughout this trying time all ranks behaved magnificently. End of first days operations.	REF MAP ZILLEBEKE 1/10,000

J.Byer Major.
O/C 17. M.G.C.

Address to:

1. MY COMPANY / PLATOON HAS REACHED .... MARK POSITION ON MAP AND GIVE MAP REFERENCE

2. I AM AT .... AND { AM CONSOLIDATING, HAVE CONSOLIDATED, AM READY TO ADVANCE TO

3. WE ARE HELD UP BY { WIRE / MACHINE GUN / RIFLE FIRE } AT ....

4. I HAVE SENT PATROLS FORWARD TO ....

5. I NEED :— S.A.A.
   BOMBS
   RIFLE GRENADES
   WATER
   VERY LIGHTS S·O·S SIGNALS, ROCKETS
   STOKES SHELLS
   STAKES, WIRE
   SPARE LEWIS GUN DRUMS
   STRETCHER BEARERS

6. ENEMY TROOPS STRENGTH ESTIMATED AT .... { ASSEMBLING AT / ADVANCING FROM / RETIRING FROM

7. I AM IN TOUCH WITH .... ON RIGHT / LEFT AT ....

8. I AM NOT IN TOUCH ON RIGHT / LEFT

9. AM BEING SHELLED FROM .... NATURE OF SHELL ....

10. I ESTIMATE MY PRESENT STRENGTH AT .... RIFLES

11. HOSTILE { BATTERY / MACHINE GUN / TRENCH MORTAR } ACTIVE AT .... AND IS SHOOTING AT ....

12. I INTEND TO

TIME .... A.M. (P.M.)   NAME ....
DATE ....   PLATOON .... COMPANY ....
                                          BATTALION ....

N.B. The R·F of Map overleaf is 1/10,000

SECRET

17th Machine Gun Company.

SKETCH MAP "A" attached.

Instructions to Section Officers for forthcoming operations.

(1.) Disposition of guns :- See attached appendix. A
    Time-Table &c :-   "   "   "   B. C

(2.) The forthcoming operations possess unique features from a machine-gunners point of view and it is therefore the duty of section officers to see that no opportunity is lost in obtaining the fullest advantage from concentrated Machine-Gun fire. This specially applies to the sections advancing with the attacking battalions. Special points to be attended to are:-

(a.) Guns to be pushed boldly forward, occupying positions and providing effective covering fire for the advance on to the BLACK and GREEN lines.

(b.) To keep a sharp lookout especially on the right flank for suitable targets, (section officers to go forward in advance of teams for this purpose.)

(c.) After the BLACK and GREEN lines are taken to take up suitable defensive positions to bring effective fire to bear on points from which the enemy are likely to counter-attack.

(d.) To send all the information possible as to the progress of operations to Company H.Q. This should include positions of our Machine-guns, the extent of the opposition on the part of the enemy, action by the enemy artillery and machine-guns. The positions of enemy machine-guns should be located if possible and compass bearings quoted.

It is the duty of section officers to see that their subordinates possess a thorough knowledge of the coming operations, of the chain of command, and the positions of the guns of other sections and method of communication with Company H.Q.

(3). **Reports.**

A system of runners will be arranged to ensure all the guns being in touch with each other.

Reports to Company hqrs from forward positions will be sent by relay runners, each section or sub section passing messages back from forward positions by relay to Company hqrs. Messages from Company hqrs will be sent in a similar manner.

(4). **Equipment.**

The following information is given for guidance.

(a). Full marching order without packs (except numbers 4 & 5 of the teams)

Omit × (b). ~~No state islands need to be carried~~

(c). Haversacks to be worn on the back (except Nºs 4 & 5 who will wear them at the side).

(d) Waterproof sheet to be carried.

(e) 2 Sandbags to be carried.

(f) Towel, soap & etc. need not be carried.

Gun teams will be arranged as follows:—

Team commander will carry first-aid case, condenser and tube, spare barrel, cleaning rod, and shovel.

Nº 1. — will carry gun with light mounting, two strips of metal belt with 50 rounds in each.

Nº 2. — 2 belt boxes
Nº 3. — 3 belt boxes
Nº 4. — 1 tin of water in pack & 1 belt box.
Nº 5. — Tripod.
(Runner) Nº 6. — 2 belt boxes
Nºs 7 & 8 — 3 belt boxes each. (if possible on Yukon packs).
(Infantry men attached).

Barrage guns to have belt-filling machines with their sections.

(5). **Rations**

On Z day every man will be in possession of one days rations and his Iron Rations.

On Z night rations for one section (Barrage guns) will be drawn at Company hqrs (HEDGE St tunnel).

10 gun teams should be rationed by the 3rd Rifle Brigade and 2 gun teams rationed by the 12th Royal Irs.

(6). **Ammunition**

Arrangements for ammunition supply, movement of guns, time, rates & periods of fire also barrage arrangements including S.O.S. will be shown on a separate appendix.

July 21st 1917.

J. Doyle Major
O/c 17th M.G.C.

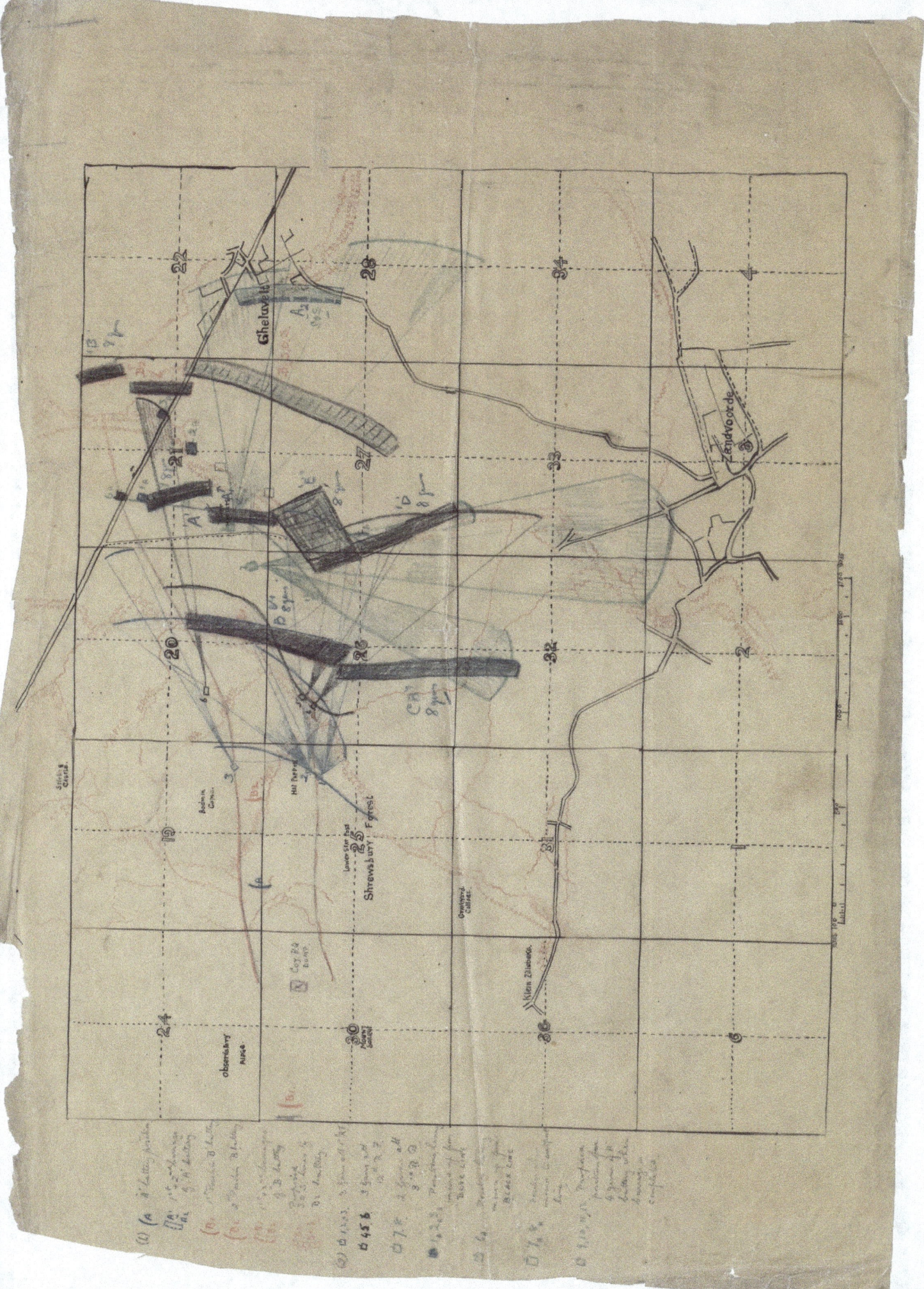

APPENDIX "B".

17th Machine Gun Company. — Company Headquarters HEDGE ST TUNNELS
Advanced Coy. HQrs. ZERO + 6 hrs. JAVA TRENCH
(About) J 26 a . 4 . 8

Disposition of guns are shown in appendix "A".
The following table shows the approximate times
by which guns should be in position, rates
of fire, movements etc.

GUN	APPROXIMATE LOCATION	FIRING FROM	FIRING TO	TARGET	RATES OF FIRE
1	J 25 b 5.3	ZERO + 60	Z + 75 / 1hr 10	JEHU TRENCH	CONTINUOUS
2	J 25 b 6.4	ZERO + 60	Z + 1 hr 25 min	JAVA / JAR TRENCH	Do.
3	J 19 d 5.3	ZERO + 60	Z + 1 hr 25 min	JASPER TRENCH	Do.

(Nos. 1, 2, & 3. Require careful elevation.)

1	Ditto	Z + 2 hrs 30	Z + 7 hrs 30	J 26 b 8.1	1 Belt per
2		Z + 2 hrs 30	Z + 7 hrs 30	J 27 a 2.3 / J 27 a 5.8	Gun per
3		Z + 2 hrs 30	Z + 7 hrs 30	J 20 b 8.7	8 minutes

These guns will after refilling belts move forward
to left flank of 3rd R.B. and take up
defensive positions on line of resistance, arriving
about Zero + 9 hrs.

4	J 26 a 5.5	Z + 2 hrs 20	Z + 7 hrs 40	J 27 c 2.5 / J 33 a 5.0	Rate of fire
5	J 26 a 4.6	Z + 2 hrs 20	Z + 7 hrs 40	J 27 a 1.8 / J 27 c 4.3	1 belt per gun
6	J 20 c 2.7	Z + 2 hrs	Z + 7 hrs 20	J 21 b 30.25	per 8 min

Nos. 4 . 5 will occupy defensive positions in this area &
keep up steady harassing fire during the night.

No. 6 will go forward Z + 8 hrs & take up defensive
position on left flank of GREEN LINE of resistance
arriving there ZERO + 9 hrs.

7	J 20 d 8.3	about Z + 7 hrs 40	Z + 8 hrs 40	Trench running South through J 27 c	
8	J 21 c 1.4	" Z + 7 hrs 40	Z + 8 hrs 40	Trench running from J 22 c b J 28 a . b CHELUVELT	

These guns will then occupy positions in line of
strong points on right flank of 3rd R.B.

9 13 ⎫ Form battery "A" for barrage scheme. 9. 10. 11 & 12 will on
10 14 ⎬ completion of barrage advance to GREEN LINE and take up
11 15 ⎪ position on left flank & should be in position by ZERO + 9 hrs.
12 16 ⎭ 13, 14, 15, 16 to be in Brigade Reserve & will keep in touch with Coy. H.Q.

17th Machine Gun Company.   APPENDIX C.

                    AMMUNITION.

Each gun will carry forward 13 belt boxes.
On arrival at positions carrying party will return
for ammunition to be drawn from a company
dump the location of which will be announced later.

The location of Brigade dumps are as follows:—
  MAIN DUMP   RUDKIN HOUSE
  FORWARD DUMPS   HEDGE ST TUNNELS. I 30 b 4. 7.
  "A" BATTERY DUMP -   at assembly positions - amount
                    to be obtained 200,000 rounds.

MACHINE GUN BARRAGE: FINAL TIME TABLE.

17th M.G.Coy.   24th Division.

Batty.	Approximate Location.	Firing from.	To.	Target.	Grid bearing of left gun Zero line.	Q.E.	Remarks.
"A"	J.19.c.4.0.	Between Zero & + 1 hr.15 mins. moves into position.					Ass.Position in HEDGE ST.TUNNELS.
		Left Sect. + 1 hr.20 mins.	+ 1 hr.45 mins.	J.21.a.5.3.to J.21.c.6.8.	73°	4°45'	Rate of fire 1 belt per gun per 4 mins.
	Ditto.	Right Sect. + 1 hr.20 mins.	+ 1 hr.50 mins.	J.21.c.4.6.to J.27.a.4.9.	83°	4° 5'	
	Ditto.	Left Sect. + 1 hr.45 mins.	+ 2hrs.30 mins.	J.21.b.1.5.to J.27.b.3.9.	73°	5°40'	On S.O.S. going up double the rate for 15 mins.
		Right Sect. + 1 hr.50 mins.	+ 2hrs.30 mins.		83°	6°40'	
	Ditto.	+ 2hrs.30 mins.*	+ 6 hours.*	Ditto.	Do.	Do.	# 2 guns per battery at half rate.
	Ditto.	+ 6hrs.20 mins.	+ 6hrs.25 mins.	Ditto.	Do.	Do.	
	Ditto.	Left Sect. + 6hrs.25 mins.	+ 7 hours.	J.21.d.5.8.to J.21.d.5.0.	82°	7°40'	
	Ditto.	Right Sect. ditto.	ditto.	J.21.d.4.1.to J.27.b.3.3.	90°	6°45'	

At Zero + 7 hours "A" Battery comes under orders of B.G.C. 17th Inf. Bde.

CONFIDENTIAL

Army Form C. 2118.

WAR DIARY
or
INTELLIGENCE SUMMARY.
(Erase heading not required.)

Sgt 19

WAR DIARY — 17th Machine Gun Company

for month of August 1917.

Volume No 20.

WAR DIARY
or
INTELLIGENCE SUMMARY

Army Form C. 2118.

Place	Date 1917	Hour	Summary of Events and Information	Remarks and references to Appendices
	August			REF. MAP. ZILLEBEKE 1/10000
MICMAC CAMP	1st		Company took over the line - Coucou was employed at HEDGE St Curreles.	
M.7.d.9.9			1 2nd d 6.0. D cais at MICMAC camp. 4.7 d.w.8. The Americans kept the company both hour in the accent on the GREEN LINE (TOWER HAMLETS Spur) as given in Diary for 31st July. The gun were on position as under.	
			No 1 gun J.19. d. 20. 40. No 6 gun, J.25. b. 4. 7	
			No 2 . J.25. t. 55. 90. 7 . J.25. a. 50. 90	
			No 3 J.25. d. 40. 98. 8 J.25. a. 40.50	
			No 4 J.25. t. 40. 90 9 . 10 J.25. a. 30.80	
			No 5 J.25. t. 30. 45. 11.12.16. Out of action	
			Guns No 11.12 & 13 were in Reserve positions at HEDGE St. linked to Junior- J.24. d. 60. 05. - J.30. b. 45. 90. - J.30. b.45. 90.	
			Owing to very bad weather, munitions came up with bodily difficulty on the Journey. Once an hour they were practically useless. They were also running by layer by the sudden water. They were - . . . difficult. The ground was splendidly.	

Army Form C. 2118.

WAR DIARY
or
INTELLIGENCE SUMMARY.
(Erase heading not required.)

Place	Date	Hour	Summary of Events and Information	Remarks and references to Appendices
Micmac Camp	1st (Cont'd)		Throughout the day our observers from A Section Report noticing the exception and spirit of the men — the refused by men one machine gun, no enemy shifting with the Coys and keeping casualties nil. Standing in a most sporting manner. Little or no firing was done. As Coys were moving up ammunition in case of a counter attack and day was spent improving and consolidating the new positions. Casualties on this date, 1 OR. Killed & 6 wounded.	Reference Map ZILLEBEKE 1/10000
Do	2nd		All guns remained in same position on or previous day. Our guns positions were heavily shelled by enemy arts. 2 OR were killed & 1 wounded. No offensive action was taken by us. Our ammunition was being moved for our entire counter-attack. Guns in same positions. They were all heavy shelling 2h.00 from	
Do	3rd	4.15 am to 5.45 am	The Left Group guns at Trig. a. 29.d.40 fired on a party of the enemy seen on the ridge at	Over

Army Form C. 2118.

WAR DIARY
or
INTELLIGENCE SUMMARY.
(Erase heading not required.)

Instructions regarding War Diaries and Intelligence Summaries are contained in F. S. Regs., Part II. and the Staff Manual respectively. Title pages will be prepared in manuscript.

Place	Date	Hour	Summary of Events and Information	Remarks and references to Appendices
MCMAC CAMP	3rd (cont.)		About T.20.C.10.15 and T.25.C.95.90 and it is believed casualties were inflicted. Enemy M.G. fire did injury Machine Guards the end of the day. As the result of our fire during the day the enemy aircraft were driven from this sector by the 73rd and 191st M.C. Companies and from Vrouwen to Moppo Corpe	Defences Nr. ZILLEBEKE J/9000
Do	4th		No patrols to enemy it was found that about 50 of the men were suffering heavily from the exposure. 10 were evacuated to Field Ambulance and the remainder were ordered rest for several days. The total casualties from 31/7/17 1 night 2/4 were 1 Officer (Lieut. W.L. JESSOPP) & 2 OR killed - 16 OR wounded & 2 missing believed killed	
Do	5th		The day was spent resting and were again requipped and cleaning up generally	JNK

WAR DIARY or INTELLIGENCE SUMMARY

Army Form C. 2118.

Place	Date	Hour	Summary of Events and Information	Remarks and references to Appendices
MICMAC CAMP	6th		Location -- Cleaning and overhaul of guns & equipment. Afternoon - parking guns etc. on lorries & getting ready to move to new camp. Transport paraded at 5.15 p.m. reveille off at 6 p.m. for M.T. Lines Dickebusch W.3 d.9.7. arriving there at 6.15 p.m.	
DICKEBUSCH	7th		The forenoon was spent in overhauling guns. Your equipment etc. Loading limbers for the move into the line. In the afternoon to relieve the 1st Machine Gun Company. Owing to casualties and sickness only 3 guns could be put into the line. These were organised by 8 Hotchkiss guns of the Yorkshire Brigade which were placed under our command. Officers moved to MICMAC CAMP. 26 purchasement from Base Depot joined on the evening.	[signature]

Army Form C. 2118.

WAR DIARY
or
INTELLIGENCE SUMMARY.
(Erase heading not required.)

Instructions regarding War Diaries and Intelligence Summaries are contained in F.S. Regs., Part II. and the Staff Manual respectively. Title pages will be prepared in manuscript.

Place	Date	Hour	Summary of Events and Information	Remarks and references to Appendices
Dieppe Camp	8th		Leonard Headquarters at LARCH WOOD-Tunnel. I.29.C.2.9. During the night enemy artillery fair was below normal. Our troops engaged in improving the gun positions. Pls. at Hispar coy. engaged slewing ammunition etc.	Reference Map ZILLEBEKE 1/10,000.
Do	9th		From midnight 9th till about 8p.m. 9th enemy artillery fairly quiet but about that hour shewing increased activity in forward and back areas. Hostile aircraft very active during the forenoon and engaged by our machine guns. 1 Physical Drill Parade for Details at camp.	
Do	10th		Heavy shelling throughout the night. At 12 noon 1st Hotchkiss gun fired at enemy aeroplane but no visible result. Parades for Details at Camp - Physical Drill - Box Resp. Drill etc.	[signature]

(A7853) Wt.W8597M1672 50,000 4/17 D.D.&L., London, E.C. Sch. 82a. Forms/C/2118/14

Army Form C. 2118.

WAR DIARY
or
INTELLIGENCE SUMMARY.
(Erase heading not required.)

Instructions regarding War Diaries and Intelligence Summaries are contained in F. S. Regs., Part II. and the Staff Manual respectively. Title pages will be prepared in manuscript.

Place	Date	Hour	Summary of Events and Information	Remarks and references to Appendices
MICMAC CAMP	11th		During the evening all leave was relieved by the 71st Batty. and proceeded to details camp at MICMAC. Casualties during this period in the line 1 O.R. Killed & 3 Wd.	
Do	12th		9 am any work in fitting & cleaning up.	
Do	13th		Parades as follows:- Forenoon - Physical training & gun drilling. Reinforcements - Gas drill. Afternoon - Foreman. Inspection and overhauling of gun equipment, ammunition etc.	
Do	14th		Parades as forenoon. Afternoon - Gun fitting inspection.	
Do	15th		Reinforcements being told on the guns. Remainder of company working parties & preparing to move to camp at DICKEBUSCH Hts.	

WAR DIARY
or
INTELLIGENCE SUMMARY.
(Erase heading not required.)

Army Form C. 2118.

Place	Date	Hour	Summary of Events and Information	Remarks and references to Appendices
MICMAC CAMP	15th (cont'd)		Company paraded at 5/30 pm and march off at 5/45 pm arriving at camp at Dickebusch at 9/30 pm.	
DICKEBUSCH	16th		Parade was carried out as follows:- Inspection - Physical Training - Gun drill. The following attended in orders of the part the ralf Commander for wearing the MILITARY MEDAL. No 31023 Pte WILKINSON H. & No 44973 Pte SMITH H. (Authority XIth Corps No 2 H.R./7/19 d/14/9/17). Lieut. M. WEST and 2/Lieut GALWAY A.T. joined company from base.	
Do	17th		Parades as follows:- Inspection - Physical Drill - Gun drill & Reinforcements - Inspection clean suppers available.	
Do	19		Reinforcements. Gun Drill & Immediate Action Gas Drill. Remainder of company overhauling guns - gun equipment.	

Army Form C. 2118.

WAR DIARY
or
INTELLIGENCE SUMMARY.
(Erase heading not required.)

Instructions regarding War Diaries and Intelligence Summaries are contained in F. S. Regs., Part II. and the Staff Manual respectively. Title pages will be prepared in manuscript.

Place	Date	Hour	Summary of Events and Information	Remarks and references to Appendices
DICKEBUSCH	18th	(Cont.)	making preparations for moving into the line on the 19.	Reference Map ZILLEBEKE 1/10,000
Do.	19		Coys proceeded to the line during the afternoon relieving the 17th M.G. Coy. Details moved to Micmac Camp at 6 pm.	
MICMAC CAMP	20		Fairly Inconspicuous at LARCH WOOD tunnels. I 29 c 2.7 Situation.- Quiet at our gun positions. Back areas shelled at 2am with relief attention forward sque at LARCH WOOD but no casualties	
Do.	21st		Guns stood to every artillery day acting on our left. During heavy shining our O.P. Gun was damaged. Our Luer at 12.30 am. Lieut. C.M. DOUGHTY M.C. was killed by shell fire and buried near Our sqne men were engaged carrying ammunition to	

WAR DIARY
or
INTELLIGENCE SUMMARY.
(Erase heading not required.)

Army Form C. 2118.

Place	Date	Hour	Summary of Events and Information	Remarks and references to Appendices
M.M.MG Coy.	21(contd)		Forward Dumps F. Barrage continuous	Reference Map LILLEGHE 1/10,000
		2pm	3 enemy aeroplanes flew over Mount Sorrel at a height of about 300 ft. They were engaged by 2 of our guns, a very large number of shots being fired at them. Considerable height 1400 rounds were fired at them.	
		5pm	The enemy shewed towards the vicinity of I.29.d.6.4 for about half an hour.	
		6.15pm	Our guns were engaged enemy aeroplanes 700 yards being fired. The remainder of the night artillery fire. During the remainder of the night was normal.	
Do	22nd	12.15 am	Our M.Guns carried out harassing fire on TOWER HAMLETS at intervals from 1000	
			Our machine guns co-operated in the morning by firing in the morning, leaving a harassing fire. Covering fire. Harassing fire.	

Army Form C. 2118.

WAR DIARY
or
INTELLIGENCE SUMMARY.
(Erase heading not required.)

Place	Date	Hour	Summary of Events and Information	Remarks and references to Appendices
MICMAC CAMP.	22			Reference map. ZILLEBEKE 1/10000

Moved through to locate on area around J.9.d – JAVA TRENCH – JAR TRENCH & TOWER HAMLETS. Area Barrage fire on

J.20 A.1.8 to J.14 A.8.12 – J.21 A.3.72 to J.14 A.27.50 – J.14 C.57.04 to J.14 A.27.50 – J.14 A.1.52 to J.20 A.60.93 – to J.14 A.27.50 – J.14 C.40.60 to J.14 A.30.55 – J.20 A.96.5 to J.20 b.6.9.

86,500 rounds of various natures expended.

The attack by 14th Bde (the larger operation of our C(?)) presented in the advance through INVERNESS COPSE & GLENCORSE WOOD.

The minor operation on our front by the 1st Royal Fusiliers was very successful. With the co-operation of the light T.M. Battery our machine gunners 1 officer and 20 men carried out a diversion attack on an enemy strong point with good results only 11 casualties to the party they captured their objective + machine gun, held it by the evening + captured 35 prisoners. They then consolidated + held the position.

Army Form C. 2118.

WAR DIARY
or
INTELLIGENCE SUMMARY.
(Erase heading not required.)

Place	Date	Hour	Summary of Events and Information	Remarks and references to Appendices
ANZAC Camp	22nd June 1916		Hostile aircraft was very active about 10 am, flying over of our guns fired 2,200 rounds at one aeroplane was observed to descend unsteadily and make towards the enemy lines. At 2:30 pm our machine gun opened fire on one Oscar aeroplane 2.0 cad a T.M.C. it hiding near supplies that the enemy were returning in this direction. 2,000 rounds were fired.	
Do.	23rd		Our machine guns carried out harassing fire during the night specially around TOWER HAMLETS - number of rounds fired 4,200. Enemy aircraft was engaged at 7.45 pm number of rounds fired 1030. During the evening flight our barn were fired by the 13th Machine Gun Company & reported to ANZAC Corp. Casualties during the 24 hours in the lines 1 officer killed 3 OR wnd.	

D. D. & L., London, E.C.
(45253) Wt W8o/M1672 350,000 4/17 Sch 52a Forms/C/2118/4

WAR DIARY
or
INTELLIGENCE SUMMARY

Army Form C. 2118.

(Erase heading not required.)

Place	Date	Hour	Summary of Events and Information	Remarks and references to Appendices
MICMAC CAMP	24		The day was spent in partly clearing up.	
Do	25	9.15 am to 10 am	Parade: Physical Drill. Reorganisation of Coy. Que classing M.G.W. PETRIE joined Coy from Tr. Depot & 22 OBn. joined Coy HQr. 14th M.G. Coy (Ce Coy to 2nd Bn post 2/27/5/17). Parade now as follows:— Physical Drill — Gas Inspection — Physical Drill — Gas Inspection of Gun, Gun equipment etc.	
Do	26		The following officers in orders of this date as attached. Lieut G.M. DOUGHTY — awarded the MILITARY CROSS. Lieut H.W. FELLS — awarded the MILITARY CROSS. No 26649 Sgt D. McCANN & No 2283 Cpl. HALL G. — awarded the D.C.M. (Authority X.th Corps. No 7/HR 249 d/30.3.17	
Do	27		Parade were carried out during the forenoon as follows:— Physical Training, Gun Drill. Mounting Paraded at 5pm marched off to DICKEBUSCH camp.	

Army Form C. 2118.

WAR DIARY
or
INTELLIGENCE SUMMARY.
(Erase heading not required.)

Place	Date	Hour	Summary of Events and Information	Remarks and references to Appendices
MOASCAR CAMP.	21		Divine Service at 6pm.	
			The following appears in orders of the day —	
			"No. 20655 L/Cpl J. Dumsty awarded the D.C.M.	
			Lately K⁽ᵗʰ⁾ Coy No.2/4.B.29 April (23.9.17) wire the following	
			in a report of a recce recce from the O.C.	
			3ʳᵈ Rifle Brigade whose Battalion L/Cpl Dumsty's team	
			was supporting asks to inform the and for	
			which he was recommended. "Please convey my	
			congratulations to No.20655 L/Cpl J. Dumsty of the Company	
			under your command on being awarded the	
			Distinguished Conduct Medal."	
	23		Parades were carried out as follows —	
			Inspection — Physical Drill Exercise —	
			Requirements being told on the gun — stoppages	
			immediate action and mechanism	

WAR DIARY
or
INTELLIGENCE SUMMARY.
(Erase heading not required.)

Army Form C. 2118.

Place	Date	Hour	Summary of Events and Information	Remarks and references to Appendices
DICKEBUSCH CAMP	29		Parade as follows:- Morning - Physical Drill - Inspection of Respirators, Gas drill. Afternoon - Kit inspection.	
Do	30		The day was spent completing guns equipment and kits generally - preparing to move into the line on the 31st.	
Do	31		During the forenoon the company was engaged packing limbers and at 3 p.m. the teams to take up positions in the line were off. The journey starting at 5/30 p.m. A Coal moved to M.2.M.A.C. Camp at 6 p.m.	

WAR DIARY
or
INTELLIGENCE SUMMARY.

Army Form C. 2118.

Place	Date	Hour	Summary of Events and Information	Remarks and references to Appendices
MEPPL CAMP	1		The foregoing message dated 31st August was received for communication to our trawlers.	
			" The Army Commander wishes to impress his appreciation and thanks to the 2nd Division for their work while with the Fifth Army. They have carried a long period in the line under most trying conditions of weather and heavy shelling."	

[signature] Major
Commanding 17. Machine Gun Company

Army Form C. 2118.

WAR DIARY
or
INTELLIGENCE SUMMARY.
(Erase heading not required.)

17 M.G. Coy
VA 20

CONFIDENTIAL

War Diary

17th Machine Gun Company

September 1917.

Volume No. 21.

WAR DIARY
or
INTELLIGENCE SUMMARY.
(Erase heading not required.)

Army Form C. 2118.

Place	Date	Hour	Summary of Events and Information	Remarks and references to Appendices
HEDGE ST Tunnels	1st		The Company moved into the line on 31st August. The positions of guns were as under. No. (1) J.19.b.10.80 (2) J.14.c.0.20 (3) J.13.d.90.65 (4) J.13.d.90.70 (5) J.19.d.15.15 (6) J.19.d.30.45 (7) J.19.c.65.95 (8) J.19.c.65.75 (9) J.13.d.90.65 (10) J.13.d.75.70 (11) J.13.c.65.15 14 guns in position in HEDGE ST tunnels 500 rounds fired by our M.G's at enemy plane flying low. At 8.15 am an enemy plane flying at a height of about 600 ft over our front line was engaged by gun at J.19.c.30.30. After 100 rounds had been fired the plane was observed to nose dive & fall about 400 yards behind the enemy line. Shelling of forward areas was below normal. 200 rounds fired at enemy planes flying low over our line at 5.30 am.	Reference chart Z ZILLEBEKE
DO	2nd		Enemy artillery & machine guns on our front	

WAR DIARY
or
INTELLIGENCE SUMMARY.
(Erase heading not required.)

Army Form C. 2118.

Place	Date	Hour	Summary of Events and Information	Remarks and references to Appendices
HEDGE ST TUNNELS	2nd (Contd)		inaction but very heavy shelling on the left of our Brigade front.	
Do	3rd		Our trenches were subjected to heavy shelling by the 13th Machine Gun Company & proceeded to Brigade camp. Relief was completed by 10.30 p.m.	
MICMAC CAMP	4th		The day was spent in cleaning up generally.	
Do	5th		The Company proceeded with the 1st Bn. Light Infy M.B. were inspected by the G.O.C. 24 Division During the afternoon the digging of trenches & erecting sandbag walls round the camp was commenced	Copy

WAR DIARY
or
INTELLIGENCE SUMMARY.

(Erase heading not required.)

Army Form C. 2118.

Place	Date	Hour	Summary of Events and Information	Remarks and references to Appendices
MICMAC CAMP	Jul. 6		Parades were carried out as follows. Forenoon - Digging of trenches and sandbagging. Drill tiddle was continued. Afternoon - Gun Drill.	
Do	7th		Parades were carried out as follows. Forenoon - Physical training. Gun drill. Parking of limbers. Afternoon - The 1 now to Dickebusch. Preparing generally for the move in the evening. Company paraded at 5 p.m. & moved off for M Camp Dickebusch arriving there at 5¼ p.m.	
DICKEBUSCH	8th		3 Officers & 1 O.R. proceeded at 5 a.m. to reconnoitre new part of line. Parades were as follows:- Physical training - overhauling of guns & gun equipment.	

WAR DIARY
or
INTELLIGENCE SUMMARY.
(Erase heading not required.)

Army Form C. 2118.

Instructions regarding War Diaries and Intelligence Summaries are contained in F.S. Regs., Part II. and the Staff Manual respectively. Title pages will be prepared in manuscript.

Place	Date	Hour	Summary of Events and Information	Remarks and references to Appendices
DICKEBUSCH	9th		Church Parade at 9 am in Dickebusch Church. 11 Officers & OR Parsons joined the Company from Base.	
Do	10th		Parades were as follows:- Physical Drill – Inspection of Gas helmets – Bar Drill. The remainder of the day was spent in preparing of generally for the move into the line on the 11th.	
Do	11th		Parades were as follows:- Foreman – Shapers Once – Iron Ration – Kit inspection. During the afternoon the Company proceeded to the line to took over new Brigade front which was from CLAPHAM JUNCTION to S.E. corner of BODMIN COPSE. It OR. were wounded before relief was complete which was at 9.50 p.m. Details moved to MICMAC CAMP. 1 Officer & 24 OR Parsons joined the Company from Base.	

D.D. & L., London, E.C.
(A983j) Wt. W80/M1672 350,000 4/17 Sch. 52a Forms/C/2118/14

Army Form C. 2118.

WAR DIARY
or
INTELLIGENCE SUMMARY.
(Erase heading not required.)

Instructions regarding War Diaries and Intelligence Summaries are contained in F. S. Regs., Part II. and the Staff Manual respectively. Title pages will be prepared in manuscript.

Place	Date	Hour	Summary of Events and Information	Remarks and references to Appendices
	11 (cont)		advanced by stages at HEDGE St trench	
HEDGE ST	12		The enemy shelled back area with gas shells between 12 midnight & 3am to which slightly affected by stages in the trench. Enemy artillery normal & rifle inactive. Work commenced on new gun emplacement at No 10 position. Remainder of gun teams engaged clearing trenches & improving gun positions. Casualties – 1 O.R. wounded.	
HEDGE ST	13		Our artillery put up a barrage at 8pm. to which the enemy replied with a counter-barrage. Our M.G's fired 1,000 rounds at enemy planes flying low over No 9 position. Enemy arty: normal. Work continued on new emplacement at No 10 position	

WAR DIARY
or
INTELLIGENCE SUMMARY.
(Erase heading not required.)

Army Form C. 2118.

Place	Date	Hour	Summary of Events and Information	Remarks and references to Appendices
HEDGE ST	14th		Enemy artillery & M.G's active at enemy planes. 500 rounds fired by our M.G's at No 8.9 position Gun at No 9 position fired on a party of the enemy near INVERNESS COPSE and it is believed 2 casualties were inflicted. 200 rounds fired at enemy planes at 7.30 pm.	Ref. map. ZILLEBEKE
Do	15th		Enemy artillery very active during the night. Our machine guns carried out harassing fire on the enemy's lines of communication during the night. 10,000 rounds were expended. During the afternoon all tires were relieved by the 10th & 19th Machine gun coys & proceeded to DICKEBUSCH CAMP. Details at MIEMAC CAMP wood up to DICKEBUSCH camp at 5 pm.	

Army Form C. 2118.

WAR DIARY
or
INTELLIGENCE SUMMARY.
(Erase heading not required.)

Place	Date	Hour	Summary of Events and Information	Remarks and references to Appendices
DICKEBUSCH	16		The Company paraded at 6 a.m. entrained with the other units of the brigade and at 6/30 a.m. proceeded to new billets in MERRIS AREA (Fr.Ay.8) arriving there at 11 a.m.	
MERRIS area (Fr.Ay.8)	17th		Parades were carried out as follows. 9 a.m. — Inspection by C.O. 9.15 a.m. to 10 a.m. — Physical training 10.15 a.m. to 12/30 p.m. Overhauling of guns & gun equipment.	
Do	18th		Parades were as follows. 9.15 a.m. to 10 a.m. — Physical Drill 10 a.m. to 12 noon. Gun Drill.	
Do	19th		Company parades with 16th M.G.C. marked 16 MERRIS & was inspected by General Daly. The new Divisional commander.	

WAR DIARY
or
INTELLIGENCE SUMMARY.
(Erase heading not required.)

Army Form C. 2118.

Place	Date	Hour	Summary of Events and Information	Remarks and references to Appendices
MERRIS Area F 2 d 8	20		The forenoon was spent in packing up limbers, cleaning up kits & preparing generally for moving off in the evening. Company paraded at 6pm. & left at 6/15 p.m. for BAILLEUL WEST Station arriving there at 7.15 p.m. Company with transport entrained & left at 11.30 p.m. for BAPAUME.	
BAPAUME	21		Arrived & detrained at BAPAUME WEST Station at 8.15 am. Marched to machine-gun camp at BUS arriving there at 2.15 p.m.	
Bus	22		Parades were carried out as follows. Forenoon:- Physical Drill - Squad & section Drill. Afternoon: - Company Drill	

Army Form C. 2118.

WAR DIARY
or
INTELLIGENCE SUMMARY.
(Erase heading not required.)

Instructions regarding War Diaries and Intelligence Summaries are contained in F. S. Regs., Part II. and the Staff Manual respectively. Title pages will be prepared in manuscript.

Place	Date	Hour	Summary of Events and Information	Remarks and references to Appendices
Bus M.C. Camp.	13th (Sunday)		Inspection by C.O. at 9.30 a.m. Afternoon – Football Match.	
Do	24th		Parades were as follows. Forenoon – Section Drill – Gun Drill – Gun Cleaning. Company Drill, gun drill. Afternoon –	
Do	25th		Parade were as follows. 9.30 a.m. – Inspection by C.O. 9.15 to 10.45 a.m. Gun Drill. 11 a.m. to 12.30 p.m. Physical training under Brigade instructor.	
Do	26th		Parades were as follows. Forenoon – Physical Drill – Overhauling of guns & gun equipment. Afternoon – Inspection by M.O. – Gas Respirators.	

Army Form C. 2118.

WAR DIARY
or
INTELLIGENCE SUMMARY.
(Erase heading not required.)

Instructions regarding War Diaries and Intelligence Summaries are contained in F. S. Regs., Part II. and the Staff Manual respectively. Title pages will be prepared in manuscript.

Place	Date	Hour	Summary of Events and Information	Remarks and references to Appendices
BUS M.G. Camp	26 (Contd)		O.O. proceeded to reconnoitre next part of line to be taken over.	
DO	27		Company paraded at 8am. & moved off at 8.15am. for camp at 1029 b3.1 arriving there at 11.25am. The remainder of the day was occupied with getting the camp in order.	
HAUT ALLAINES 1029 b 3.1	28		Parades were as follows:- Reveille. Inspection by M.O. Physical Drill & General Cleaning. Advance parts of 1 Wks & 2 Cos. proceeded by motor to take over new front near BERNES.	
1029 b 3.1	29		Company paraded at 8 am & marched to Brigade embussing point & moved off from there by motor bus at 9.30am. Arrived at BERNES at 11.30 am. & took over camp.	

Army Form C. 2118.

WAR DIARY
or
INTELLIGENCE SUMMARY.
(Erase heading not required.)

Place	Date	Hour	Summary of Events and Information	Remarks and references to Appendices
BERNES	29.July.17		During the afternoon 12 horse & gun proceeded to the lines & took over from the 11th Battery WK. Squadron relieving a mounted number of guns. The part of the line taken over from LE VERGUIER to the left of the french line at PONTRUET. Advanced Troop Hqrs formed at SMALL FOOT WOOD.	Ref Sheet 62 C N.E.
Do	30.		Situation very quiet at over gun positions.	
			Casualties during the month.	
			2/Lieut A.J. GALWAY wounded 27. 7/17	
			Lieut W WEST to UK sick. 4/9/17	
			1 O.R. Died of wounds & 9 O.R. wounded	
			Compiled 30.7.17	
				J.N.G. Major
				Commanding "J" W.V. Kempany
Strength of			10 Officers 194 O.R.	

Army Form C. 2118.

WAR DIARY
or
INTELLIGENCE SUMMARY.
(Erase heading not required.)

Vol 21

Place	Date	Hour	Summary of Events and Information	Remarks and references to Appendices
Cambrin			War Diary	
			17th Machine Gun Company	
			October 1917.	
			Volume 22.	
			Joy. Major	
			17th M.G. Coy	
			Commanding	

Instructions regarding War Diaries and Intelligence Summaries are contained in F. S. Regs., Part II. and the Staff Manual respectively. Title pages will be prepared in manuscript.

Army Form C. 2118.

WAR DIARY
or
INTELLIGENCE SUMMARY.
(Erase heading not required.)

Reference Sheet 62cNE

Place	Date	Hour	Summary of Events and Information	Remarks and references to Appendices
BERNES	Oct 1		Transport lines & Details remain at BERNES.	
			Advanced Hdqs. at SMALL FOOT WOOD - B.8.b.75.40.	
			The Company moved up to the line on the 29th September	
			relieving the 11th Cavalry M.G. Squadron	
			12 M.Gs. were in the line and disposition as follows.	
			Gun N° Position Gun N° Position	
			1. M.13.b.2.7 5. R.12.b.0.8 9. L.34.a.5.9	
			2. M.8.c.3.3 6. R.5.d.3.4 10. G.31.d.8.4	
			3. M.7.d.8.0 7. R.4.b.3.5 11. G.31.b.3.8	
			4. R.12.a.2.3 8. L.3a.d.2.8 12. L.20.a.6.8	
			The first of the line advanced was from	
			LE VERGUIER to the left of the Tower Wood at PONTRUET.	
			One machine-gun fired on enemy work parties (L.21 & L.27)	
			1,000 rounds expended.	
			Enemy M.Gs. & artillery active.	

WAR DIARY
or
INTELLIGENCE SUMMARY.
(Erase heading not required.)

Army Form C. 2118.

Reference Sheet 62 C NE 1/20000

Place	Date	Hour	Summary of Events and Information	Remarks and references to Appendices
BERNES	2nd		Enemy M.G's & artillery were active on occasions engaged in firing positions	
Do.	3rd		The enemy fired a few shells near our no 9 position and also shelled the French on our immediate right, who retaliated.	
Do.	4th		French Artillery active during the night. The enemy in retaliation fired a few shells on BERTHAUCOURT. Our M-Guns fired on enemy wire and all gun teams engaged enemy gun positions during the night shelling	
Do.	5th		A quiet day at all gun positions. Enemy fired a few shells near no 9 position at 11 am. Enemy M-Guns active. Owing to the extreme heat &c	

Army Form C. 2118.

WAR DIARY
or
INTELLIGENCE SUMMARY.
(Erase heading not required.)

Instructions regarding War Diaries and Intelligence Summaries are contained in F.S. Regs., Part II. and the Staff Manual respectively. Title pages will be prepared in manuscript.

Regiment 62nd Bde M.G.C. 1/10,000

Place	Date	Hour	Summary of Events and Information	Remarks and references to Appendices
PERNES.	5.		of the Brigade it was decided to bring the 4 reserve guns into the line, these were put in position at R.5.d.3.1 - L.29.c.2.8 - L.29.d.8.9 - L.29.c.1.9	
Do.	6.		Our gun-teams in the right sector "stood to" during the night in expectation of a local attack by the enemy on the French. But nothing occured. Enemy Artillery & M.Guns inactive.	
Do	7.		Enemy shewed twelve on our right during the afternoon & night, also fired a few gas-shells. Our machine-guns fired a barrage & SOS barrage at 12. noon which appeared to do to satisfaction. 4,500 rounds were fired. Enemy M.G. was fairly active	
Do	8.		Enemy shelled Tournes at 3 p.m. French artillery fairly active	

(A783) Wt. W.26/M1672 350,000 4/17 Sch. 52a Forms/C/2118/14

WAR DIARY
or
INTELLIGENCE SUMMARY.
(Erase heading not required.)

Army Form C. 2118.

Reference sheet. 62 c N.E 1/10,000.

Place	Date	Hour	Summary of Events and Information	Remarks and references to Appendices
BERNES	8 (cont)		Active at 1.30 p.m. Everything quiet at all our own positions and areas except enemy positions dug-outs shelling.	
Do	9		Lewis gun heard firing in No Man's Land at 2.30 am evidently our patrols engaging the enemy. Eleven Torpedos intermittently during the day. Enemy Machine-gun fire on enemy back areas.	
Do	10		Enemy shewd Torpedos also our front posts intermittently during the day. Enemy M.Guns inactive.	
Do	11		Our Machine guns fired on area G26 a G20 also on ELEVEN TREES at 3.30, 5. 5.30, 9.5-9.45 p.m. 11,500 rounds expended. Enemy M.Guns inflicted firstly.	99

WAR DIARY
or
INTELLIGENCE SUMMARY

Army Form C. 2118.

Reference Cher 62cNE 1/20,000

Place	Date	Hour	Summary of Events and Information	Remarks and references to Appendices
BERNES	12		The day passed quietly. Enemy Machine Guns ranging waiting All gun. teams engaged improving positions & shelters	
Do	13		Enemy artillery fire on Jns. shelter to Toppers & huts of 3mSh fire at 3 & 5 a.m. At 5.45 p.m. enemy Machine guns fired on Does that at C.26.a — 1500 rounds expended. Enemy machine guns did not reply. "Lieut H.W. FELLS MC. attended a special parade at Brigade with other sergeants of the Brigade & was decorated with the MILITARY CROSS by the Corps Commander.	
Do	14		Artillery activity by both sides much above normal. Much intermittently during the day.	

Army Form C. 2118.

WAR DIARY
or
INTELLIGENCE SUMMARY.
(Erase heading not required.)

Reference Sheet 62, c N.E. 1/10,000

Place	Date	Hour	Summary of Events and Information	Remarks and references to Appendices
BERNES	15		Information having been received that an enemy relief was to take place on machine-gun fire on the following targets – BIG BILL – LITTLE BILL – VICTORIA X ROADS – ELEVEN TREES – SOMMERVILLE WOOD – MAX WOOD (M2t) – WATLING ST – FISHER CRATER and G.29.c & d central. Hours of firing 10 p.m. till 12 midnight. 18,000 rounds expended. Guns teams of the night sub-sector were relieved during the afternoon & evening by a similar number of teams from Details Camp BERNES.	
Do	16		Enemy artillery & M.G's very quiet. Both the enemy's planes & ours much more active than usual. Enemy planes flying too high to be engaged by our machine-guns.	
Do	17		At 6 p.m. our machine guns fired on "BIG BILL" and	

WAR DIARY
or
INTELLIGENCE SUMMARY

Army Form C. 2118.

Reference Sheet 62cNW. 1/10,000

Place	Date	Hour	Summary of Events and Information	Remarks and references to Appendices
PERNES	17		"LITTLE BILL". L.A.A. expended - 750 rounds. About 30 small shells fell in area around GRAND PRIEL FARM and in valley forward of that B.team. Enemy aeroplanes very active but flying too high to be engaged by our Machine Guns.	
PERNES	18		Heavy shelling by the enemy during the afternoon on valley forward of GRAND PRIEL FARM, particularly heavy around JOE POST & RED FARM. Aerial activity again around our area. Numerous fights 550 rounds at enemy planes between 11 a.m. and 12 noon. Enemy machine guns active during the evening.	
Do	19		Enemy artillery quieter. Enemy M.G. fired intermittently during the evening on PONTRO. Owing to the Brigade front being extended on the left	

Army Form C. 2118.

WAR DIARY
or
INTELLIGENCE SUMMARY.
(Erase heading not required.)

Instructions regarding War Diaries and Intelligence Summaries are contained in F. S. Regs., Part II. and the Staff Manual respectively. Title pages will be prepared in manuscript.

Reference Sheet 62c.N.E.

Place	Date	Hour	Summary of Events and Information	Remarks and references to Appendices
PERNES	19	(cont'd)	to the S.W. end of BUISSON SPUR our machine guns were moved from N°s 1, 8 & 9 positions & placed in position at L.29.a.2.8 - L.23.d.5.9 - L.24.c.30.95 and re-numbered 14, 15, 16 respectively.	
Do	20		Enemy artillery active - firing on SUNBEAM ROAD (near N°9 position) intermittently during the day. Enemy machine gun fires bursts between 5 & 6 p.m. on our right sub sector.	
Do	21		Enemy artillery and machine guns quiet. For situation of the Trench spr flank our machine guns at N°1, 2, & 3 positions were moved BERTHAUCOURT to LE BEUX trench to provide direct fixed of fire across the Trench front now co-ordinates ① & M.9.c.7.8. ② M.9.c.5.8. ③ M.9.c.3.8.	Off

Army Form C. 2118.

WAR DIARY
or
INTELLIGENCE SUMMARY.
(Erase heading not required.)

Reference Sheet 62cNE 1/40,000

Place	Date	Hour	Summary of Events and Information	Remarks and references to Appendices
PERNES	22		Scattered shelling during the day particularly ASCENSION FARM. Enemy MG's active. During the afternoon & evening gas shells at No 8 to 15 inclusive were fired by a number of rounds from hostile cann.	
Do	23		Enemy artillery quiet. Enemy machine guns active between 6 & 7 pm. 2/Lieut B. LOCKE joined the battery from Base depot.	
Do Sep			About 20 smoke shells fired around DRAGOON POST between 5 & 6 pm. Enemy machine guns fired in Nab Fork Valley to No 1 Por activity 5 - 6 pm.	
Do 25			Enemy shelled BERTHAECOURT between 11.30 am & 1 pm. Torpedos & forward posts intermittently during the day. Enemy	

Army Form C. 2118.

WAR DIARY
or
INTELLIGENCE SUMMARY.
(Erase heading not required.)

Reference Sheet 62c N.E. 1/10,000

Instructions regarding War Diaries and Intelligence Summaries are contained in F.S. Regs., Part II. and the Staff Manual respectively. Title pages will be prepared in manuscript.

Place	Date	Hour	Summary of Events and Information	Remarks and references to Appendices
BERNES	25 (contd)		Machine Guns fired on Huns Trench or Dragoon Post at "Sheldon" Lehere	
DO	26		Enemy machine guns fired intermittently into BESTHACOURT.	
		6-7 pm	Enemy artillery fired several shells on TRANCHEE LE BEUX. No. 1 & 2. positions and enemy machine fire intermittently on Barré Place.	
			Our machine-guns co-operating with the guns by the 72nd Bn. on our left made a demonstration on the following points G.14.c.8. to C.11.c.70 (Final Zn.) & BUISSON GADLAINE FARM, 15,000 rounds expired.	
			Enemy reply to our M.G. barrage was feeble. The demonstration had the desired effect of inducing the enemy & drawing his attention away from the point which the successful raiding party entered. The raid was a successful because of the enemy being killed and an important identification obtained.	

WAR DIARY
or
INTELLIGENCE SUMMARY

Army Form C. 2118.

Place	Date	Hour	Summary of Events and Information	Remarks and references to Appendices
BERNES	27		Enemy Machine gun fired across Nº 6 Post. At times. 5.30 to 7pm. Enemy Artillery active shelling forward posts, BERTHAUCOURT & TOMBOIS intermittently. 12 command a better defensive position guns attached to Nº 1 Post (C.21 & 3.9) was moved to Nº 6 Post (S.2 d 7.5).	
Do	28		Enemy artillery very active. Enemy guns shelled on near neighbourhood immediately N.W. of LE VERGUIER shells with 5.9 from 1/30pm to 5/15pm and forward posts, TOMBOIS & BERTHAUCOURT intermittently during the day. Enemy M-guns fired bursts on and around Nº 6 Post from 1:30 am. to 3:45am. M.G. fire then became intense and was accompanied by Rifle grenade fire. No Man's Land. This continued for about a quarter of an hour. No Infantry action followed.	

Army Form C. 2118.

WAR DIARY
or
INTELLIGENCE SUMMARY
(Erase heading not required.)

Reference Sheet 62 c N.E. 1/10000

Place	Date	Hour	Summary of Events and Information	Remarks and references to Appendices
BERNES	28 (cont)		and no casualties were caused.	
Do	29		Our Aeroplanes very active, patrolling the enemy's lines & were heavily shelled by enemy O.a. A few shells fell near PLEUMER WOOD (Brigade hqrs) between 2.30 & 4 p.m. Occasional bursts of M.G. fire by the enemy on Nº 6 & Nº 9 posts also on the L night post. Patrol from 10 pm. till midnight. 4 am. to 5.30am.	
Do	30		Everything quiet on our sector. Enemy Mortar the French batteries in afternoon. The 51 guns found in the night detection during the afternoon & evening were followed by a similar number of rounds from the Mortar about BERNES.	98

Army Form C. 2118.

WAR DIARY
or
INTELLIGENCE SUMMARY.
(Erase heading not required.)

Reference Sheet 62c NE 1/40,000

Instructions regarding War Diaries and Intelligence Summaries are contained in F.S. Regs., Part II. and the Staff Manual respectively. Title pages will be prepared in manuscript.

Place	Date	Hour	Summary of Events and Information	Remarks and references to Appendices
BERNES	31		Enemy artillery and gun very quiet. All guns crews engaged improving gun positions, Dug-outs etc.	
			NOTE: Casualties during the month. NIL.	
			Strength of Company on 1st of Month. 10 Officers 184 O.R.	
			" " 31st of Month. 10 " 183 O.R.	

Jones Major
Commanding 17th Wilts Company

WAR DIARY
or
INTELLIGENCE SUMMARY.

Army Form C. 2118.

Place	Date	Hour	Summary of Events and Information	Remarks and references to Appendices
BERNES (Q.4) Sheet 62c	Nov. 1st 1917		Transport lines and details camp were at BERNES. Forward hqrs at SMALL FOOT WOOD R.8.b.35.10. The Company came in to this sector on Sept. 22nd the Tank of the line been was from LE VERGUIER to the top of the culvert front at PONTRU. Owing to the extensive front line by the Brigade the 16 guns of the Company were in the line in the following positions.	Reference Sheet 62 N.E.

Map Ref. Sheet N° Map Ref. Sheet N°

1. M.9.c.7.8.   5. R.17.a.2.3.   9. G.25.d.27.53.   13. L.30.a.6.3.
2. M.9.c.5.8.   6. R.5.d.8.4.   10. R.35.b.6.1.   14. L.29.a.2.3.
3. M.9.c.3.8.   7. R.5.b.3.1.   11. L.27.c.2.5.   15. L.29.c.5.9.
4. M.7.d.95.85.   8. G.31.d.5.4.   12. L.29.c.1.9.   16. L.24.c.30.95.

Enemy MGuns fired a few bursts at dusk & occasional bursts on N° 6 post during the night.
Enemy Artillery inactive.

Army Form C. 2118.

WAR DIARY
or
INTELLIGENCE SUMMARY.
(Erase heading not required.)

Confidential   M 22

WAR DIARY.

17th Machine Gun Company

November 1917.

Volume No. 23.

Remarks and references to Appendices

Reference sheet 62 e N.E.

Foster, Major
Commanding 17 M.G. Coy

Army Form C. 2118.

WAR DIARY
or
INTELLIGENCE SUMMARY.
(Erase heading not required.)

Instructions regarding War Diaries and Intelligence Summaries are contained in F.S. Regs., Part II, and the Staff Manual respectively. Title pages will be prepared in manuscript.

Place	Date	Hour	Summary of Events and Information	Remarks and references to Appendices
BERNES	2nd		The enemy fired a few shells in the vicinity of the CHATEAU at 4.30 pm (L-22d)	Reference Sheet 62 N.E.
			Our Machine-gun fired 950 rounds on SOMERVILLE WOOD G.26.c.d	
Do	3rd		Enemy M. guns very active between 4.30 & 5.30 pm.	
			Enemy artillery inactive.	
			Our teams engaged in improving gun positions L.6	
Do	4th		Enemy machine-guns very active at dusk.	
			In retaliation our M.G's fired on Area G.27.d.1.1 to G.27 central – 1000 rounds expended.	
Do	5th		Enemy machine-guns active on our Left Sector at 5 pm & up to 12.30 am, also our our Right Sector from 8 to 11 pm.	
			Our M.G's in retaliation fired 950 rounds on our around G.27 cent.	

WAR DIARY
or
INTELLIGENCE SUMMARY.
(Erase heading not required.)

Army Form C. 2118.

Place	Date	Hour	Summary of Events and Information	Remarks and references to Appendices
BERNES	6th		Details moved to HANCOURT, transport remaining at BERNES.	Reference
			Enemy M. Guns not so active, only firing at Jus bursts over our No. 3 post between 12 & 12.30 a.m.	shot over G.S.
			Our Machine guns fired 1000 rounds on area around G27 central.	
			Enemy artillery inactive.	
HANCOURT	7th		Enemy M.Guns fired a few bursts over our area around G27 central. Our M.Guns fired 150 rounds at 4.30 a.m.	
			One of our patrols engaged an enemy patrol at 1.15 a.m. in ASCENSION WOOD.	
			Enemy shelled VADENCOURT between 9 & 9.30 a.m. Otherwise enemy artillery quiet.	
	8th		Enemy M.Guns active at morning "evening" Stand to".	85

Army Form C. 2118.

WAR DIARY
or
INTELLIGENCE SUMMARY.
(Erase heading not required.)

Instructions regarding War Diaries and Intelligence Summaries are contained in F. S. Regs., Part II. and the Staff Manual respectively. Title pages will be prepared in manuscript.

Place	Date	Hour	Summary of Events and Information	Remarks and references to Appendices
HANCOURT	8th (cont.)		Our M. Guns fired 950 rounds on G.27.d.1.1 to G.27 central. Enemy artillery inactive. Only some desultory shelling during the day.	
Do	9th		Enemy machine-guns active during the night firing over our forward posts. Our M. Guns fired 750 rounds on G.27.d.1.1 to G.27 cent. Enemy artillery shelled BERTHAUCOURT at 4.30 pm.	Reference Sheet 62 c NE.
Do	10th		Enemy artillery active during the evening 6 heavy shells fell near TWIN CRATER between 6.15 & 6.30 pm Y near our Right Section M.G. (M.17.a.75.85) at 8.30 pm. Enemy M. Guns active firing over our Right Sector at dusk.	
Do	11th		Enemy artillery active between 10-12 midday, firing on Enc R. Area evidently counter battery work. Also between 1 & 2 pm D.D. on ASCENSION FARM & GRAND PRIEL FARM.	

Army Form C. 2118.

WAR DIARY
or
INTELLIGENCE SUMMARY.
(Erase heading not required.)

Instructions regarding War Diaries and Intelligence Summaries are contained in F. S. Regs., Part II. and the Staff Manual respectively. Title pages will be prepared in manuscript.

Place	Date	Hour	Summary of Events and Information	Remarks and references to Appendices
HANCOURT	11th (contd)		Enemy M guns very active at dusk, firing on our Right flank	Reference Year
Do.	12th		Bombing rifle fire heard in SOMERVILLE WOOD at 4.45 am, evidently our patrols engaging the enemy.	6 CNE
Do	13th		Enemy patrol threw bombs & fired shots near No. 8 post at 12.45 am. 9 4.2's fired on LE VERGUIER at 11.15 am and 3 more in same place at 3.45 pm. Enemy M guns fairly active at dusk.	
Do	14th		Desultory shelling of LE VERGUIER during the afternoon. The enemy artillery opened & kept up rapid fire from 5.5 to 5.20 pm. From information received this was covering fire for a raiding party which was successful in its object, an identification being	

Army Form C. 2118.

WAR DIARY
or
INTELLIGENCE SUMMARY.
(Erase heading not required.)

Instructions regarding War Diaries and Intelligence Summaries are contained in F. S. Regs., Part II. and the Staff Manual respectively. Title pages will be prepared in manuscript.

Place	Date	Hour	Summary of Events and Information	Remarks and references to Appendices
HANCOURT	14th (cont.)		Obtained & all the loading tank returning.	Reference sheet
Do	15th		About 30 shells fell near the Sugar Factory PONTRU between 2.30 & 4 p.m. and considerable shelling of the same place during the early part of the night. A few shells were fired on BERTHAUCOURT at intervals between 4.15 and 10.15 pm. Our Machine-guns fired 780 rounds on trench at G 21 c 3.0 & G 20 d 80 40.	65 CN 6
Do	16th		Enemy artillery machine-gun inactive during the day, but fairly active on our left sector between 9.30 & 10.30 pm. Our M.Guns fired 500 rounds on LILY TRENCH (G7994).	
Do	17th		Enemy artillery and machine-guns inactive. A few	

WAR DIARY
or
INTELLIGENCE SUMMARY.

(Erase heading not required.)

Army Form C. 2118.

Place	Date	Hour	Summary of Events and Information	Remarks and references to Appendices
HANCOURT	17 (cont)		Heavy shells fell near VADENCOURT between 1.30 & 2 p.m.	Reference sheet 62c N.E.
Do	18		There was a heavy artillery bombardment by both sides on our immediate left between 5.30 & 6-15 a.m. Heavy artillery fire on our right between 5 & 5.30 p.m. the French raiding the enemy's line. Our machine-guns fired 750 rounds on bends of 27a 9.4. All guns teams employed in carrying S.A.A. and constructing new barrage positions for coming operations. Our aeroplanes very active.	
Do	19		A few shells fell in Jerry near N°11 Pontoon (L27c28) & Second near MUSTARD CRATER between 9 & 9.45 p.m. Our aeroplanes very active - patrolling the enemy's lines. All gun teams again employed carrying S.A.A. & completing new barrage emplacements.	

Army Form C. 2118.

WAR DIARY
or
INTELLIGENCE SUMMARY.
(Erase heading not required.)

Instructions regarding War Diaries and Intelligence Summaries are contained in F. S. Regs., Part II. and the Staff Manual respectively. Title pages will be prepared in manuscript.

Place	Date	Hour	Summary of Events and Information	Remarks and references to Appendices
HANCOURT	20		Our machine guns in co-operation with the operations on our left fired 124,500 rounds on enemy areas around BUISSON GADLAINE FARM – WATLING St – G.27.c.7.d – TRENCH TN G.33.a – BELL COPSE – PEARL WOOD and communication trenches between these points. Firing commenced at 6/20 am and lasted for 2½ hours. Enemy artillery and machine guns did not retaliate. Our machine guns carried out harassing fire on the same objectives between 6.25 pm & 8.35 pm. 8,750 rounds expended. Enemy M.G's & artillery did not respond.	Reference Sketch & RENG
Do	21		Our machine guns continued the harassing fire programme on the same targets as the previous day. Ammunition expended 51,750 rounds and hours of firing 6/35 am to 6/35 am. Enemy MG's did not retaliate.	

Army Form C. 2118.

WAR DIARY
or
INTELLIGENCE SUMMARY.
(Erase heading not required.)

Place	Date	Hour	Summary of Events and Information	Remarks and references to Appendices
HANCOURT	22		Our machine guns again continued the programme of harassing fire, on the same targets, as entrusted during the day. 33,500 rounds expended. Enemy M.Guns did not respond.	Reference Sht Event
Do	23		About 2 a.m. our No. 2 post was raided by the enemy. They did not succeed in entering the post and casualties were inflicted on the raiders. 1 German officer (wounded) was brought in. Enemy fired a few gas shells around No. 12 position (L.29.c.1.9) about 1 a.m. There was some irregular shooting of our guns during the day.	
Do	24		Our machine-guns carried out harassing fire during the night on the following objectives, WATLING ST.—	

WAR DIARY
or
INTELLIGENCE SUMMARY.

(Erase heading not required.)

Army Form C. 2118.

Place	Date	Hour	Summary of Events and Information	Remarks and references to Appendices
HANCOURT	24 (contd)		BELL COPSE - G.14 central - G.14 central - G.20 G.7.7 - and communication trenches. Various shell points. 6,750 rounds expended. Enemy machine-guns did not reply.	Reference Sheet 62 c NE
Do	25		Several heavy shells fired into LE VERGUIER between 9 & 10 a.m. All gun teams engaged in removing guns &c. back to the old positions and clearing up generally.	
Do	26.		Enemy M.G. and artillery fire normal. Gun teams engaged overhauling guns & gun equipment & filing ammunition belts.	
Do	27		The enemy shelled LE VERGUIER during the afternoon. Gun teams engaged in cleaning guns &c.	

Army Form C. 2118.

WAR DIARY
or
INTELLIGENCE SUMMARY.
(Erase heading not required.)

Place	Date	Hour	Summary of Events and Information	Remarks and references to Appendices
HANCOURT	28		Enemy artillery active between 2:30 pm and 3:30 pm firing heavy shrapnel over APPLE TREE ROAD - BERTHAUCOURT & VADENCOURT. Enemy machine-guns were active during the night. All spare men engaged carrying S.A.A. gun reserve ammo to gun positions.	Reference Sheet 62cNE
Do	29		A few shells fell near 2 of our gun positions at 2.30 pm. All spare men again engaged in carrying S.A.A. to gun positions.	
Do	30		6 heavy shells fell 100 yards forward of TUPULUS between 3 & 3.30 pm. Our aeroplanes very active all day. No enemy attacked the Division on our left this morning. Our positions precautions were taken in case [...]	

Army Form C. 2118.

WAR DIARY
or
INTELLIGENCE SUMMARY.
(Erase heading not required.)

Place	Date	Hour	Summary of Events and Information	Remarks and references to Appendices
HANCOURT	30		the attack developed South towards our Lines	Reference Sheet 62cNE.
			All gun teams "Stood to" & arrangements made to strengthen our M.G. defences on our Left flank and additional S.A.A. placed at the gun positions for the purpose. No further development took place during the day.	
			Strength of Company on November 1st - 10 off 173 O.R. Casualties during the month NIL. Strength on 30th November 10 off. 173 OR.	

JE?? Major
O.C. 17th M'Gun Company

Army Form C. 2118.

WAR DIARY
or
INTELLIGENCE SUMMARY.
(Erase heading not required.)

Confidential   No 23

1st Machine Gun Company

December 1917.

Volume No 24.

WAR DIARY

E. M. Tibbitt Lieut
for O/o 1st Machine Gun Coy

Army Form C. 2118.

WAR DIARY
or
INTELLIGENCE SUMMARY.
(Erase heading not required.)

Place	Date	Hour	Summary of Events and Information	Remarks and references to Appendices
	December 1st		Transport lines at BERNES – Details and Recce Headquarters at HANCOURT	Ref. Nr sheet 62C NE
HANCOURT			Forward Headquarters at SMALL FOOT WOOD R.8.6.35.40.	
			The front of the line held was from LE VERGUIER to the left of the French at PONTRU.	
			Owing to the extensive frontage held by the Brigade the 16 guns of the Company were in the line in the following positions:-	
			(1) M.9.c.4.8. (5) R.12.a.7.3. (9) Q.25.d.2.4.53. (13) L.30.a.6.8.	
			(2) M.9.c.5.8. (6) R.5.d.5.4. (10) R.35.6.6.9. (14) L.29.c.2.8.	
			(3) M.9.c.3.9. (7) R.5.6.3.1. (11) L.29.a.2.8. (15) L.29.c.5.9.	
			(4) M.7.d.7.5.3.5. (8) Q.31.d.5.4. (12) L.29.c.9. (16) L.24.c.30.9.5.	
			The enemy attacked the Division on our left on the morning of the 30th ultimo – all possible precautions were taken in case the attack developed south towards our lines but no further developments took place.	
			15" Heavy shells fell near DAWES QUARRY between 7/30 & 7/45 pm.	
			Enemy artillery very active during the night	

Army Form C. 2118.

WAR DIARY
or
INTELLIGENCE SUMMARY.

(Erase heading not required.)

Instructions regarding War Diaries and Intelligence Summaries are contained in F. S. Regs., Part II. and the Staff Manual respectively. Title pages will be prepared in manuscript.

Place	Date	Hour	Summary of Events and Information	Remarks and references to Appendices
HANCOURT	December 2nd		Some 6 shells fell near our No 6 post between 8 and 8/30 A.M.	
			The enemy shelled LE VERGUIER intermittently during the day	
			Enemy machine gun fire normal	
	3rd		There was some desultory shelling by the enemy during the day. All gun teams were "standing to" but no further development has taken place.	
	4th		Owing to the charge on the front of the left division and the expectation of an attack by the enemy on our Brigade front the following alterations were made in the H.Q. destinations:-	
			– No 9 Bur. – Old Position – New position	
			9. – L 25 d 27.53 (No 6. Ost) L 23 a 6.1.	
			13. – L 30 a 1.8 (No 9 Post) L 23 a 6.3 } Round CHATEAU	
			15. – L 29 c 5.9 L 23 a 3.0.	
			16. – L 24 c 30.95 (S.3 Host) L 25 a 3.8 (J.H.9 E. corner of GRAND PRIX WOOD)	

Army Form C. 2118.

WAR DIARY
or
INTELLIGENCE SUMMARY.

(Erase heading not required.)

Instructions regarding War Diaries and Intelligence
Summaries are contained in F. S. Regs., Part II.
and the Staff Manual respectively. Title pages
will be prepared in manuscript.

Place	Date	Hour	Summary of Events and Information	Remarks and references to Appendices
HANCOURT (Continued)	4th		Heavy artillery fire commenced on our immediate Left at dawn.	Ref sheet 62 C.N.E.
			Everything quiet at all our positions	
			Gun teams engaged moving guns and equipment to new positions	
Do.	5th		Situation unchanged at all gun positions. Enemy machine guns and artillery fire normal	
			Officers then engaged surveying A.A. to new gun positions	
Do.	6th		Situation unchanged	
			Enemy artillery inactive	
			All gun teams finishing to hand over to the relieving company on the 7th.	
Do.	7th		Our machine guns carried out a demonstration on the enemy lines firing on the following objectives—	(signature)

WAR DIARY
or
INTELLIGENCE SUMMARY.

Army Form C. 2118.

(Erase heading not required.)

Place	Date	Hour	Summary of Events and Information	Remarks and references to Appendices
HANCOURT (continued)	7th		WATLING ST - BELL CORSE - G.14 central - G.27 C & D - Ypres junction (G.33.A Notchees)	Notchees b.2.3 N E
			PEARL WOOD and communication trenches between these points.	
			Hours of firing 12.10 A.M. to 12/20 AM	
			S.A.A. Expended 15,500 rounds	
			Enemy machine-guns did not reply.	
			During the afternoon and evening 12 guns were relieved by the 8th Cavalry M.G. Squadron, the 4 guns forming the M.G. strong point behind the CHATEAU remaining in the line. The relieved teams proceeded to VRAIGNES where details had moved to during the day.	
VRAIGNES	8th		Instructions times remained at BESNES. The remaining 4 guns in the line were relieved by 4 guns of the 8th Cavalry M.G. Squadron and joined the remainder of VRAIGNES	
			The day was spent in sorting out guns and gun equipment	

Army Form C. 2118.

WAR DIARY
or
INTELLIGENCE SUMMARY.
(Erase heading not required.)

Instructions regarding War Diaries and Intelligence Summaries are contained in F. S. Regs., Part II. and the Staff Manual respectively. Title pages will be prepared in manuscript.

Place	Date	Hour	Summary of Events and Information	Remarks and references to Appendices
VRAIGNES	9th		The day was spent in cleaning guns and gun equipment and refitting men requiring new clothing	Ref sheet 62 e NE
Do.	10th		Parades were carried out as follows:— 9am to 12/30pm — Training on the range 2/30pm to 4pm — Elementary gun training	
Do.	11th		Parades were as follows:— 9 - 9.45 am — Kit inspection 10am - 11.30am — Overhauling of guns and gun equipment 12/15 - 3pm — Baths Parade	
Do.	12th		Parades were as follows:— 9 - 9.45 am — Physical Training 10am - 11am — Inspection of respirators and bus drill 11.15 to 12/30pm — Immediate Action — 2pm - 4pm — Football	

Army Form C. 2118.

WAR DIARY
or
INTELLIGENCE SUMMARY.
(Erase heading not required.)

Instructions regarding War Diaries and Intelligence Summaries are contained in F. S. Regs., Part II. and the Staff Manual respectively. Title pages will be prepared in manuscript.

Place	Date	Hour	Summary of Events and Information	Remarks and references to Appendices
VRAIGNES	13		Parades were as follows:—	
			9am to 9.45 AM. — Physical Training	
			10 AM to 12/30 pm — Elementary Gun training	
			2 pm to 3 pm — Company and Section Drill	
			3 pm to 4 pm — Squad Drill with box respirators on	
Do	14		Parades were as follows:—	
			9 AM. to 9.45 AM. — Physical Training	
			9.45 AM. to 12/30 PM — Elementary Gun training	
			2 pm to 3 pm — Company and Section Drill	
			3 pm to 4 pm — Squad Drill and Gas Drill.	
Do	15		9 am to 12/30 pm — Firing on the range	
			2 pm to 4 pm — Football	
Do	16		9.30 AM. — Digging of M.G. emplacements	

Army Form C. 2118.

Army Form C. 2118.

WAR DIARY
or
INTELLIGENCE SUMMARY.
(Erase heading not required.)

Place	Date	Hour	Summary of Events and Information	Remarks and references to Appendices
VRAIGNES	14		Parades were as follows:-	R/R List
			9am to 10am - Physical Training	12 O.N.E.
			10am to 11/30am - Advanced Squad Drill.	
			11/30 to 12/30 am - Gas Drill	
			2pm to 4pm - Overhauling of gun equipment.	
VRAIGNES	16		The morning was spent in preparation for the line	
			The company moved into the line in the course of	
			the afternoon relieving the 43rd Machine Gun Company	
			the front of the line defended was the HARGICOURT SECTOR:-	
			13 guns were in position and 3 guns in Reserve at	
			Company H/Q TEMPLAIRE (G.1.C.46.21).	
			Disposition of guns as follows:-	
			F.1. G.1.C.46.21. F.4. F.29.c.45.72. S.3.F.29.d.69.52. R.1. L.40.c.90.19.	
			F.2. E.30.d.40.46. F.5. F.24.c.12.67. S.4. F.29.d.40.98. R.4. L.C.90.10.	
			F.3. F.29.c.65.56. S.2. L.5.b.99.93. S.5. F.29.d.85.88. R.2. F.28.b.42.30.	
				R.Z. F.29.d.31.
				M. [signature]

WAR DIARY or INTELLIGENCE SUMMARY.

Army Form C. 2118.

(Erase heading not required.)

Place	Date	Hour	Summary of Events and Information	Remarks and references to Appendices
VRAIGNES	18 (continued)		Situation quiet. Company detail moved to transport lines BERNES during the evening	Vraignes 7616 to BERNES
BERNES	19"		Situation unchanged. 2 guns in reserve at Company HQrs. relieved two guns of the 42nd Machine Gun Company in the line during the day in the following positions:- ① T.6.b.35.53 ② L.10.c.09.53	
Do	20"		Situation unchanged. Our M.G.s fired 1000 rounds on RUBY WOOD, 500 rounds on MALAKOFF WOOD and 1000 rounds on QUENNEMONT FARM. The enemy fired several minniewerfers in the vicinity of our F1 position (G.I.E.46.21)	

WAR DIARY
or
INTELLIGENCE SUMMARY.
(Erase heading not required.)

Army Form C. 2118.

Place	Date	Hour	Summary of Events and Information	Remarks and references to Appendices
BERNES	21st		Our M. Guns fired 2000 rounds on the following targets	Ref. sheet 62C N.E.4
			RUBY WOOD, QUENNEMONT FARM and X roads.	
			Enemy M. Guns and artillery inactive.	
Do	22nd		Situation unchanged.	
			The enemy shelled TEMPLAIRE S.W. intermittently throughout the day.	
			Our M. Guns fired 2000 rounds on the following objectives	
			QUENNEMONT FARM and X ROADS also MALAKOFF WOOD.	
			During the day teams we reserve positions relieved those in forward positions.	
			The three guns in position at F.29.b.65.56, T.29.6.95.42 and F.2H.c.12.64 were withdrawn to Company H/Qrs.	
			One gun in position at G.1.c.46.31 was withdrawn to L.6a.55.15.	
			Enemy M. Guns inactive.	

Army Form C. 2118.

WAR DIARY
or
INTELLIGENCE SUMMARY.
(Erase heading not required.)

Instructions regarding War Diaries and Intelligence Summaries are contained in F. S. Regs., Part II. and the Staff Manual respectively. Title pages will be prepared in manuscript.

Place	Date	Hour	Summary of Events and Information	Remarks and references to Appendices
BERNES.	23		Situation unchanged.	
			The enemy shelled TEMPLEUX.S.W during the forenoon.	
			Our M. Guns fired 1000 rounds on MARRIONS WOOD (A 25.2)	
Go.	24		Enemy Artillery and M. Guns very active throughout the night but no attack was attempted.	
			Our M. Guns fired 1030 rounds at enemy aircraft flying low over our lines during the day	
			Our M. Guns fired 1000 rounds on QUINNEMONT FARM and X Roads (A200)	
Go.	25		Situation Quiet.	
			Enemy Artillery and M. Guns inactive.	
			Gun at R2 position (F.28.c.42.20) fired 750 rounds on QUENNEMONT FARM.	
Go.	26		The enemy fired a few heavy shells in the vicinity of gun	

WAR DIARY
or
INTELLIGENCE SUMMARY
(Erase heading not required.)

Army Form C. 2118.

Place	Date	Hour	Summary of Events and Information	Remarks and references to Appendices
BERNES	26th (continued)		S१ position COLOGNE FARM. Firing carried out by our M. guns on the following targets MALAKOFF WOOD and QUENNEMONT FARM and X ROADS. The squdns. of the Cavalry M.G. Squadron under our command were taken over by the 73rd Machine Gun Company. 1000 rounds fired at enemy aircraft flying low over our lines between 9ᵃᵐ and 11ᵖᵐ. Our M. guns fired 1500 rounds on QUENNEMONT FARM and X Roads also MALAKOFF WOOD. The command was relieved in the line by the 73rd M.G. Coy. 4 of our guns remaining in to take over reserve positions vacated by the 73rd M.G. Coy. These were situated as follows — 4 guns in reserve at F.2.b. y.15 and H guns viz position at ① F.28.a. c.5 ② F.28.a. 15.15 ③ F.27.a.90.50 ④ F.27.b.15.50	Ref: sheet 62ᵃ NE.H.

Army Form C. 2118.

WAR DIARY
or
INTELLIGENCE SUMMARY.
(Erase heading not required.)

Instructions regarding War Diaries and Intelligence Summaries are contained in F. S. Regs., Part II. and the Staff Manual respectively. Title pages will be prepared in manuscript.

Place	Date	Hour	Summary of Events and Information	Remarks and references to Appendices
BERNES	27th		The remainder of the company proceeded to HERVILLY	Ref/Ops 52 even
(continued)			which was the area of the Brigade in support	
			4 guns were held in readiness to move at one hour's	
			notice in the event of alarm	
HERVILLY	28th		The day was spent in cleaning w/o generally	
Do	29th		The day was spent in cleaning guns and gun equipment	
			The following names appeared in the list of those mentioned in despatches — London Gazette:—	
			MAJOR T. Joyce M.C.	
			No 265654 Sgt. Hambley J.W.	
			No 20590 Sgt. Condon J.	
Do	31st	9.30 p.m.	Parades were as follows:— Kit inspection	

Army Form C. 2118.

WAR DIARY
or
INTELLIGENCE SUMMARY.
(Erase heading not required.)

Place	Date	Hour	Summary of Events and Information	Remarks and references to Appendices
HERVILLY	30th (Continued)		the remainder of the day was spent in refitting & requiring new clothing	Kit but is a new issue
do	31st		Parades were as follows:— 9.30 am to 12.30 pm — Belt filling. Afternoon — Baths.	
			Strength of Company on December 1st. 10 Off. 193 O.R.	
			Casualties during the month. Nil.	
			Strength on 31st December 10 Off. 170 O.R.	
			G.M. Tillett Lieut for O/C 14th Machine Gun Company	

Army Form C. 2118.

WAR DIARY
or
INTELLIGENCE SUMMARY.
(Erase heading not required.)

YN 24
Confidential

WAR DIARY
14th Machine Gun Company.

January 1918.

Volume No 25.

Jones Major.
Commanding 14th M.G. Coy.

Place	Date	Hour	Summary of Events and Information	Remarks and references to Appendices
				Reference Sheet 62d East.

Instructions regarding War Diaries and Intelligence Summaries are contained in F.S. Regs., Part II and the Staff Manual respectively. Title pages will be prepared in manuscript.

WAR DIARY
or
INTELLIGENCE SUMMARY.
(Erase heading not required)

Army Form C. 2118.

Place	Date 1918	Hour	Summary of Events and Information	Remarks and references to Appendices
HERVILLY	January 1st		Company and Company H/Qu at HERVILLY (K.23d.S.4) which was the crest of the Brigade in Support. Transport lines remained at BERNES (Q.4.e.90.20). 8 of our guns attached to the 93rd Machine Gun Company in reserve positions in the line. Parades were as follows:- 9/30 A.M. - Company inspection. The remainder of the day was spent in overhauling guns and gun equipment.	Reference sheet 62.C
60.	2nd.		The Company moved to VRAIGNES (Q.19d.90.50) which was the area of the Brigade in Reserve. The remaining 8 teams of the 92nd Machine Gun Company were relieved by teams of the 92nd Machine Gun Company and rejoined the company in reserve.	

Army Form C. 2118.

WAR DIARY
or
INTELLIGENCE SUMMARY.
(Erase heading not required.)

Place	Date	Hour	Summary of Events and Information	Remarks and references to Appendices
VRAIGNES	3rd		Parades were as follows:—	Ref: Sheet 62C
			9 A.M. to 9.45 A.M. — Physical Training	
			10 A.M. to 11.15 A.M. — Elementary gun drill.	
			11.30 A.M. to 12.30 p.m. — Mechanism.	
			2 p.m. to 3 p.m. — Squad Drill.	
			3 p.m. to 4 p.m. — Elementary gun training.	
Do.	4th		Parades were as follows:—	
			9 A.M. to 9.45 A.M. — Physical Training.	
			10 A.M. to 11.15 A.M. — Immediate Action.	
			11.30 A.M. to 12.30 p.m. — Elementary gun drill.	
			2 p.m. to 4 p.m. — Recreational Training.	
Do.	5th		Parades were as follows:—	
			9 A.M. to 9.45 A.M. — Physical Training.	
			10 A.M. to 11.15 A.M. — Squad Drill.	
			11.30 A.M. to 12.30 p.m. — Gun Drill.	
			2 p.m. to 4 p.m. — Football.	

Army Form C. 2118.

WAR DIARY
or
INTELLIGENCE SUMMARY.
(Erase heading not required.)

Place	Date	Hour	Summary of Events and Information	Remarks and references to Appendices
VRAIGNES.	6th		Church Parade.	Ref. Sheet 62c.
			Honours & Awards – The following appeared in the List of Officers awarded decorations – London Gazette Supplement of 1/1/18 – Lieut C.E.E. Gilbert – Awarded MILITARY CROSS.	
Do.	7th		Parades were as follows –	
			9.30 A.M. to 12.30 p.m. – Firing on the range.	
			2 pm to 4 pm – Revolver Practise.	
Do.	8th		The Company moved to HERVILLY and relieved the 73rd Machine Gun Company in support.	
			9 Hour guns relieved a similar number of the 73rd Machine Gun Company in the line during the day. The Company also took over 2 A.A. positions at MONTIGNY FARM from the 73rd Machine Gun Company.	

Army Form C. 2118.

WAR DIARY
or
INTELLIGENCE SUMMARY.
(Erase heading not required.)

Instructions regarding War Diaries and Intelligence Summaries are contained in F. S. Regs., Part II. and the Staff Manual respectively. Title pages will be prepared in manuscript.

Place	Date	Hour	Summary of Events and Information	Remarks and references to Appendices
Hervilly	9th		Parades were as follows:-	Ref Sheet 62.C.
		9.30 A.M.	- Company instruction	
		10.30 A.M. to 12.30 P.M.	- Gun Drill.	
		2 P.M. to 4 P.M.	Inspection of Box respirators and gas drill	
Do.	10th		Parades were as follows:-	
		9.30 A.M.	- Instruction	
		9.45 A.M. to 10.15 A.M.	- Physical training	
			The remainder of the day was occupied in building splinter proof protection against enemy aircraft	
Do.	11th		Parades were as follows:-	
		Forenoon	- Continuation of work on aircraft protection of huts.	
			The remainder of the day was spent in instructions for the line.	

Army Form C. 2118.

WAR DIARY
or
INTELLIGENCE SUMMARY.
(Erase heading not required.)

Place	Date	Hour	Summary of Events and Information	Remarks and references to Appendices
HERVILLY.	12th		The company moved into the line and relieved the 92nd Machine	Ref. Sheet
			Machine Company. Company H/Qrs TEMPLEUX (G.1.C.46.21)	HARGICOURT
			The sector of the line defended was the HARGICOURT SECTOR	1A.
			Dispositions of guns as follows :-	
			(1) F.30.c.40.55. (5) F.23.c.35.90. (10) L.11.c.c.8.38. (14) L.4.c.10.45.	
			(2) L.6.d.00.70. (6) F.23.c.45.99. (11) L.11.c.08.38. (15) L.4.c.90.17.	
			(3) F.29.d.75.48 (7) L.6.d.55.15. (12) F.28.c.45.22. (16) L.10.c.op.53	
			(4) F.29.d.35.90. (8) L.6.c.45.60. (13) F.24.d.26.00.	
			1 gun held in reserve at Company Hqrs (G.1.C.46.21)	
BERNES.	13th		Important lines and details carrying were at BERNES.	
			Our M.Guns fired 1500 rounds on enemy back areas	
			during the night. Enemy M.Guns inactive.	
			500 rounds fired at enemy aircraft active during the	
			forenoon.	
			Desultory shelling of TEMPLEUX S.W. throughout the day.	

Army Form C. 2118.

WAR DIARY
or
INTELLIGENCE SUMMARY.
(Erase heading not required.)

Instructions regarding War Diaries and Intelligence Summaries are contained in F. S. Regs., Part II. and the Staff Manual respectively. Title pages will be prepared in manuscript.

Place	Date	Hour	Summary of Events and Information	Remarks and references to Appendices
BERNES.	14th		Enemy artillery fairly active firing in the vicinity of ORCHARD POST	Ref Sheet HARGICOURT 1A.
			HILL POST and HUSSAR POST	
			Several gas shells fired near the ROISEL-TEMPLEUX Road between	
			5/30 p.m and 6 p.m.	
			Our M.Guns carried out harassing fire during the night	
			on the following enemy areas ① G.30.33.18 ② A.20.56.98. ③ A.20.c.56.98.	
Do	15th		Our M.Guns fired 1000 rounds during the night on enemy	
			areas A.24.c.10.20 and A.20.c.56.98.	
			Enemy artillery shelled TEMPLEUX village and Quarries	
			at intervals day and night.	
			Enemy M.Guns fired short bursts throughout the night.	

Army Form C. 2118.

WAR DIARY
or
INTELLIGENCE SUMMARY.

(Erase heading not required.)

Instructions regarding War Diaries and Intelligence Summaries are contained in F. S. Regs., Part II. and the Staff Manual respectively. Title pages will be prepared in manuscript.

Place	Date	Hour	Summary of Events and Information	Remarks and references to Appendices
BERNES.	16th		Teams in forward positions were relieved by those in reserve.	Ref. Sheet HARGICOURT 1A.
			1500 rounds expended in harrassing fire on enemy back areas, A27.c.45.16, A.20.c.56.98 and A.20.c.56.98.	
			Several gas shells fired into TEMPLEUX between 8pm and 9pm.	
			Enemy MGuns inactive.	
Do.	17th		Enemy MGuns were very active during the night firing in the vicinity of F.30.c.40.60 to F.29.d.80.20.	
			Enemy artillery active firing on our back areas intermittently.	
			1500 rounds expended in harrassing fire on the following enemy points - (1) G.2.b.20.60, (2) A.20.c.56.95 & (3) A.20.c.56.98.	

Army Form C. 2118.

WAR DIARY
or
INTELLIGENCE SUMMARY.
(Erase heading not required.)

Instructions regarding War Diaries and Intelligence Summaries are contained in F.S. Regs., Part II. and the Staff Manual respectively. Title pages will be prepared in manuscript.

Place	Date	Hour	Summary of Events and Information	Remarks and references to Appendices
BERNES.	18th		Several 5.9's fired on the vicinity of COLOGNE FARM between 2pm and 4pm. Enemy M.Guns active at Doyzeel. Enemy views G.3.c.20.50, A.2.a.56.95 and A.2.a.56.95 fired on during the night by our M.Guns — 1500 rounds expended.	Ref. Sheet. HARGICOURT 1/A
	19th		Enemy artillery active on ridge S.W. of RONSOY. Our No 9 position (L.C.c.45.60) shelled during the forenoon with heavies.	
	20th		6.45 A.M. Enemy front and support lines were raided at from A.23.d.30.10 to A.25.d.15.45. by a raiding party of the 2nd Batt: the Rifle Brigade, in co-operation our M Guns fired a concentrated barrage on this sector — Ammunition expended 40,250 rounds.	

WAR DIARY
or
INTELLIGENCE SUMMARY.

(Erase heading not required.)

Army Form C. 2118.

Place	Date	Hour	Summary of Events and Information	Remarks and references to Appendices
BERNES.	20th (continued)		Retaliation by Enemy Artillery and M.Guns very feeble. The raid was in every way a success as a result of which valuable identifications were obtained. During the day all teams were relieved by the 43rd Machine Gun Company and proceeded to VRAIGNES in RESERVE. Transport lines remained at BERNES as heretofore.	Ref. Sheet HARGICOURT 1A.
VRAIGNES.	21st		The day was spent in sorting out guns and gun equipment.	Ref. Sheet 62.c.
Do.	22"		Parades were as follows :— 9am to 9.45 A.M. — Physical Training. 10 A.M. to 11.15 A.M. — Overhauling guns and gun equipment	

WAR DIARY
or
INTELLIGENCE SUMMARY.

(Erase heading not required.)

Army Form C. 2118.

Place	Date	Hour	Summary of Events and Information	Remarks and references to Appendices
VRAIGNES	22nd	11.30 a.m. to 12.30 p.m.	Squad Drill	Ref: Sheet 62 C.
(continued)		2 p.m. to 3 p.m.	Kit inspection.	
		3 p.m. to 4 p.m.	Lecture by Section Officers – Trench Routine	
Do.	23rd		Parades were as follows:–	
		9 a.m. to 9.45 a.m.	Physical Training.	
		10 a.m. to 11 a.m.	Stoppages and Immediate Action.	
		11.15 a.m. to 11.45 a.m.	Revolver Drill.	
		11.45 a.m. to 12.30 p.m.	Squad Drill.	
		2 p.m. to 4 p.m.	Recreational Training.	
Do.	24th		Parades were as follows:–	
		9 a.m. to 9.45 a.m.	Physical Training.	
		10 a.m. to 11 a.m.	Gas Drill.	

Army Form C. 2118.

WAR DIARY
or
INTELLIGENCE SUMMARY.
(Erase heading not required.)

Place	Date	Hour	Summary of Events and Information	Remarks and references to Appendices
VRAIGNES	24th		Parades (continued)	Ref: sheet 62c.
(continued)		11.15 A.M. to 12/30 p.m.	Advanced gun drill.	
		2 p.m. to 3 p.m.	Company drill.	
		3 p.m. to 4 p.m.	Lecture by Section officers - "Indirect Fire"	
Do	25th		Parades were as follows:	
			Forenoon - Baths.	
		12.15 A.M. to 3 p.m.	Firing on the range.	
Do.	26th		Parades were as follows:	
		9 a.m. to 9.45 a.m.	Physical training.	
		10 a.m. to 11 a.m.	Stoppages and Immediate Action.	
		11.15 a.m. to 12.30 p.m.	Gun drill.	
		2 p.m. to 4 p.m.	Recreational training.	

Army Form C. 2118.

WAR DIARY
or
INTELLIGENCE SUMMARY.
(Erase heading not required.)

Instructions regarding War Diaries and Intelligence
Summaries are contained in F. S. Regs., Part II.
and the Staff Manual respectively. Title pages
will be prepared in manuscript.

Place	Date	Hour	Summary of Events and Information	Remarks and references to Appendices
VRAIGNES	27th		Church Parade.	Ref. Sheet 62a.
Do	28th		Parades were as follows:-	
			9am to 9.45am - Physical Training.	
			10 A.M. to 11 A.M. - Stoppages and Immediate Action.	
			11.15 A.M. to 12.30 P.M. - Advanced Gun Drill.	
			2 pm to 3 pm - Section Drill.	
			3 pm to 4 pm - Revolver Drill.	
Do	29th		Parades were as follows:-	
			9am to 9.45 A.M. - Physical Training.	
			10 A.M. - Inspection by the C.O.	
			10.30 am to 11.30 - Mechanism.	
			11.30am to 12.30pm - Gun Drill.	
			2 pm to 3 pm - Lecture by the C.O.	

WAR DIARY
or
INTELLIGENCE SUMMARY.
(Erase heading not required.)

Army Form C. 2118.

Place	Date	Hour	Summary of Events and Information	Remarks and references to Appendices
VRAIGNES	30th		All available men engaged on working parties.	Ref. Sheet 62.C.
do.	31st		Parades were as follows:-	
			9 a.m. to 12.30 p.m. - Range Practice.	
			2 pm to 4 pm - Recreational Training.	
			Strength of Company on January 1st. - 10 Officers 170 O.R.	
			Casualties during the month NIL.	
			Strength on 31st January. - 10 Officers 143 O.R.	
			J.W. [signature] Major	
			Commanding 14th Machine Gun Coy.	

Army Form C. 2118.

WAR DIARY
or
INTELLIGENCE SUMMARY.
(Erase heading not required)

CONFIDENTIAL

Vol 25

REFERENCE SHEETS.
62e. Ed. 1.
HAREICOURT.
1A.

17th Machine Gun Company

February 1918

Volume No. 26

Jones
Major.
Commanding 17th Machine Gun Coy.

— WAR DIARY —

Army Form C. 2118.

WAR DIARY
or
INTELLIGENCE SUMMARY.

(Erase heading not required.)

M.G.

Place	Date 1918	Hour	Summary of Events and Information	Remarks and references to Appendices
VRAIGNES (Q19d.90.50)	February 1st		Company and Company H/Qs situate at VRAIGNES (Q19d.90.50) in RESERVE. Transport lines remained at BERNES - (Q16c.90.20) The day was spent in, Physical training gun Drill, Mechanism and Company Drill. Special N.C.O's class in Compass Bearings and Map Reading.	Ref Sheet 62 c.
Do.	2nd		The day was spent in Physical training, Fire direction with Practical demonstrations, Range finding and Visual training. The remainder of the day was devoted to Recreational training.	
Do.	4th		The day was spent in Physical training, Mechanism Advanced M.G. drill and Section drill.	Yes

Army Form C. 2118.

WAR DIARY
or
INTELLIGENCE SUMMARY.
(Erase heading not required.)

Instructions regarding War Diaries and Intelligence Summaries are contained in F. S. Regs., Part II. and the Staff Manual respectively. Title pages will be prepared in manuscript.

Place	Date	Hour	Summary of Events and Information	Remarks and references to Appendices
VRAIGNES Q.19.d.90.30	5th		The day was spent in preparations for the line.	Ref Sheet 62c
Do.	6th		The company moved into the line during the afternoon and relieved the 42nd Machine Gun Company. Details moved to transport lines which remained at BERNES - Q.4.c.90.20. Company H/Qrs situate in HARGICOURT TRENCH (L.4.c.90.20) Disposition of guns as follows:- (1) F.22.d.10.60. (6) F.29.d.35.95. (11) L.4.c.90.20 (2) F.28.b.40.30. (7) L.6.a.60.70. (12) L.10.b.10.55. (3) F.23.c.20.95. (8) L.5.a.50.30 (13) L.11.b.05.45. (4) F.29.a.40.10 (9) L.6.a.55.15. (14) L.11.b.05.45. (5) F.29.d.35.95. (10) L.6.c.40.30 Reserve guns in positions (2) at L.4.c.90.20 and L.10.b.10.55 respectively	HARGICOURT /A

Army Form C. 2118.

WAR DIARY
or
INTELLIGENCE SUMMARY.
(Erase heading not required.)

Instructions regarding War Diaries and Intelligence Summaries are contained in F. S. Regs., Part II. and the Staff Manual respectively. Title pages will be prepared in manuscript.

Place	Date	Hour	Summary of Events and Information	Remarks and references to Appendices
BERNES. Q.H.C.90.20	7th		Enemy artillery inactive.	Ref. Sheet HARGICOURT 14
	8th		Enemy M.guns active during the night - our guns retaliated successfully reducing their fire to a minimum.	
			Indirect fire carried out by our M. guns on the following targets - A 20 c. 56. 95, A20 c. 56.95 and A 24 c. 10. 20.	
			Enemy artillery and M. guns inactive.	
	9th		Enemy fired several trench mortars in the vicinity of our OP position (L 6c. 55.15) between 1AM and 2AM.	
			Harassing fire carried out on the following targets.	
			(1) A 20 C. 56. 95.	
			(2) A 20 C. 56. 95.	
			(3) A 24 C. 45. 16.	

Place	Date	Hour	Summary of Events and Information	Remarks and references to Appendices
BERNES. Q.4e.9a.20.	9th (continued)		Enemy aeroplane appeared over our lines flying low at 4/30pm and again at 4/40pm and was successfully engaged by our M. Guns and forced to rise	Ref Sheet HARGICOURT 1A
Do.	10th		At 5/5pm in response to our "S.O.S." signals, our M. Guns immediately opened fire on "S.O.S" lines commencing with intense fire for 10 minutes and continuing with medium fire until the artillery ceased - no enemy attack developed Harassing fire carried out on the following targets:-	
			(1) A.26.a.60.60.	
			(2) A.20.c.56.98.	
			(3) A.20.c.56.95.	
			(4) A.27.c.10.20.	

Army Form C. 2118.

WAR DIARY
or
INTELLIGENCE SUMMARY.
(Erase heading not required.)

Place	Date	Hour	Summary of Events and Information	Remarks and references to Appendices
BERNES. Q.40.90.20.	11th		Enemy heavily shelled over OH position – F.29.d.94.18. about 8am wounding two men of the team. Enemy artillery more active throughout the day shelling our back areas intermittently. Programme of harassing fire carried out during the night on the following enemy areas :- (1) A.26.a.60.60 – (2) A.20.c.56.95 – (3) A.20.c.56.98 – (4) Q.3a.30.50 (3) A.26.a (Track) and (6) A.25.t (Track)	Ref. Sheet HARGICOURT 1A
Do.	12th		The Brigade on our right made two very successful raids during the night. Nothing unusual occurred on our Brigade front.	

Army Form C. 2118.

WAR DIARY
or
INTELLIGENCE SUMMARY.

(Erase heading not required.)

Instructions regarding War Diaries and Intelligence Summaries are contained in F.S. Regs., Part II. and the Staff Manual respectively. Title pages will be prepared in manuscript.

Place	Date	Hour	Summary of Events and Information	Remarks and references to Appendices
BERNES. Q.4.c.90.20.	13th		Enemy artillery active shelling over back areas intermittently.	Ref Sheet MARQ. 1.100RT 1A
			30, 4.2s fired in the vicinity of our O.H. position - F.29.a.99.48.	
			Enemy M. Guns inactive.	
	14th		Enemy artillery active in the vicinity of our M.G. position Hussar Post.	
			Our M. Guns successfully engaged enemy M. Gun activity during the night reducing their fire to a minimum.	
			Enemy shelled our M.G. position Hussar Post wounding two of our men	
	15th		The Company was relieved in the line by the 43rd Machine Gun Company and proceeded to take over anti-aircraft positions vacated by them.	O.O. No 3. attached. JW

Army Form C. 2118.

WAR DIARY
or
INTELLIGENCE SUMMARY.

(Erase heading not required.)

Instructions regarding War Diaries and Intelligence Summaries are contained in F. S. Regs., Part II. and the Staff Manual respectively. Title pages will be prepared in manuscript.

Place	Date	Hour	Summary of Events and Information	Remarks and references to Appendices
HERVILLY K.23.d.9.4.	15th		Company HQs and Details succeeded to HERVILLY - K.23.d.9.4. the area in SUPPORT.	Ref. Sheet HARGICOURT 7A
	16th		4 guns remained in the line in "Battle Zone" positions. The day was spent overhauling guns, gun equipment and refitting men requiring new clothing.	Ref. Sheet 62C.
	18th		The day was devoted to Physical training and overhauling of guns and gun equipment.	
	19th		Available men engaged on working parties.	
	20th		All available men engaged on working parties.	
	21st		The day was spent in preparations for the line.	

WAR DIARY
or
INTELLIGENCE SUMMARY.

Army Form C. 2118.

Place	Date	Hour	Summary of Events and Information	Remarks and references to Appendices
HERVILLY. K.23d.5.4	22nd		The company moved into the line and relieved teams of the 191st Machine Gun Company. Company H/Qrs - HARGICOURT TRENCH - L.4.c.90.20. Details remained at HERVILLY (K.23d.5.4) in SUPPORT. Transport lines remained at BERNES - Q.4.c.90.20. Disposition of guns as follows:— (1) L.6a.50.05 (2) L.6c.35.30. (3) L.11.b.10.35. (4) L.4.b.10.50. (5) L.4.b.10.30. (6) L.4.c.90.20. (7) L.10.b.10.45. (8) L.6a.90.00. (9) L.8.b.10.40.	Ref: Sheet HARGICOURT 1A. O.O. Not attached
do.	23rd		The sector of the line defended was the HARGICOURT Sector. A further 4 teams of the company relieved teams of the 191st Machine Gun Company in barrage positions at L.11.A.30.25. Enemy artillery and M. Guns inactive.	

Army Form C. 2118.

WAR DIARY
or
INTELLIGENCE SUMMARY.

(Erase heading not required.)

Place	Date	Hour	Summary of Events and Information	Remarks and references to Appendices
HERVILLY K.23.d.8.4.	24th		Programme of harrassing fire carried out on the following targets:- ① G.2c.45.85 (Trench Junction) ② G.2c.65.55 (Trench and Road) ③ G.20.c.70.30 (Trench and Road) ④ G.2d.15.45 (Road) Inspected E. M.Guns at about A.26a.30.15 and A.26a.40.35 harrassed by our M.Guns which were successful in neutralising their fire.	Ref: Sheet 44&91COURT 1.A.
	25th		Enemy artillery and M. Guns inactive. Our M.Gs in BOBBY QUARRY (L.11a.31.18) harrassed QUENNEMONT TRENCH (A.2.o.c) throughout the night. Enemy shelled our position at TEMPLEUX FARM wounding two gunners.	Day

Army Form C. 2118.

WAR DIARY
or
INTELLIGENCE SUMMARY.
(Erase heading not required.)

Instructions regarding War Diaries and Intelligence Summaries are contained in F. S. Regs., Part II and the Staff Manual respectively. Title pages will be prepared in manuscript.

Place	Date	Hour	Summary of Events and Information	Remarks and references to Appendices
HERVILLY. R.23.d.8.4.	26th		Artillery activity on both sides. At 11/50 pm. the enemy put up a fairly heavy barrage on our RIGHT front. Our Artillery immediately opened out and at 12/5 am. the "S.O.S." signal went up from our lines. Our M. guns immediately opened fire on "S.O.S." lines co-operating with intense fire and continued with medium fire until the artillery ceased and the "stand-down" signal given. Considerable aerial activity on both sides.	HERVILLY/100/1 1A.
do	27th		Enemy M. guns and artillery active. Heavy artillery bombardment on our left between 5am & 6/30am. Our aircraft very active over the enemy's lines between 3pm and 5/30 pm.	

Army Form C. 2118.

WAR DIARY
or
INTELLIGENCE SUMMARY.
(Erase heading not required.)

Place	Date	Hour	Summary of Events and Information	Remarks and references to Appendices
HERVILLY. K23d94.	28th		The Company was relieved in the line by the 203rd Machine Gun Company and took over billets for one night at ROISEL preparatory to entraining on the 1st morning for the BOVES area. Strength of Company on February 1st — 10 Officers 193. O.R. Casualties during the month — 6. O.R. Strength of Company on February 28th — 10 Officers 187. O.Rs. On the 20th inst. the following were transferred and joined the Company from General wings the Battalions in the Brigade:— 8th Batt. The Queens — 8 O.Rs 3rd Batt. the Rifle Brigade — 6 " 1st Batt. Royal Fusiliers — 6 " Total 20 O.Rs.	Ref Maps: WARGINOURT 1A. O.O. No 5 attached. [signature] Major. Commanding 17th Machine Gun Coy

SECRET.   Wardowy: Copy No. 7

17th Machine Gun Coy.
OPERATION ORDER No. 3.

1. The 17th Machine Gun Company will be relieved in the FORWARD ZONE by the 73rd M.G. Coy on the 15" inst.

2. On relief the company will take up SUPPORT positions and anti-aircraft positions from the 73rd M.G. Coy.

3. Relief will be carried out in accordance with table.

4. S.A.A. belts and boxes will be handed over to relieving teams and receipts obtained.

5. All trench stores, work programme, maps, range cards and S.O.S. and fire orders must be carefully handed over and receipts obtained.

6. 2/Lieut G.W. PETRIE will proceed from BERNES and take over teams and positions at L.4.c.0.10.

7. Teams proceeding to ROISEL (A.A. positions) will meet guides at entrance to ROISEL on TEMPLEUX - ROISEL Road at 7 km.

   Remaining A.A. teams will proceed to MONTIGNY and HANCOURT direct.

8. Transport will be detailed as per attached table.

9. Completion of relief to be notified by code word CORBY.

10. Company H/Qrs will move to HERVILLY on completion of relief.

Copies. 1 - 17th Bn.
2 - 73rd MGC.
3 - T.O.
4) Section Commanders.
5)
6)
7 - War Diary.
8 - File.

Joy
Major
O/C. 17th Machine Gun Coy

SECRET.

TABLE to O.O. No 3. — 14th Machine Gun Company.

Gun Position	Rendezvous for Guides	Times for Guides	New Positions	Remarks
ORCHARD POST.	ORCHARD POST.	11.30 pm	(8) TEMPLEUX FARM. L5a.80.50 9pm	Guide 93rd M.G. Coy. will meet team at L26.20.30 12/30 p.m.
TOINE POST.	— Do —	Do.	(7) — do —	do
HILL TOP.	— Do —	Do.	(3) F.24.c.62.45.	Guide 93rd M.G.C. at TOINE POST 1pm.
PELLICOURT Rd.	— Do —	Do.	A.A. HANCOURT	1 Limber at ORCHARD POST 12 noon to proceed to HANCOURT.
HUSSAR POST	— Do —	Do.	— do —	do
(8) L.10.c.15.	Coy. 1110.	2 pm	(6) L.4.b. – 10.50	Guide 93rd M.G.C. from Coy. 1110.
(6) RESERVE TEAM	Do.	3 pm	(4) F.28.d.20.60	at 2/30 pm to remain at (8) Position until 5pm — meet 93rd M.G.C. guide at Coy 1110. 5/30 pm
CEMETERY	Do.	2/30h.	(5) F.28.d.80.10.	(4) Position from Coy 1110. 4/45 pm to take place at dusk.
(1) L.4.c.90.20. Reserve Team	Do.	tush	A.A. MUNTIGNY FARM.	1 Limber at Coy 1110. to MUNTIGNY
BOBBY FARM 2 guns.	Do.	5/30h.	A.A. ROISEL STATION.	1 Limber at BOBBY FARM 6pm to proceed to ROISEL.
(2) L.4.00.90. (3) F.2.d.y.40.	HARGICOURT DUMP (3).	6pm	Company H.Q. HERVILLY.	1 Limbers at HARGICOURT and proceed to Coy 1110.
COLOGNE RESERVE (L.6.a.50.05)	— do —	do.	do	2 Limbers at HARGICOURT Dump 6/45 pm HERVILLY.
COLOGNE FARM. L.5.c.30.20.	— do —	do.	do	do

17th M.G. Company

Operation Order No 4

Ref. sheet
Hargicourt Ed. 1a.

① The 17th M.G. Coy. will relieve 6 Guns of the 73rd M.G. Coy on the right of the Hargicourt Sector on the 22nd inst., and 4 guns of 191st M.G. Coy. in Bobby Quarry on the 23rd inst.

② The moves will be carried out in accordance with the attached table.

③ The three teams at Nos. 3, 4, & 5 positions will be relieved by the 73rd M.G. Coy, & on relief will return to Bernes where they will remain as reserve guns in readiness to move at 30 mins. notice.

④ Teams proceeding to Bobby Quarry to relieve the 191st M.G. Coy will vacate the A.A. positions at Hancourt & Montigny taking steps that all guns, equipment etc. are removed.

⑤ The 2 guns now at TEMPLEUX FARM remain in positions until further orders.

(CONTD)

Sheet 2.

(6) Trench stores including belt boxes will be carefully handed over & receipts obtained. These receipts will be forwarded to Coy. H.Q. not later than 24 hrs after completion of relief.

(7) (a) 2nd Lieut. Locke will relieve the Officer at L.5.d.30.90 & will be in charge of guns at Cologne Farm & Cologne Reserve.

(b) 2nd Lieut. Falls will relieve the Officer of the 191st M.G. Coy. at Bobby Quarry on the 23rd inst. & will be in charge of the 4 guns at Bobby Quarry & 2 guns at Bobby Farm.

(c) 2nd Lieut. Kirkby will relieve the Officer at Coy. H.Q. Hargicourt Trench & will be in charge of the following guns Nos. 6, 7 & 8.

(d) 2nd Lieut. Petrie will be relieved by an Officer of the 173rd M.G. Coy. & on relief will return to transport lines Ronssoy reporting at Coy. H.Q. Hargicourt Trench on his way out.

(9) Completion of relief will be notified by code word "PERHAPS".

21.2.18.

E. L. Tibbitt Lieut.
p. O.C. 17th M.G. Company

8. Company H.Q.
will move to
Hargicourt Trench
L40 90 10 at 2.30 p.m.
9.

A

DATE	FROM	TO RELIEVE	GUIDES TIME	GUIDES PLACE	REMARKS
22.2.18	ROISEL A.A. Positions	① Teams at No.1 Bohain ② Teams at No.8 positions	4 PM	Coy. HQ. Hargreaves Trench	① Guide from A.A. positions to Hy on ROISEL–TEMPLEUX Road at Kr.10a, 30.80 at 11am to meet 3 teams from Bhd M.G. Coy who will take over A.A. positions. The 2 teams of 17th M.G. Coy will move to ROISEL at 2.15pm with carts & equipment. These will bivouac or limber which will arrive at A.A. positions at 1.45pm.
"	Heuvilly Coy HQ 2 Teams of No.2 Bohain	Teams at Bobby Farm	5 PM	Coy. HQ. Hargreaves Trench	Teams will move off from Heuvilly at 3pm & equipment less kit harves to be packed on limber or Heuvilly.
"	Heuvilly Coy HQ 1 Team of No.1 Bohain	Team at Cologne Reserve	6 PM	Bivouac Behind Script Road Bohain	Teams will move off from Heuvilly at 4pm. Guns & equipment & Lewis kit boxes to be packed on remaining limber at Heuvilly.
"	1 Team of No.2 Bohain	Team at Cologne Farm	6 PM	B.D.	

B

Date	From	Relieved By	Guides		Remarks
			Time	Place	
22.2.18	No 3 Parkin	73rd M.G Coy	4.30pm	Coy. H.Q Hargicourt Trench	When relieved teams will rendezvous at crucifix on TEMPLEUX — HARGICOURT ROAD L.3 C.6.5. 70 at 6.30pm. On arrival limber will be waiting for guns etc. Teams will then proceed to BERNES reporting to 2/Lt Copeland on arrival.
"	No 4 Parkin	Do	5.30pm	Cross Rd Hargicourt L.5.C.15.30	Do
"	No 5 Parkin	Do	5.30pm	Do	Do

C

Date	From	To Relieve	Guides		Remarks
			Time	Place	
23.2.18	A.A. Perkins Hancourt 2 Teams.	To relieve 2 teams of 191st M.G. Coy, nr. BOBBY QUARRY.	12 noon	Bn. HQ Hollycourt Trench	Teams will leave Hancourt at 9.30am, all gun equipment including Bell boxes will be packed on limber which will arrive at Gun* Bell boxes will not be taken into the position may be left on limber to be returned to transport lines.
Do.	A.A. Perkins Muchy-lez-teams 2 Teams.	Do.	Do	Do	Teams will leave Muchy at 10am, all gun equipment including Bell boxes will be packed on limbers which will arrive at 9.30am. Bell boxes will not be taken into the position may be left on limber to be returned to transport lines.
	NOTE: *	These times are liable to be altered			

Secret.   Copy No. 1

17th Machine Gun Company.

Operation Orders No. 5.

Ref Sheet HARGICOURT Ed. 1A.

1. The 17th Machine Gun Coy. will be relieved out of the line on the 28th inst. by the 203rd. M.G. Coy.
2. The move will be carried out in accordance with attached table.
3. Transport details as shown on the attached table.
4. 2nd Lt. H.D. Fell's M.C. + 4 man guns will remain in the line for 24 hrs. after relief of teams, after which they will proceed to ROISEL.
5. All Limber Boxes, gun work programmes + alternative positions must be carefully handed over to the incoming teams. Receipts must be obtained for all stores handed over, forwarded to Company H.Qrs. All emplacements dug-outs + abris must be left scrupulously clean + Section Officers will be held responsible that this be done.
6. After relief teams will proceed to ROISEL the following day will entrain to the BOVES area. Entraining orders will be issued separately.
7. Completion of relief will be notified by the code word "ATLAST".
8. Company H.Qrs. will move from the line to ROISEL at 7pm on the 28th inst.

Operation Order No 6.

1. The 17th Machine Gun Coy. will entrain from ROISEL on the 1st March to the BOVES area.
2. The Company will be billeted at BERTEAUCOURT or THENNES until the 6th March, after which it will probably be billeted at VAIRES.
3. A billeting party of 1 Officer, 1 N.C.O. + 3 men (under Lt. C.P. Gilbert M.C) will proceed in advance to take over billets for Company. Instructions will be issued later.
4. Transport of the Company will move in 2 Sections. Section A under 2nd Lt. D.S. Couplands with the Brigade Groups on the 28th inst. Section B under Transport Sergt. will move on the 1st proximo. Instructions to be issued later.
5. The billets at ROISEL must be left scrupulously clean. Section Officers will see that this is carried out.

Copy No. 1.   17th. O.B.
  "   " 2.   203rd. M.G.Coy. → O.O. No. 5 only.
  "   " 3.   Section Officers
  "   " 4.
  "   " 5.   Transport Officer.
  "   " 6.   War Diary.
  "   " 7.   File.

J. Hoyle
Major.
O/c. 17th Machine Gun Coy.

APPENDIX A

GUN POSITION	GUIDES		LIMBERS	REMARKS
	TIME	PLACE		
Cologne Reserve. Cologne Farm.	5.45 pm	Company H. Qrs.	One.	Limbers to be at forward ration dump Hargicourt. 7pm.
Bobby Farm 2 Guns.	5.45 p.m	Company H. Qrs	One.	Limbers to be at Bobby Farm 6.45 p.m.
Bobby Quarry 4 Guns.	5.30 pm	Company H. Qrs.	Two.	Limbers to be at Bobby Quarry 6.15 pm.
6, 7 + 8.	5 pm	Company H. Qrs.	Two.	Limbers to be at Company H.Qrs. 6 pm.
Templeuse Farm 2 Guns.	4.30 p.m	Entrance to "B" track. ROISEL-TEMPLEUX ROAD.	One	Limbers to be at Templeux Farm 5 pm.
				Mess cart to be at Company Headquarters at 4.30 pm.
Company H.Qrs.				All teams on relief to proceed to ROISEL.